1001 WAYS

TO REWARD

EMPLOYEES

BY BOB NELSON, Ph.D.

WORKMAN PUBLISHING
NEW YORK

Library of Congress Cataloging-in-Publication Data is available.

ISBN-13: 978-0-7611-3681-1
ISBN-10: 0-7611-3681-9

Cover design by Lisa Hollander
Cover and interior illustrations by Stephen Schudlich

Workman books are available at special discounts when purchased in bulk
for premiums and sales promotions as well as for fund-raising or educational use.
Special editions or book excerpts can also be created to specification.
For details, contact the Special Sales Director at the address below.

Workman Publishing Company, Inc.
708 Broadway
New York, NY 10003-9555

First printing: May 2005
Manufactured in the United States
10 9 8 7 6 5 4 3 2

ACKNOWLEDGMENTS

This revision would probably still be in progress if it were not for the tireless efforts of Nick Swisher, administrative assistant extraordinaire, who personally contacted everyone and every place referenced in the original book to update, correct, or delete information as necessary and then went on to contact thousands of additional organizations in search of the best recognition practices in use today.

I'd also like to thank:

The 1,000 or so organizations I've worked with on this topic since the original publication of *1001 Ways to Reward Employees* and especially those Nelson Motivation Inc. clients who submitted examples of their recognition practices, techniques, and programs for potential inclusion in this revision.

Dr. Joe Maciariello of The Peter F. Drucker Graduate Management School of The Claremont Graduate University in Los Angeles for giving me the initial inspiration for this book; my doctoral committee: Drs. Don Griesinger, Harvey Wichman, and David Drew for their help in shaping my research and thinking on why managers do and do not use recognition with their employees; and Dr. Peter Drucker for his advice to first learn the insights of the topic through client fieldwork and then to prove those insights through research.

At Workman Publishing: editor Richard Rosen, editor-in-chief Susan Bolotin, and CEO Peter Workman for their vision and support of this book; Yanfei Shen and Anne Cherry for their tireless editorial attentions; and the incredible marketing and promotions people who have helped make the book so successful, including Jenny Mandel, Kim Cox-Hicks, Katie Workman, James Wehrle, and Page Edmunds. I can truly say working with you all has been, and continues to be, a joy.

My long-time friend, associate, and spouse, Jennifer, and our wonderful children, Daniel and Michelle, for their ongoing love, support, and encouragement.

12-7-05

FOREWORD

If there's one thing I've learned in my life, it's the fact that *everyone* wants to be appreciated. This goes for managers as well as employees, parents as well as children, and coaches as well as players. We never outgrow this need, and even if it looks like we are independent and self-sufficient, the fact is we need others to help us feel valued.

Although this might sound like common sense, so often I've found that common sense is not common practice in organizations today. We're often too busy or too stressed to remember that the recognition we crave, others crave as well. For that reason, this book is a godsend to every well-intentioned manager or frustrated employee. It makes a compelling case that recognition, rewards, and positive reinforcement all do work and that they can work for you.

With *1001 Ways to Reward Employees,* praising, recognizing, and rewarding employees just became a little easier. You can now provide the rewards and recognition that people in your life so richly deserve. Bob Nelson highlights the research that demonstrates the success of proven principles through a multitude of potent examples from companies across the country. He provides a treasure chest of ideas, inspiration, and resources to enable you to make praising, recognition, and rewards a permanent part of your management repertoire. This is one book that should be on every manager's desk!

No longer can managers deny the power and practicality of praising. No longer can they fail to recognize a deserving employee because they couldn't think of something to do to show their appreciation. No longer will using praise, recognition, and rewards be optional in managing people.

No employee seeks to be mediocre; all seek to be magnificent. With this book they can be. And in the process, any job or work environment can be made more productive, motivating, and fulfilling.

—Ken Blanchard,
coauthor of *The One Minute Manager*

PREFACE TO THE REVISED EDITION

In the decade since this book was originally published, I've learned a great deal about employee recognition, and have continued to be excited by the topic's potential. I continue to be intrigued by the richness and power of the concepts of recognition and rewards, not just at work, but within all our relationships. I continue to be surprised by the creativity and variation that people bring to the successful practice of reward and recognition. I continue to be impressed by the fact that the simplest, easiest, and least expensive options for recognizing employees often work the best to make them feel valued.

Perhaps the most important lesson I've learned is that it works better to use recognition with a sense of purpose—to systematically link it to the performance and behavior you are most seeking. It's the contingent use of recognition that is the most powerful and meaningful to others. Other things that I've learned include:

- It can be difficult for managers and executives to take the first step in believing in the power of recognition, but once they do, a momentum quickly builds, creating substantial benefits for the organization.

- Although a wide range of behaviors and activities can serve as recognition, its true power comes from how it is used—its timing, context, symbolism, modeling, and leveraging—to bring out the best in any person and situation.

- There's a power and excitement that comes from variety, freshness, and spontaneity. Motivation is a moving target, and what works today may not work tomorrow—and probably won't work if you keep doing exactly the same thing!

In today's business climate, rewards and recognition have become more important than ever for several reasons:

- Managers have fewer ways to influence employees and shape their behavior. Coercion is no longer an option; managers must increasingly serve as coaches who influence rather than demand desired behavior.

- Employees are increasingly asked to do more and to do it more autonomously. To support looser controls, managers need to create work environments that are both positive and reinforcing.

- Demographics predict that fewer workers will be available in the post–baby boom era and that those who do exist will likely have fewer skills than their predecessors. This new pool of employees have different values and expect work to be both purposeful and motivating.

Since its initial publication, many readers have reported to me that they use this book as a personalized motivation handbook by simply passing it around to their staff and having each person initial the ideas they like. When someone does a good job, you can then surprise them with something you already know they will value.

My hope is that you will use this book to experiment and learn the power of recognition and that, as a result, your workplace—and the employees in it—will become more positive, productive, and enjoyable. Better yet, once you see the value of this topic, I hope you start using it in other aspects of your life to make *all* your relationships more rewarding.

—Bob Nelson, Ph.D.
San Diego, California

THE RECOGNITION-AND-PERFORMANCE LINK

A fundamental reinforcer for the use of employee recognition is its impact on improving employee job performance, which in turn reinforces managers to provide additional recognition. In my doctoral research I found evidence to support the recognition-performance link in at least three ways.

First, several performance-related variables were broadly supported by all managers in the study, the majority of whom agreed or strongly agreed with the following statements:

• Recognizing employees helps me to better motivate them. (90 percent)

• Providing nonmonetary recognition to my employees when they do good work helps to increase their performance. (84 percent)

• Recognizing employees provides them with practical feedback. (84 percent)

• Recognizing employees for good work makes it easier to get the work done. (80 percent)

• Recognizing employees helps them to be more productive. (78 percent)

• Providing nonmonetary recognition helps me to achieve my personal goals. (69 percent)

• Providing nonmonetary recognition helps me to achieve my job goals. (60 percent)

Second, 73 percent of managers reported that they received the results they expected when they used employee recognition either immediately or soon thereafter, and 99 percent said they felt they would eventually obtain the desired results.

Third, of the thousands of employees who reported to the managers in my study, 78 percent said that it was very or extremely important to be recognized by their manager when they do good work. Fifty-three percent of employees expected recognition to occur soon thereafter.

INTRODUCTION

Results of a survey by the Council of Communication Management confirm what almost every employee already knows: that recognition for a job well done is the top motivator of employee performance.

Yet most managers do not understand or use the potential power of recognition and rewards. This is true even though 33 percent of managers themselves report that they would rather work in an organization where they could receive better recognition. When a manager is apprised of the importance of this fundamental principle of human behavior, the typical reaction is to insist that employees would appreciate only rewards that directly translate to their pocketbooks—raises, bonuses, or promotions, for example.

While money is important to employees, research shows that what motivates them really to perform—and to perform at higher levels—is the thoughtful, personal kind of recognition that signifies true appreciation for a job well done. Numerous studies have confirmed this. The motivation is all the stronger if the recognition creates excitement, an enhanced sense of value and respect, and a story the employee can tell to family, friends, and associates, possibly for years to come.

A note about terminology. The term *recognition* typically refers to an intangible activity, such as thank-yous, pats on the back, and positive gossip. The term *reward,* on the other hand, refers to something tangible, such as money, merchandise, or travel. In practice, however, these two terms are sometimes used interchangeably. For example, you can give someone an on-the-spot reward of $20 while also verbally thanking them. An *award* is a combination of these terms that typically takes the shape of a trophy, plaque, or certificate. It is a specific item that serves as an honor for a certain achievement, but almost always involves a presentation of some sort that captures the recognition aspect of the occasion. An *incentive* is most often thought of as a planned reward, that is, advance knowledge that if you do a certain thing, you will be given a certain reward.

Most forms of reward and recognition fall into two categories: *formal* and *informal*. Formal rewards tend to be planned, structured programs that are typically repeated over time and continue for years, such as employee-of-the-month or years-of-service awards. Informal rewards are the more here-and-now, spontaneous forms of sincere thanks and appreciation for doing good work. They are often fresh and fun and can be used to acknowledge a specific behavior, such as customer service, cost-saving ideas or teamwork, or for specific achievements ranging from completion of an interim report to finishing a project or closing a key sale.

In general, the most highly valued forms of recognition have shifted from the formal to the informal and spontaneous, and from the tangible to the intangible and interpersonal. Motivation for today's employees has become increasingly personal and situational. When it comes to recognition, it's increasingly true that one size no longer fits all!

The first four parts of this book deal primarily with informal forms of recognition: Day-to-Day Recognition (Part I), Informal Intangible Recognition (Part II), Tangible Recognition & Rewards (Part III), and Group Recognition, Rewards & Activities (Part IV). The last two parts deal with more formal types of recognition: Rewards for Specific Achievements (Part V), and Formal Organizational Reward Programs (Part VI). The appendixes include lists of companies that can help you customize rewards and plan recognition activities, as well as a listing of all companies featured in the book.

The recognition and rewards in these categories can cost little or nothing or a great deal; they can be private or public; and they can focus on a wide variety of desired behaviors and achievements or be geared to a few significant objectives in the organization. The most effective informal rewards ultimately link to formal programs of some type and vice versa. For example, a thank-you letter or public praise can be a significant way of acknowledging a person's efforts and achievements, but if it is the only form of recognition a manager uses, it will soon lose effectiveness.

Regardless of the cost, scope, or complexity of effective rewards and recognition, the guidelines are simple:

1. Match the reward to the person. Start with the individual's personal preferences, and reward the person in ways he or she will truly find rewarding. Such rewards may be personal or official, informal or formal, public or private, and may take the shape of gifts or activities. To take guesswork out of effective recognition, ask your employees what they most value, perhaps even giving them an index card to list forms of recognition they like, which is what several organizations do.

2. Match the reward to the achievement. Effective reinforcement should be customized to take into account the significance of the achievement. Obviously, an employee who completes a two-year project should be rewarded in a more substantial way than one who simply does a favor for you. And, of course, the reward should be a function of the amount of time you have to plan and execute it and the money you have to spend.

3. Be timely and specific. To be effective, rewards need to be given as soon as possible after the desired behavior or achievement. Those that come weeks or months later do little to motivate employees to repeat their actions. You should always say why the reward is being given—that is, provide a context for the achievement. Once you have consistently rewarded desired performance, your pattern of recognition may become more intermittent as the desired behavior becomes habitual. In fact, research shows that intermittent reinforcement becomes more effective in sustaining performance in the long run.

Catherine Meek, president of Meek and Associates, Los Angeles compensation consultants, adds that reward and recognition programs should reflect the company's values and business strategy, and that employees should participate in their development and execution. In addition, Aubrey Daniels recommends that leaders be held accountable for effectively recognizing employees and that organizations avoid using blanket or "silver bullet" approaches to motivation. "Jelly bean" motivation—giving the same reward to every member of the organization—not only does not inspire employees to excel, but it may actually damage performance as top achievers see no acknowledgement of the exceptional job they have done, while other employees receive recognition just for showing up at work.

Here is a good rule of thumb: For every four informal rewards (e.g., a special thank-you), there should be a more official acknowledgment (e.g., a letter of recognition), and for every four of those, there should be a still more official reward (e.g., a plaque or public praise at a company meeting), leading ultimately to more traditional rewards such as raises, bonuses, promotions, and special assignments.

Any moment of recognition can be made more valuable with some simple forethought as to what is done, who does it, who should be present, the context of the achievement, and the stories that are shared to give relevance and bring the achievement to life for everyone involved. With a little attention and practice any manager (or employee) can become skilled at capturing the recognition value of any situation, achievement, or occasion.

We often think of recognition and rewards as what managers do for employees, but increasingly the power of recognition can be attained in any relationship, including peer-to-peer, employee-to-manager, customer-to-employee, employee-to-vendor, and even manager-to-family on the home front. Part of the power of recognition is leveraging these different possibilities, as you will see in examples throughout this book.

CONTENTS

1001 WAYS
TO REWARD
EMPLOYEES

PART I

DAY-TO-DAY RECOGNITION

I n my doctoral research on why managers use or don't use recognition with their employees, I found the top variable distinguishing those managers who use recognition was that they felt it was their responsibility—not corporate's or human resources'—to create the motivational environment for *their* people. They truly believed that recognizing their deserving employees played an integral part in how those workers felt about their jobs.

This finding coincides with what my research shows are the most important ways that employees prefer to be recognized when they do good work—that is, simple day-to-day behaviors that any manager can express with their employees, the most important of which is praise. The best praise is done soon, specifically, sincerely, personally, positively, and proactively. In a matter of seconds, a simple praise conveys, "I saw what you did, I appreciate it, here's why it's important, and here's how it makes me feel"—a lot of punch in a small package!

Four out of the top ten categories of motivators reported by employees in my research are forms of praise, and these categories make up the four chapters in Part I: personal praise, written praise, electronic praise, and public praise. Now, you might say, "Are these really different types of praise? Don't they all have the same effect?" This was my initial thought, too, but I learned that these types of praise are in fact distinct from one another. Praising someone in person means something different to that person than writing him or her a note, and these forms of praise are both different from praising the person in public. To get the maximum impact out of this simple behavior, vary the forms you use, and use them all frequently.

Research by Dr. Gerald Graham of Wichita State University supports these observations. In multiple studies, he found that employees preferred personalized, instant recognition from their direct supervisors more than any other kind of motivation. In fact, in another survey of American workers, 63 percent of the respondents ranked "a pat on the back" as a meaningful incentive.

In Graham's studies, employees perceived that manager-initiated rewards for performance were done least often, and that company-initiated rewards for presence (that is, rewards based simply on being in the organization) occurred most often. Dr. Graham concluded, "It appears that the techniques that have the greatest motivational impact are practiced the least, even though they are easier and less expensive to use."

Graham's study determined the top five motivating techniques reported by employees to be:

1. The manager personally congratulates employees who do a good job.

2. The manager writes personal notes about good performance.

3. The organization uses performance as the basis for promotion.

4. The manager publicly recognizes employees for good performance.

5. The manager holds morale-building meetings to celebrate success.

Ideally, you should vary the ways you recognize your staff while still trying to do things on a day-to-day basis. For example, Robin Horder-Koop, manager of programs and services at Amway Corporation, the distributor of house and personal-care products and other goods in Ada, MI, uses these inexpensive ways to recognize the 200 people who work for her on a day-to-day basis:

- ✔ On days when some workloads are light, the department's employees help out workers in other departments. After accumulating eight hours of such work, employees get a thank-you note from Horder-Koop. Additional time earns a luncheon with company officials in the executive dining room.
- ✔ All workers are recognized on a rotating basis. Each month, photos of different employees are displayed on a bulletin board along with comments from their coworkers about why they are good colleagues.
- ✔ Horder-Koop sends thank-you notes to employees' homes when they do outstanding work. When someone works a lot of overtime or travels extensively, she sends a note to the family thanking them for their support.
- ✔ At corporate meetings, employees play games such as Win, Lose, or Draw and The Price Is Right, using questions about the company's products. Winners get prizes such as tote bags and T-shirts.

Other inexpensive ideas Horder-Koop uses to recognize employees include giving flowers to employees who are commended in customers' letters, having supervisors park employees' cars one day a month, and designating days when workers can come in late or wear casual clothes to the office.

According to author and management consultant Rosabeth Moss Kanter, "Recognition—saying thank you in public and perhaps giving a tangible gift along with the words—has multiple functions beyond simple human courtesy. To the employee, recognition signifies that someone noticed and someone cares. To the rest of the organization, recognition creates role models—heroes—and communicates the standards, saying: 'These are the kinds of things that constitute great performance around here.'" Following are some guidelines Kanter offers for successfully recognizing employees:

Principle 1: Emphasize success rather than failure. You tend to miss the positives if you are busily searching for the negatives.

Principle 2: Deliver recognition and reward in an open and publicized way. If not made public, recognition loses much of its impact and much of the purpose for which it is provided.

Principle 3: Deliver recognition in a personal and honest manner. Avoid providing recognition that is too "slick" or overproduced.

Principle 4: Tailor your recognition and reward to the unique needs of the people involved. Having many recognition and reward options will enable management to acknowledge accomplishment in ways appropriate to the particulars of a given situation.

Principle 5: Timing is crucial. Recognize contribution throughout a project. Reward contribution close to the time an achievement is realized. Time delays weaken the impact of most rewards.

Principle 6: Strive for a clear, unambiguous, and well-communicated connection between accomplishments and rewards. Be sure people understand why they receive awards and the criteria used to determine awards.

Principle 7: Recognize recognition. That is, recognize people who recognize others for doing what is best for the company.

Personal Praise & Recognition

The most important type of recognition is that which occurs on a day-to-day basis—where the rubber meets the road. In my research with employees, 99.4 percent reported it was somewhat, very, or extremely important for them to be recognized by their managers when they did good work, and 73 percent expected recognition to occur either immediately or soon thereafter. *Personal* praise is generally considered to be the most important, and employees rank four forms of personal praise thus: "being personally thanked for doing good work" (88 percent); "being given a verbal praising" (86 percent); "being sought out by a manager to be commended" (82 percent); and "praising an employee for good work in front of another person" (61 percent).

The gap between the amount of praise managers think they give their employees and the amount employees report receiving is unfortunately wide. Bob Levoy, president of Success Dynamics, Inc., reports: "I've asked more than 2,500 doctors to rank on a scale of 1 to 5 (1 = never, 5 = always) the following statement: 'I let my employees know when they're doing a good job.' Their average response is 4.4. I then asked their staff members to rank this statement: 'The doctor lets me know when I'm doing a good job,' and their average response is only 1.7. This difference between what doctors say they give and what employees say they get is often the underlying cause of employee resentment, diminished productivity, and turnover. This 'feedback gap' is present in almost every manager-employee relationship."

How do you close that gap? Management consultant Marshall Goldsmith offers the following advice:

One of my clients who was using 360-degree feedback scored very low in the area of "Provides Adequate Positive Recognition." What he did to improve was a great strategy for leaders everywhere.

First, he listed the key groups of people that impacted his life: his friends, family, direct reports, colleagues, and customers. Then he listed the names of each of the people who were in that group. Then twice a week, once on Wednesday and once on Friday, he would look at the list and ask himself, 'Did anyone on this page do anything I should recognize?' If they did, he'd send them a little note, an e-mail, or a voice-mail to say thank you. He didn't do anything that took more than a couple of minutes. If nobody on the list did something he should recognize, he did nothing. He didn't want to appear to be false, to be a phony.

By following this simple technique, in one year he went from a 6 percentile in giving recognition to a 94 percentile. I have recommended this strategy to many leaders and have never seen it *not* work. It can help you, too, to do a great job in providing more positive recognition to those that are most important to you in your life.

It's the daily interactions that add up to define our relationships at work. It's the little things that managers do or do not do that can end up making a big difference in how others feel about working with and for them and about being a part of the organization. A systematic focus on the positives serves as a foundation and buffer to negative challenges— problems, complaints, stress, and so on.

Although most positive day-to-day interactions are apt to be smaller in focus with little or no cost, with some thought and planning you can be prepared to do more significant things as well. For example, if someone closes a big sale or finishes a significant project, you can ask your president or CEO to phone the person to personally thank him or her. While you might not be able to do that every day, it's an out-of-the-ordinary yet simple form of thanks you can call upon for special circumstances.

Remember: the best personal praise is timely, sincere, and specific. Create time to connect with each of your employees—even if it's over coffee or lunch—to see how they are doing and to thank them for all they've done. You could even, on occasion, personally praise each of your employees when your staff gets together for a meeting. (If you use this tactic, make sure you find something positive to say about everyone present so that no one feels left out.)

You can praise employees directly, in front of others, or when they are not around (a concept known as "positive gossip") knowing that this indirect praise will get back to them. For some employees, indirect recognition is the most credible because it is done without any expectation in return. It essentially says: "My boss must have thought what I did was important to have brought it up to the entire management team!"

Try working sincere thanks into your daily activities on an ongoing basis. For example, make it a habit to greet people with 100 percent focus, as if you had all the time in the world for them, even if you only have a few minutes. Give them your undivided attention and if that is not possible, tell them that you're distracted and would like to get back to them when you could better focus on them, their needs, and your conversation.

When someone leaves the office at the end of the day, say good-bye and thank them for their effort that day. When asking employees about great managers they have worked for, I've had more than one person tell me how such a manager would thank them for being there every day before they went home. A simple courtesy, yes, but one that employees noted and valued. Nothing beats simple, day-to-day recognition for building a foundation of trust and goodwill.

A survey by the Minnesota Department of Natural Resources found that recognition activities contributed significantly to employees' job satisfaction. Most respondents said they highly valued day-to-day recognition from their supervisors, peers, and team members. Other findings from the survey include:

✔ 68 percent of the respondents said it was important to believe that their work was appreciated by others.

✔ 67 percent agreed that most people need appreciation for their work.

✔ 63 percent agreed that most people would like more recognition for their work.

✔ Only 8 percent thought that people should not look for praise for their work efforts.

Nancy Branton, project manager for the survey, says, "Recognition is more important now than in the past. Employees increasingly believe that their job satisfaction depends on acknowledgment of work performance as well as on adequate salary. This is especially true of employees who are highly interested in their work and take satisfaction in their achievements."

Organizations can greatly influence the use of positive recognition on a daily basis by providing training, tools, activities, and programs to foster that behavior, examples of which will be provided throughout this book. The Tennant Company, a manufacturer in Minneapolis, has a Positive Feedback Committee that each year sponsors a Positive Feedback Day, on which all employees receive "That-A-Way" notepads, pens printed with the phrase "Positive Strokes Only," balloons, and signs. At holiday time, the committee sponsors an open house with cider and cookies and invites employees to drop by at scheduled breaks.

> **❝I can live for two weeks on a good compliment.❞**
>
> —Mark Twain

Randy Niendorff of Lucent Technologies/Audya Communications in Denver, stops by employees' desks "just to see how things are going today." He reports that it's a pleasant surprise for employees to see him, even when things are going well, and that they appreciate his accessibility.

———

When Greg Peel, a zone manager for Paychex in Dallas, sees an employee working really hard, he calls that person's mother and thanks her.

———

Tyler Bracey, president and CEO of the Atlanta Consulting Group, places five coins in one of his pockets each day. During the day, he transfers a coin to his other pocket every time he recognizes an employee for good work. That technique has helped him make praise a habit.

———

One store manager for Long's Drugs brings a silver dollar to work on Monday mornings and gives it to a supervisor, who is asked to praise one of his employees and then hand the coin off to another supervisor. If the coin gets around to all the supervisors by the end of the week, the manager brings in donuts to the supervisors' meeting.

———

Top military officers in several branches of the military use coin medallions as personal recognition items. One bank president gold-plates quarters and hands them to deserving employees. Other companies have used wooden nickels, regular nickels, or even green glass pebbles as symbolic recognition items for work well done.

———

A task-oriented, top manager at Qwest Communications in Denver reminds himself to recognize others by listing his employees' names on his to-do list each week. Then, he crosses names off the list when he has had a chance to acknowledge those people for some aspect of their performance or behavior, such as reaching project milestones or delivering exceptional customer service. He says it's his way to "turn the people aspect of my job into manageable tasks I can focus on each week."

———

> **"There are two things people want more than sex and money . . . recognition and praise."**
>
> —MARY KAY ASH,
> Founder,
> Mary Kay, Inc.

ASAP-Cubed Guidelines for Effective Praise

- As Soon
- As Sincere
- As Specific
- As Personal
- As Positive
- As Practical

... as possible!

Baltimore Orioles manager Ray Miller didn't get much personalized attention from his coaches as a minor league pitcher back in the '60s and '70s. "The way I was treated hurt me," he recalls. Miller learned from experience that paying attention to players is important, whether they are performing well or not. To be sure that he communicates with all players, he keeps a "talk-to" list on a yellow legal pad. "Just talking really matters," he says. "Take Cal Ripken. If he is playing great and for some reason you don't talk for four or five days, he looks at you and says, 'What's wrong?'" Miller has learned an important lesson: Feedback and recognition go a long way.

———

Store managers at the St. Ann branch of Famous-Barr department stores, based in St. Louis, MO, go to each employee at the end of the day to see what went well for them that day, rather than wait for a weekly or monthly report. Those positive items are worked into the next morning's store rally. "It's been a very effective way to reinforce good news on a timely basis and charge employees up to do their best every single day," says Dan Eppler, merchandise sales manager for the company.

———

Joe DeLuce, director of recreation for Champaign Park District in Champaign, IL, says it's important to bring up the topic of praise with your staff: "In our department staff meetings we recently asked everyone to say when they last thanked someone. Every one of the thirty people in the room talked about how they had thanked one of their staff or someone else in our department that day or within the last week. One staff member talked about one of her staff members going above and beyond, and since that staff person was in the room, it became very emotional. We talked about how important it is to thank people for doing outstanding work and that we want to be a department that appreciates others."

———

R obert Maurer, in his book *One Small Step Can Change Your Life,* describes working with a reluctant manager, Michael, to get him to start praising his employees:

"I asked him to imagine giving a person from his department a specific, detailed compliment in an enthusiastic tone of voice, as if there were no problems at all with this person's work. He was to imagine how he would stand in front of the person, how it would feel to approach the person with a relaxed, open posture, how his voice would sound, and what any ambient sounds or smells there might be.

"I wanted Michael to start with compliments for a couple of reasons. Like most people, Michael found it easier to give criticism than compliments. But I also knew that a likely result of letting trouble in his department percolate for too long was that Michael would see his employees as nothing but a collection of problems. And from another perspective, psychological research clearly shows that people who feel underappreciated tend to resent criticism and

> **"The way positive reinforcement is carried out is more important than the amount."**
>
> —B. F. SKINNER,
> Psychologist

> **❝Recognition is so easy to do and so inexpensive to distribute that there is simply no excuse for not doing it.❞**
>
> —ROSABETH MOSS KANTER,
> Author and
> Management Consultant

ignore the advice they're given. By practicing giving compliments, Michael was not only learning to feel comfortable doing something that felt unnatural to him. He was also developing a skill that would increase the satisfaction and productivity of his employees.

The small, active steps of mental rehearsal taught Michael a new set of skills, as well as a sense of the ease and reward of offering praise. At the end of three months, Michael found himself frequently stopping in hallways to give fifteen- or twenty-second recognition to deserving employees."

———

A ccording to Phoebe Farrow Port, vice president of Estée Lauder, founder Leonard Lauder spent a limited amount of time with executives on store visits, preferring to meet with floor people. Phoebe says, "One day, I saw him reach across a counter and say, 'Sorry to interrupt. My name is Leonard Lauder. I hear you are one of the beauty advisors. Thank you for everything you are doing for Estée Lauder.'" As they walked away on one such occasion, Phoebe said, "Mr. Lauder, you're so good at this." He said, "I put myself on a quota of three thank-you's a day years ago. I suggest you do the same." Phoebe adds, "Everywhere the man goes, he writes a personal note to whomever he meets."

———

Written Praise & Recognition

Written praise, considered by employees to be the next most valued type of praise, comes in several varieties. Here is how employees ranked different forms in terms of importance: "letters of praise are placed in the employee's personnel file" (72 percent); "being given written praise" (61 percent); "being given a written note of thanks" (59 percent); and "being given a thank-you card" (48 percent).

A survey by the International Association of Administrative Professionals (IAAP) revealed that as many as 30 percent of professional secretaries would be happy with a simple letter of appreciation from their managers, but only 7 percent of respondents reported having ever received such a letter. In another study, positive written communication was found to be very important in motivating employees; however, this technique was used by only 24 percent of managers.

Writing notes to employees who have performed well at the end of the day is an effective recognition strategy, claims Steve Wittert, president of Paragon Steakhouse Restaurants, based in San Diego. Wittert finds that his days are so busy that he seldom has time to personally recognize his staff. Instead, he keeps a stack of note cards on his desk, and when the pace slows down at the end of the day, he takes a few minutes to jot personal notes to the individuals who made a difference that day.

At the end of each year, I write an individual letter to each of my employees, specifically listing highlights of their performance that I was proud of over the past year. This takes less time than you might think, and the impact on employees is more significant than you might imagine!

Joe Floren of Tektronix, Inc., a manufacturer of oscilloscopes and other electronic instruments located in Beaverton, OR, likes to tell the story of the "You Done Good Award." A former communications manager, Floren recalls having coffee a number of years ago with his boss, a vice president. The boss said he'd been mulling over a problem stemming from the company's rapid growth. He thought the company was getting so big that it needed a formal recognition program. He had read some personnel handbooks on the subject and began telling Floren about several variations on the gold watch traditionally given for good work.

The boss's proposition sounded ludicrous to Floren. So he challenged Floren to come up with something better. Floren suggested drawing up a card called the "You Done Good Award" and letting employees give it to fellow employees.

To his surprise, the vice president agreed. Floren had some note cards printed and started distributing them. They caught on, and the informal awards have become part of life in the company. "Even though people say nice things to you," Floren says, "it means something more when people take the time to write their name on a piece of paper and say it. Employees usually post them next to their desks."

Janis Allen, a performance management consultant, tells the story of a group of officers she was training in the Department of the Army. One person in particular, a colonel, showed great resistance to the use of any reinforcers. A week or so after the seminar, the colonel's manager—a general—wanted to praise him for his handling of an important presentation. The general found a piece of yellow construction paper, folded it in half, and wrote "Bravo" on the front. Then he wrote his reinforcing remarks inside.

The colonel was called in, praised, and given the card. "He took it and read it," Allen says, "and didn't even look up when he finished. He just stood up abruptly without making eye contact, turned, and walked out of the office." The general thought, "Wow, I've done something wrong now." He thought maybe he had offended the colonel.

However, when the general later went to check on the colonel, he found that he had stopped at every office on the way out and was showing off the "Bravo" card. He was smiling and everybody was congratulating him.

The colonel subsequently printed his own recognition cards with "Wonderful" on the front. They became his signature reinforcers.

———

At SeaWorld San Diego, team leaders give "spotlight cards" to employees when they see them doing something well. They write down what they observed and what they liked about it, get at least two other leaders or supervisors to sign the card, and then present it to the employee. A copy is also posted on the employee bulletin board.

———

SAY IT IN WRITING

- *Make a thank-you card by hand.*

- *Post a thank-you note on the employee's office door.*

- *Write a "letter of praise" to employees to recognize their specific contributions and accomplishments; send a copy to your boss or higher managers and to the personnel department.*

- *Provide managers with specially printed packets of thank-you cards to hand out to employees who do exceptional work.*

- *Ask your boss, a very senior manager, or the CEO to send a letter of acknowledgment or thanks to individuals or groups who make significant contributions.*

> 66Recognition is the most inexpensive, easy-to-use motivational technique available to management. Yet the degree to which this essential improvement tool is underused by most otherwise intelligent managers is bewildering.99
>
> —JIM CLEMMER,
> Author and President,
> The Clemmer Group

Kelly McNamara at Raytheon Aircraft Company wanted to cut down on all the red tape before an employee could be rewarded. So she and her team brought back an award—employee-to-employee thank-you notes featuring the "Beechcraft Busy Bee" cartoon (used many years ago by Beechcraft, a company that Raytheon acquired in the early 1980s)—which could be given to anyone by anyone in the company with no approval required.

———

In Marietta, GA, Wellstar Health System created a simple peer-to-peer leadership recognition program called "The Seven Attributes of Stars." According to Wellstar, these attributes are: communicating, global thinking, people-developing, lifelong learning, innovating, goal-achieving, and service-leading. Managers are given printed notepads and asked to check off the attributes that are embodied by fellow leaders and describe why they should be recognized for them. Any leader who is recognized for five or more attributes is publicly acknowledged at the next quarterly leadership meeting and gets to select a book from among five choices.

———

A CASE STUDY IN WRITTEN PRAISE

When it comes to recognizing employees, most companies have trouble holding their managers accountable. After all, how can you force someone to be nice to their employees? Plus, if you do make them do something they don't want to do, won't they resent it and undermine your effort anyway?

They didn't think so at Bronson Healthcare Group in Kalamazoo, MI, currently ranked as one of the "Best Places to Work in America" by *Fortune* magazine. Six to seven years ago, the organization decided to stop focusing on the small number of people who do not conform to their expectations and to start focusing, recognizing, and rewarding the 95 percent who are doing good work. It took some four years to ingrain this philosophy, but a systematic focus on their recognition practices has clearly made them an employer of choice.

For example, they asked all managers to write twelve thank-you notes per quarter, and to show them to their own managers as proof that they were indeed recognizing their employees. Additionally, human resources did random spot-checks on managers, asking to see copies of thank-you notes, and if a manager didn't have them, he or she was asked to schedule a "little talk" with the senior leader of the group. They've never had to schedule more than one talk before managers quickly got the message that the organization was serious about this activity.

Better yet, managers who started writing notes quickly discovered that they were being

> **❝**The most important factor is individual recognition—more important than salaries, bonuses, or promotions. Most people, whether they're engineers, business managers, or machine operators, want to be creative. They want to identify with the success of their profession and their organization. They want to contribute to giving society more comfort, better health, more excitement. And their greatest reward is receiving acknowledgment that they did contribute to making something meaningful happen.**❞**
>
> —PAUL M. COOK,
> Founder and CEO,
> Raychem Corporation

MAKE USE OF NEWSPAPERS TO PRAISE EMPLOYEES PUBLICLY

■ *Write and publish a personal ad or publicity article in the local newspaper or company publication praising the person for a job well-done.*

■ *Send information about an accomplishment to the appropriate trade publication and the individual's home-town newspaper.*

■ *Take out a full-page advertisement in a local newspaper every year and thank every employee by name for his or her contribution.*

rewarded by their employees for those very notes! Now, new leaders in the organization are oriented to the practice from the very start of their jobs.

The thank-you note program has since expanded so that managers now send notes to employees' families or even to their children (sometimes with coupons for ice cream so they can take their parents out), and employees are increasingly writing more thank-you notes to their peers.

As a result of all this focus (and related activities), Bronson Healthcare Group's turnover has dropped drastically, and they now have a waiting list for employees who want to work at the hospital. They have also been named a "best practice" in several national databases for nurse retention, as well as listed on *Fortune*'s "Working Mothers' Best Employer" lists.

Following are other real-life examples of effective written recognition.

———

Markeeta Graban, associate director of the department of psychiatry at the University of Michigan Health System, reports: "It's really true that anything can be a significant form of recognition. Over three years ago I drew a star on a piece of scrap paper, colored it, and gave it to someone for helping me out that day. They in turn gave it to someone else. It took on special significance with each use. Now we have it on a magnetic backing and pass it on to someone who has helped or is having a rough day. People love it!"

———

"We try to emphasize peer-to-peer recognition on our Organizational Development Team," reports Debbie Liles, supervisor of OD at EMC Mortgage Corporation. One of the ways they do that is by using a form called the Appreciation/Recognition Form. Teammates complete the form when they observe someone exhibiting the behavior(s) EMC Mortgage values. These are deposited in a beautifully decorated box throughout the month. At every monthly team meeting, all the certificates are read out loud. Certificate recipients get to pick their favorite candy bars or healthy snacks from the reward grab bag.

"A more informal way that we recognize/ appreciate team members at EMC Mortgage Corporation in Irving, Texas, is through 'Notes to My Terrific Teammate,'" reports Debbie Liles. They post notes on colored paper on teammates' walls, and do it when they're not around, so they can be pleasantly surprised by the latest "fan mail." When the sheets are filled up, more sheets are passed out.

CalPERS, the California Public Employees' Retirement System, based in Sacramento, uses "Steady as a Rock" note cards shaped in the image of a rock, as well as mounted, pass-around rocks, to recognize behind-the-scenes daily performance by coworkers.

> "Recognition is something a manager should be doing all the time; it's a running dialogue with people."
>
> —RON ZEMKE,
> Senior Editor,
> *Training*

The New England Aquarium allows employees to recognize coworkers with a "thank-you cod" (a card shaped like a codfish)—a play on the New England accent. "Half the card goes to the employee and the other half goes into a quarterly lottery for gift certificates for paid time off, the company store, and local restaurants," reports Linda Hower, learning technologist for Gilbane University in Providence, RI.

Ginny Heard, supervisor of member correspondence at an AARP office in Lakewood, CA, has a simple yet effective recognition technique she developed when previously employed by Airborne Express. She cut an apple out of construction paper, wrote "Look for Teachable Moments" on it, and used the note as an icebreaker for discussing learning points or lessons in an employee's job performance. The award became very popular, and many other managers followed her lead. Everyone liked receiving the apples, and the notes became collectibles.

If one of Marty Stowe's employees at the New England Regional Office for Paychex in Boston is working extremely hard, Stowe sends a handwritten note to inform his or her spouse. If this employee really outdoes him- or herself, Stowe gives the husband and wife a gift certificate for dinner for two.

At Lands' End in Dodgeville, WI, CEO Mike Smith personally reviews all of his mail. If he finds a letter from a customer who mentions an employee by name, he jots a simple note to the employee and forwards a copy of the letter to him or her. Employees love these personal kudos from the CEO and post them up in their work cubicles.

———

Jimmy Collins, president of Chick-fil-A, the Atlanta-based restaurant chain, writes personal notes of thanks on P&L sheets that he returns to owner-operators.

———

Doubt that little acts of recognition mean a lot? In her book *What I Saw at the Revolution,* former president Ronald Reagan's speechwriter Peggy Noonan writes about a personal note she received from the president. She had been writing for him for four months, and had not yet met him, when one day President Reagan wrote "Very Good" on one of her speech drafts. First she stared at it. Then she took a pair of scissors and cut it off and taped it to her blouse, like a second-grader with a star. All day, people noticed it and looked at her and she beamed back at them.

———

Joan Padgett of the learning resources center at Veterans' Medical Center in Dayton, OH, reports, "I recently decided to take the time to give a welcome card to a new employee and

> **❝**Men and women want to do a good job, a creative job, and if they are provided the proper environment, they will do so.**❞**
>
> —BILL HEWLETT,
> Cofounder,
> Hewlett-Packard

> **❝**In the twenty years I have been doing this and the thousands of employees I have interviewed, if I had to pick one thing that comes through to me loud and clear, it is that organizations do a lousy job of recognizing people's contributions. That is the number one thing employees say to us. 'We don't even care about the money; if my boss would just say thank you, if he or she would just acknowledge that I exist. The only time I ever hear anything is when I screw up. I never hear when I do a good job.' Recognition programs are a very important element of your total compensation program.**❞**
>
> —CATHERINE MEEK,
> President,
> Meek and Associates

wrote a personal note, saying, 'At the end of some days you'll feel elated; after some you'll feel completely drained; but may you always leave your office knowing you contributed to our organization.' The employee was thrilled and said she would keep the card always. Her emotional response convinced me of the value of giving cards to thank, congratulate, welcome, and celebrate employees."

———

Angela Gann at Kaiser Permanente sends personal notes to anyone she interviews for a job, but saves a really special greeting for the new hire, decorating the person's workstation on the first morning with glitter stars or banners.

———

According to the Department of Organization, Development, and Training at Busch Gardens-Tampa, the company gives a "Pat on the Back Award" to employees who do an outstanding job, and places a notice of the award in the employee's file.

———

The *San Francisco Business Times* had paper tablets printed with different headlines, such as "Saved the Day," "Bit the Bullet," and "Went Above and Beyond," which they gave to employees whenever they did an exceptional job. Soon, everyone had lots of the notes, and people were feeling more appreciated.

———

John Plunkett, director of employment and training for Cobb Electric Membership Corporation in Marietta, GA, says, "People love to collect other people's business cards. Simply carry a supply of your cards with you and as you 'catch people doing something right,' immediately write 'Thanks,' 'Good job,' 'Keep it up,' and what they specifically did in two to three words. Put the person's name on the card and sign it."

———

"An engineer on my staff spent an extended amount of time on the road doing environmental evaluations of companies," reports Michael L. Horvath, director of environmental projects for FirstEnergy Corporation, headquartered in Akron, OH: "I sent a letter to his three school-age children explaining why their dad was gone so much lately and that he was doing special 'secret agent' work that was very important for our company. His wife called the next day to say how excited their kids were that Dad was a 'secret agent!'"

———

The "Reward of Excellence" program at Herbalife, the health and nutrition company based in Inglewood, CA, uses two-part cards, called "WOW!" cards, to recognize employees. Employees fill them out to praise coworkers for service, teamwork, etc. One part goes to the honoree, the other goes into a recognition box, and the contents are reviewed each month by a six-member recognition committee. The committee

> **"**If human beings are perceived as potentials rather than problems, as possessing strengths instead of weaknesses, as unlimited rather that dull and unresponsive, then they thrive and grow to their capabilities.**"**
>
> —ROBERT CONKLIN,
> American Teacher,
> Author & Speaker

> **❝I try to remember that people—good, intelligent, capable people—may actually need day-to-day praise and thanks for the job they do. I try to remember to get up out of my chair, turn off my computer, go sit or stand next to them and see what they're doing, ask about the challenges, find out if they need additional help, offer that help if possible, and most of all, tell them in all honesty that what they are doing is important: to me, to the company, and to our customers.❞**
>
> —JOHN BALL,
> Service Training Manager,
> American Honda
> Motor Company

selects the best "WOW!" card employee, and posts the card on the "WOW!" bulletin board. The winner then gets points toward merchandise purchases, as well as raffle tickets for a cruise drawing, which is held at the end of every six months. All honorees are also automatically entered into the company's "All Star" program for additional recognition and visibility.

To make the program as successful as possible, Herbalife started with a three-month trial period, during which they collected feedback and suggestions. For example, when they discovered that employees didn't like paying shipping and handling for the merchandise they selected, the company built those amounts into the awards and slightly increased the number of points required. Besides increasing recognition, other benefits emerged as well. Ana Franklin, senior manager of the Order Support Department, identified three: (1) the program helped employees set more specific goals and provided systematic tracking of results; (2) it costs less than previous programs, yet has a longer-term impact, replacing what had previously been a hit-and-miss approach (such as occasional distribution of gas cards and gift certificates); and (3) employees can now include their families in selecting merchandise, which is an added motivational incentive.

———

Jeffrey S. Wells, senior vice president of human resources for Circuit City Stores, Inc., based in Richmond, VA, has his administrative assistant place note cards on his desk each month for him to write personal notes to employees who have anniversaries with the companies. It's a time commitment, but well worth the effort, and he enjoys keeping in touch with his employees in this small way.

———

Don Eggleston, director of organizational development at SSM Healthcare in St. Louis, says, "I mark my calendar and then send cards or flowers to employees on the anniversary of important events in their lives. For example, I've sent cards on the anniversary of a parent's death or for a child's graduation or birthday. These are subtle ways of letting employees know I'm interested without prying into their lives. After all, we're working with human beings, and we can all be more effective and sensitive if we understand one another better."

———

> ❝I consider my ability to arouse enthusiasm among men the greatest asset I possess. The way to develop the best that is in a man is by appreciation and encouragement.❞
>
> —CHARLES SCHWAB,
> Founder,
> The Charles Schwab
> Corporation

Electronic Praise & Recognition

Electronic praise is similar to written praise, but it is transmitted more readily and often with less effort than the latter. Praising via e-mail, voice-mail, cell phone, pager, fax, or other forms of technology is increasingly important to today's employees, who are spending more and more time on "electronic leashes," interfacing more with their computers and less with their bosses or coworkers. Although today's office technology can make us more efficient, it also tends to have an alienating effect, creating more distance in work relationships and more stress as we are increasingly expected to be "available" 24/7.

A recent study by Pitney Bowes on messaging tools and practices reveals that U.S. workers are now receiving over 200 messages per day—more than ever before. What's the impact of this constant bombardment of messages and increased use of office technology? How can managers best recognize employee performance when an employee may not even have physical contact with his or her manager for weeks or months at a time?

Managers must take a proactive role in fostering a sense of teamwork by establishing regular, mutually agreed-upon communication times. Telephone calls, e-mail, teleconferences, videoconferences, and chat areas can all be conducted at an agreed-upon time. Additionally, message boards can be used for ongoing communication about progress on critical aspects of teamwork. Communicating in these ways gives virtual employees the opportunity to exchange ideas with team members, talk about problems, discuss ways to improve, evaluate the team's progress, share ideas, get feedback, brainstorm new ideas, discuss strategies, and acknowledge success.

For these reasons, it is increasingly important to use technology in positive ways to reinforce good work and encourage the human spirit. Employees increasingly perceive electronic praise as a critical motivator in their jobs. For example, in research I've conducted, over 70 percent of employees indicate that having a positive e-mail forwarded to them is very or extremely important to them, followed by "being copied on positive e-mail messages" (65 percent); "being given a praising via e-mail" (43 percent); and "being given a praising on voice-mail" (26 percent).

Here's some additional advice that can help keep the human element at work even as we make a greater use of technology:

1. Get to know people before you communicate electronically. All rapport comes from shared experiences. Trust and respect are difficult to establish through the exclusive use of electronic exchanges. Since an estimated 90 percent of all communication occurs at the nonverbal level, what you don't see in your interactions might hurt your relationships.

2. Be aware of technology's limitations when you communicate. Don't have electronic communication replace a personal meeting just for the efficiency of it. Think of when it works well to use voice-mail or e-mail, for example, and when a personal meeting would be better. Avoid the use of electronic communication for dealing with sensitive or complex issues, which would be better dealt with in face-to-face interaction.

3. Use electronic communication to enhance relationships. I know one manager who makes a point of using his cell phone to leave "thank-you" voice-mails for others as he commutes home each evening, reflecting on the day's events. He keeps his messages 100 percent positive and avoids rolling them over into work problems or additional assignments. I know another manager who copies *his* manager on all complimentary e-mails he sends to any of his employees. When it comes time for performance reviews and salary actions, his manager always agrees with his recommendations because he's been kept in the loop the entire year.

4. Use technology to expand your scope of recognition. In discussions and decision making, technology can help you include others who might have been cumbersome to incorporate in the past. For example, Home Depot has weekly satellite feeds to every store that they call "Breakfast with Bernie and Arthur," their chairman and CEO. It's a chance for everyone to hear what's new and how things are going. A.G. Edwards, the financial services company, has a weekly audio conference that includes every employee on-line. I know of another company that audiotapes a monthly message to employees, which they can listen to at their convenience. Web chats, message boards, and dedicated phone lines for employee access to top management are other possibilities companies are using today to keep employees more connected and to allow them to play an integral role in their organizations.

5. Use the power of technology to amplify good news. Find ways to pass on positive information to your staff, such as forwarding them the news or publicly thanking them via e-mail. At a Hughes Network Systems office in San Diego, for example, they use an "Applause" electronic pop-up bulletin board on their Intranet system, to which any employee can post thanks and recognition to any other employee. Employees get to see the latest praise each time they log on to their computers. In these days of relentless pressure and change in most organizations, hearing what's going well becomes a salve to relieve our stress and frustrations. Use technology to highlight any good news as it occurs and don't forget to use e-mail and voice-mail to leave a positive word of thanks.

Since there tends to be a fine line between stress and excitement in most jobs today, a positive use of technology can go a long way toward creating more positive work relationships and a more human and supportive work environment.

———

Chris Higgins, senior vice president of project planning at Bank of America's Services Division in Virginia, says, "It is so important to give everyone credit. I always try to find out who is going above and beyond the call of duty. My team is usually spread out over the country, so I wander over the telephone wires or pop in unexpectedly on conference calls. It is not a huge effort; it mainly takes discipline, but has tremendous payoff."

> ❝The more high technology around us, the more the need for the human touch.❞
>
> —JOHN NAISBITT,
> Author,
> *Megatrends*

Barbara Green, office manager for Buckingham, Doolittle & Burroughs, LLP, in Canton, OH, reports: "We sent an e-mail to our entire staff asking everyone to applaud the great efforts of our office services department at 4 P.M. at their desks. Members of that department work throughout the building and are rarely in one place at the same time, so this was a terrific way for each staff member to receive the benefit of the praise at exactly the same time and in the same way."

At Business First in Louisville, KY, the advertising department sends a broadcast voice-mail daily with a motivational message, joke, success story, or whatever helps the team get excited about its workday.

Edward Nickel, regional training and development manager for Nordstrom, Inc., in Oak Brook, IL, reports that some Nordstrom stores

> **"**We can invest all the money on Wall Street in new technologies, but we can't realize the benefits of improved productivity until companies rediscover the value of human loyalty.**"**
>
> —FREDERICK REICHHELD,
> Director,
> Bain & Co.

recognize employees over the store intercom system before the store opens by sharing great letters they have received from customers about exemplary service. Letters are then posted on an employee bulletin board for all to read. Each store manager has his or her own routine, but there is never a dearth of material, and hearing the examples motivates other employees to do the same.

———

Fargo Electronics, based in Eden Prairie, MN, uses an electronic newsletter to keep in touch with employees daily. Information about sales and production figures, customer feedback, and profit-sharing updates with employees are shared daily. At the end of each workday, department heads send information into the company's e-mail system.

———

At a division of General Mills in Plymouth, MN, photos of top achievers are posted on the Web site as "champions," according to retail coupon activity manager Carl Bisson.

———

At Metro Honda in Montclair, CA, the name of the Employee of the Month is posted on the electronic billboard over the dealership. Similarly, the City of Philadelphia used an electronic message board that runs around all four sides of a downtown skyscraper to honor the head of the local school system: "Philadelphia congrats Dr. Constance Clayton on 10 years."

———

Public Praise & Recognition

I n my research, *public* praise ranked as one of the top recognition pref-erences by today's employees. This included the following items being ranked as either very or extremely important to them: "customer letters are publicly shared or posted" (62 percent), "employee is praised in a department/company meeting" (54 percent), "employee is recognized at a company awards ceremony" (46 percent), and "employee is acknowl-edged in the company newsletter" (39 percent). This supports other research that indicates that 76 percent of American workers rank recog-nition at a company meeting as a meaningful incentive.

Most employees perceive the use of public recognition as highly desirable. Performance management consultant Janis Allen notes that it's easy to leverage positive feedback when you hear it by passing it on to others. "When someone says something good about another person and I tell that person about it," Allen says, "she seems to get more reinforce-ment value from it than if she had received the compliment firsthand."

There is almost an endless variety of ways to acknowledge employ-ees publicly. Sharing good news such as positive letters from customers at the beginning of a staff meeting or posting them on a "Good News Bulletin Board" along with other positive information from members of the department can be effective. For example, Childress Buick-Kia, in Phoenix, AZ, focuses its monthly meetings on sharing goals and results, and on publicly recognizing employees who have been nominated by customers or other employees for good service. You could even bring in key customers to your organization to acknowledge deserving employ-ees and send a powerful message about the importance of customer service.

Dr. Jo-Anne Pitera, director of corporate education and training for Florida Power and Light in Juno Beach, suggests putting a flip chart next to the elevator door where people can list thank-you's and successes for all to see. Pitera also recommends soliciting and announcing nominations for recognition awards for outstanding efforts at department meetings, perhaps in conjunction with a drawing for gifts or money. You can even create a "wall of fame" to show appreciation for top achievers, as they do at the headquarters of KFC.

You can take time at the beginning of department or company-wide meetings to recognize employees as they do at Honeywell Inc.'s industrial fibers plant in Moncure, NC, where employees exchange public praising as part of morning plant-wide meetings. Or you can use the end of meetings for employee recognition. Norman Groh, a customer service manager at a Xerox Corporation office in Irving, TX, ends his management staff meetings on a high note by asking that all managers share one thing they have done to thank their employees since they last met. Besides generating a surge of energy and an exchange of practical ideas, he gives them broader visibility by putting the stories in the employee newsletter.

Allowing employees to acknowledge one another at group meetings can also be very effective. Petro Canada, a large energy company based in Calgary, Alberta, hosts "bragging sessions" to allow employees to share progress they were making against goals with upper management. The meetings have a fun and celebratory feel and generate high energy to continue efforts.

Many companies have a year-end awards banquet, which of course provides lots of opportunities to spotlight individuals and groups. You can bring such ceremonies alive with stories about people's successes and the obstacles they had to overcome to achieve their goals. Tag on to any holiday celebrations you have planned some extra time to thank your staff for their dedication and performance. Look to the future as well, and share the signs you've seen of good things to come.

Most organizations also use company newsletters to recognize employees for a wide range of performance, to thank project teams, and even to share information about employee interests and hobbies.

A division of Hewlett-Packard in San Diego held a day of appreciation for an exceptional employee, computer scientist Jennifer Wallick. Fellow employees reserved 10-minute time slots to visit her, present her with flowers, and thank her for something she had done for them. She was praised every 15 minutes throughout the day.

———

Peter Economy reports that when he worked as a manager for the City of San Diego Housing Commission, all participants at week-long management-training workshops would write down one positive thing on an index card for every other person in the session, an activity they called a "strength barrage." Each individual would then receive his or her index cards and read what everyone else had to say about them out loud.

———

Connie Maxwell of West Des Moines Community Schools says, "I post notes from other departments that have something positive to say about any of us; this way, people who work with me are more inclined to write one to someone else, so there's a mutual sharing of thanks. It's become a point of pride to have a note that one wrote posted."

———

When she worked for Time Warner in Milwaukee, Noelle Sment used an effective stress strategy: a "Bad Day Board," which

> **"Outstanding leaders go out of their way to boost the self-esteem of their personnel. If people believe in themselves, it's amazing what they can accomplish."**
>
> —SAM WALTON,
> Founder,
> Wal-Mart, Inc.

was a list of everyone's names with a magnet that could be moved to indicate who was under a lot of stress, experiencing personal problems, struggling with difficult customers, etc. Initially meant to serve as a warning system for others, the group soon started cheering up anyone who was having a "bad day," and having a lot of fun in the process!

_____

Xerox Corporation, headquartered in Stamford, CT, gives Bellringer Awards: when an employee is recognized, a bell is rung in the corridor. Pacific Gas & Electric rings a ship's bell every time someone makes a noteworthy achievement. And the special markets department at Workman Publishing in New York City uses a cheap party noisemaker when any employee wants to share good news with the group. Everyone within earshot comes running.

_____

Chris Giangrasso, director of management and organizational development for Philadelphia's ARAMARK Corporation, which provides food and leisure services and textile rentals, suggests organizing a day of appreciation for a worthy person. ARAMARK schedules a day in honor of the person (for example, Bob Jones Day), and sends a notice to all employees announcing the date and the reason for the honor. The honoree enjoys all sorts of frills, such as computer banners and a free lunch.

_____

Chris Ortiz, at NASA's Johnson Space Center in Houston, reports: "After reading *1001 Ways to Reward Employees,* I created an award for all my team members who helped me. I call it my Thanks-a-Million Award. It contains a thank-you note taped to ten $100 Grand candy bars. Recipients break them up and pass them on to others who have helped them."

The president of a teacher's union in Vancouver explains that when he worked in the construction industry, what started as a joke became a coveted honor each workday. One morning, a foreman placed a yellow rubber ducky on the desk of the person who had done a great job the previous day. The tradition continued and soon everyone looked forward to seeing who would receive the day's honor.

A government contractor based in Pensacola, FL, tells us, "I'm the maintenance manager supervising sixty-four jet mechanics for a company that contracts out to the U.S. Navy's flight school. These rough-and-tough men love it when I tape a pinwheel or a balloon to a plane they're working on, signifying that the jet engine has passed every test with flying colors."

At San Francisco–based Jossey-Bass, Inc., a division of publisher John Wiley & Sons, all employees have nameplates from their first day on the job. They are made with an etching

> **"In an environment where there is a shared vision of excellence, where people can be the best they can be on a daily basis, where they know what is expected of them, understand that reward is linked to performance, and believe they can make a difference because they will be heard, they will make a difference. They will go beyond our expectations and great things will start to happen."**
>
> —FREDERICK W. SMITH,
> CEO,
> FedEx Corporation

> **❝We realized that our largest asset was our workforce and that our growth would come from asset appreciation.❞**
>
> —LARRY COLIN,
> President,
> Colin Service Systems

machine and slipped into a slot on the employee's door or desk. This not only makes newcomers feel welcome, but also helps their colleagues to remember their names.

———

Whenever possible, allow employees to connect their names with their work. Home Depot posts workers' names on signs, such as "This aisle maintained by Jerry Olson."

———

At a Bloomington, IN, hospital cafeteria, sandwiches are named in honor of the "Employees of the Month" and those who have received the most commendations from patients. Items stay on the menu for six months.

———

Wells Fargo Bank has developed some unusual no-cost rewards, such as renaming an item in the cafeteria after a deserving employee or presenting a bag of fertilizer, supplied by the keepers of the Wells Fargo stagecoach horses themselves.

———

All employees at Apple Computer in Cupertino, CA, who worked on the first Macintosh computer had their signatures placed on the inside of the product. Employees at Cooper Tire & Rubber Company of Findlay, OH, are allowed to stamp their names on the inside of the tires they produce so they can be recognized for their contributions.

When Southwest Airlines achieved the best on-time performance and baggage-handling, and the fewest complaints per customer for the fifth year in a row, it dedicated an airplane to all of its 25,000 employees and placed all of their names on the outside of the overhead bins.

———

Federal Express in Memphis used to inscribe the name of an employee's child in large letters on the nose of each new airplane it purchased. The company held a lottery to select the name and flew the child's family to the manufacturing plant for the christening.

———

Ford Motor Company, AT&T, and Meridian Health in New Jersey use their employees in commercials.

———

A CASE STUDY IN PUBLIC RECOGNITION

In the Electro-Optics Division of Honeywell Inc., in Minneapolis, financial difficulties were causing a serious dip in morale that was leading to additional problems. The company needed to turn the situation around, but had to do so on a very low budget, given the state of the division. Seeking a creative solution, managers developed a recognition program called Great Performers. "The division was looking for top performance from its employees," says Deborah van Rooyen, program director, "and that got me thinking that top performance comes from top performers, and

---

THE MOST BEAUTIFUL SOUND ... YOUR NAME

■ *Use the person's first name when delivering a compliment.*

■ *Greet employees by name when you pass their desks or in the hall.*

■ *When discussing an employee's ideas with other people, make sure you give credit.*

■ *Acknowledge individual achievements by using employees' names when preparing status reports.*

■ *Name a continuing recognition award after an outstanding employee.*

■ *Ask five people in your department or company to go up to the person during the day and say, "[Your name] asked me to thank you for [the task or achievement]. Good job!"*

CAPTURE THE MOMENT

■ *Create a Hall of Fame wall with photos of outstanding employees.*

■ *Take a photo of the person being congratulated by his or her boss's boss. Place photographs of top performers in the lobby.*

■ *Make a photo collage about a successful project that shows the people who worked on it, its stages of development, and its completion and presentation.*

■ *Create a "yearbook" to be displayed in the lobby that contains everybody's photograph, along with his or her best achievement of the year.*

■ *Create a "Good Tries" booklet to recognize those whose innovations didn't achieve full potential. Be sure to include what was learned during the project so that this information can benefit others.*

that got me thinking about top performers everyone is familiar with."

Van Rooyen spent a month in the local library researching the lives of great performers in politics, education, social work, business, science, and the arts. All the people she studied had one characteristic in common: They succeeded by overcoming obstacles.

Van Rooyen's idea was to put together a program in which these people's well-known accomplishments would be celebrated alongside those of division employees. She hoped that the possibility of being named a Great Performer would inspire employees to put forth their best efforts.

"Turnaround begins with small accomplishments," van Rooyen says, "so we wanted to convey the idea that every job is important. For example, we wanted to encourage secretaries to type a letter only once, and to encourage employees in the shipping department to be careful enough that nothing would get broken, and so forth."

Management accepted the idea, and van Rooyen worked with the division's staff to finalize the list of forty celebrity Great Performers, being careful to include men, women, minorities, and teams.

A teaser campaign then followed featuring the celebrity Great Performers with memorable quotes. Employees were invited to nominate Great Performers in the company and were asked to explain the reasons for their nominations. A committee of volunteers reviewed the nominees. All were given pins in the shape of the letter *G* (for great) and the committee selected five employees they thought best exemplified the spirit of the program. These winners were interviewed, and stories were created to use on posters that looked just like the ones featuring the celebrities. Each included the employee's photo, a quote, and a description of the employee's achievements and contributions.

"The posters were a visible way to help boost self-esteem," says Chuck Madaglia, division public relations manager. "The idea was to catch employees doing something right and get them feeling good about themselves."

The response was overwhelmingly positive. The Great Performers became corporate celebrities overnight, and everyone wanted to be one. Many more individuals had the chance: five new employees were selected each month during the year the program was in place. Morale improved dramatically, and the ongoing program encouraged employees to make changes in work habits, make successful proposal bids, begin recycling scrap, and improve quality control. Within six months, the division was in the black, thanks in part to the success of the program.

Bob Gaundi, human resources manager of Mental Health Systems in San Diego, says: "Certainly recognition from supervisors is important, but praise from fellow employees is of the highest order, so we allow employees to recognize coworkers through a monthly newsletter. We ask employees to write a short statement about laudable efforts they witness from fellow

> **"Provide positive, immediate, and certain consequences for people's behaviors, and they will do what you want."**
>
> —BARCY FOX,
> Vice President,
> Performance Systems,
> Maritz, Inc.

☑ *Introduce top management to individuals and groups who have made significant contributions.*

☑ *Use charts or posters to show how well an employee or group is performing.*

☑ *Develop a Behind the Scenes Award for those whose actions are not usually in the limelight.*

☑ *Name a space after an employee and put up a sign (The Suzy Jones Corridor, for example).*

☑ *Honor peers who have helped you by recognizing them at meetings. Mention the outstanding work or idea brought to your attention by an employee during your staff meetings or at meetings with your peers and managers.*

☑ *Recognize people who recognize others.*

employees. All of the examples are published in a special section of our monthly newsletter. Employees always turn to this section first!"

———

At Stew Leonard's in Norwalk, CT, the company newsletter overflows with news of accomplishments, customer comments, and employee contests, such as the offer of a $5 reward to the first employee who deciphered the meaning of a performance chart that measured some aspect of the store's operation.

———

Jackson, MI, Chick-fil-A marketing coordinator Tara Hayes produces a newsletter highlighting individual accomplishments both at work and in the community. She also includes feature stories on deserving teams.

———

At Label House Group Limited, a medium-sized brand identity and packaging solution company located in Trinidad and Tobago, one of the most frequent ways of recognizing employees is through the internal newsletter, under the heading "Caught You Doing Something Right," according to Shelly-Ann Jaggarnath, human resources officer for the company. On a quarterly basis, employees caught exhibiting the desired behaviors and attitudes, or going beyond the call of duty, are profiled in the newsletter and given small tokens of recognition, such as cooler bags.

———

At H. J. Heinz, based in Pittsburgh, routinely shares information about employees at all levels of the organization in its internal publications and annual reports, including personal details about their lives, their off-the-job pursuits, and even their poetry. At Collins & Aikman Floorcoverings, a carpet manufacturer in Dalton, GA, the company recognizes and lists the achievements of employees' children in its newsletter.

———

Publix Super Markets, based in Lakeland, FL, publishes a biweekly bulletin that lists the births, deaths, marriages, and serious illnesses of employees and their families. For more than twenty years, the president sent personalized cards to the families of everyone listed in the bulletin.

———

Chuck King of the East Longview and Longview Mall Chick-fil-A's in Longview, TX, highlights employee success in the local newspaper and offers Chick-fil-A sandwiches to all students who provide proof of perfect school attendance.

———

At Claire's in Wood Dale, IL, district managers reward a manager by working his or her store on a Saturday. The regional managers also have a traveling trophy cup, which they fill with goodies (and items related to the award) as it is passed from one district manager to another.

> **"Everyone who works gets paid—but not everyone gets recognition. That's why it means so much to people."**
>
> —Bob Nelson

At Kragen Auto Parts, based in Phoenix, AZ, the president and other top executives served dinner to all store managers at their annual meeting as a thanks for a job well done.

RHC (Resident Home Company), a nonprofit agency that supports individuals with developmental disabilities in Cincinnati, sets up a quarterly car wash for its 200 employees (and the general public) on a Friday when they are getting their paychecks. "We feel that this is a great motivating tool that the administrative team will take three hours of their day to serve them like they serve others," says Larry Mullins, human resources director. "We also feel this is a great way to show the general public around us that we are a great organization to work for, and it gives us time to discuss with them what we are about—important aspects for a nonprofit agency that depends on financial and volunteer support from the local community." RHC also hosts "Massage Days" twice a year, when they bring in a massage therapist and allow employees to sign up for 15-minute slots.

☑ Present "State of the Place" reports periodically to your employees, acknowledging the work and contributions of individuals and groups.

☑ Establish a place to display memos, posters, photos, and so on, recognizing progress toward goals and thanking individual employees for their help.

When Norwest Banks (now a part of Wells Fargo) hosted a sales and service conference in Orlando, FL, all the executives lined up on the sidewalk and applauded employees as they disembarked from the buses and entered the resort. "It really made everyone feel very special," reported Victoria Gomez, a bank vice president from Columbia, MD.

PART II

INFORMAL INTANGIBLE RECOGNITION

This section concerns informal recognition that goes beyond mere praise: support and involvement, autonomy and authority, flexible work hours and time off, learning and career development, and manager availability and time—all presented in order of importance, as reported by today's employees. Surprisingly, this category of nebulous concepts and activities represents one of the greatest sources of motivation for employees today, underscoring a basic trust and respect between an employee and manager that defines their relationship.

Few managers think of the intangibles discussed in this section as "recognition," yet they matter increasingly to today's employees. As Dr. Gerald H. Graham, professor of management at Wichita State University, has observed: "Managers have found that simply asking for employee involvement is motivational in itself." It is also motivational to

involve someone in setting goals, giving them a choice of work assignment, being accessible to them when they most need you, and supporting them when they make a mistake.

The suggestions in this section will be all the more motivational if you are clear about how and when they are used. For example, having an employee attend a meeting for you could at first blush seem like an attempt on your part to dodge yet another boring meeting (and maybe it is!). But if you position the assignment as a form of recognition, and an opportunity for learning and gaining visibility, it can be extremely motivating to the employee you're sending.

In all my research, and that of others, *informal* recognition and reward activities show up as more important than traditional, formal rewards. Their immediacy helps to underscore the importance of the behavior or achievement. When provided by a person the employee holds in high esteem, be it his or her immediate manager, a colleague, or a customer, informal recognition helps to give context and meaning to one's work, leading in turn to increased pride in one's job and an increased affiliation with the organization.

As in all forms of reward and recognition, the ideas in this section and in the rest of the book will be most effective if they are tailored to the individual preferences of the employees being recognized. You can ask people what motivates them one-on-one or by having them share that information in a group setting, thus allowing for a broader range of people knowing how to thank one another in the work group. You can also incorporate recognition into your work plans by asking, "If we attain our goals (finish this project, etc.), what would be rewarding to you (or the group)?" Or you can rotate the responsibility for recognition among individuals on your staff, allowing each member to decide who should be recognized, for what, and how.

Most people think spontaneity means acting without planning, yet it is possible to plan for spontaneity. In fact, when it comes to employee recognition, the better you plan, the better the chance that you will be able to take advantage of recognition opportunities as they arise—rather than thinking weeks or months later that you "probably should have done something."

Information, Support & Involvement

Numerous motivational studies show that employees typically place a high value on getting information about their job, their performance, and how the company is doing. Such information helps employees on both an emotional and practical level. Feeling "in" on things helps them to feel like a valued member of the team—someone who is worth keeping informed. On a practical level, having such information helps them to better perform their responsibilities. When the information is communicated in a personal and timely manner, the experience is even more highly valued.

In my research, the category of "information, support, and involvement" was ranked the highest in importance to employees, with the following items cited as very or extremely important: "manager provides employee information he or she needs" (95 percent); "manager supports employee when he or she makes a mistake" (95 percent); "manager asks employee for his or her opinion or ideas" (92 percent); and "manager involves employee when making decisions" (89 percent). According to a Gallup survey, 61 percent of respondents agreed that having input in company decisions was more important than a share in the ownership of the company.

> **"**An individual without information cannot take responsibility; an individual who is given information cannot help but take responsibility.**"**
>
> —JAN CARLZON,
> CEO,
> SAS

Crillon Importers of Paramus, NJ, the importers of Absolut vodka, and Air France recently started a joint program called Team Talk, designed to improve communication between employees and managers. Employees can call an 800-number to answer surveys and to leave comments and suggestions for managers. Callers gain "air points" redeemable for travel on Air France; some callers are "instant winners," capturing prizes such as personal stereos and phones.

———

Bronson Healthcare Group in Kalamazoo, MI, created a monthly thought-a-day calendar of information related to their hospital and its programs, with entries such as: "Do you know that over $2 million was paid in employee benefits in 2002?" In their internal communications, the organization, uses a "hand" icon next to any idea that initially stemmed from an employee suggestion, signifying "You had a hand."

———

To improve the morale of its drivers, who feel "out of things" because they are often off-site, Barr-Nunn Transportation of Granger, IA, publishes a newsletter and hands out a four-hour cassette tape with industry and company news, information on benefits, and personalized messages such as birthday announcements. Since starting this, the company has experienced a 35 percent reduction in turnover.

———

The Hydraulic Specialty Company in Fridley, MN, shares sales and revenue results with employees. Everyone pulls together without any pressure from management now that they can see how improvements pay off for the bottom line.

———

Terry O'Neal, manager of the Oak Ridge, TN, Chick-fil-A restaurant, opens the books to employees, helping them see how their performance affects the profits, and links performance to month-to-month bonuses.

———

Enterprise Rent-A-Car, headquartered in St. Louis, encourages friendly rivalry between its branch offices by posting the financial results of every branch office and region. New Jersey manager Woody Erhardt explains, "We're this close to beating out Middlesex. If they lose, they have to throw a party for us, and we get to decide what they wear."

———

Employees are invited to make presentations at corporate meetings at Republic Engineered Products in Akron, OH. Videotapes are made and shown at the shareholders' meeting.

———

Each morning at Precision Metalcraft in Winnipeg, Manitoba, management holds "huddles" to pass out the day's work assignments. The huddles end in a cheer as people disperse to get to work. To show they are all on the

> **"**Nothing creates more self-respect among employees than being included in the process of making decisions.**"**
>
> —JUDITH M. BARDWICK
> Management Consultant
> and Author,
> *The Plateauing Trap*

same team, Sheldon Bowles, chairman of the company, moved executives to the shop floor and used their offices to store the company's finished products.

———

Akili Systems Group in Dallas issues mock passports, and new recruits must acquire at least twenty stamps from fellow workers, which they receive for attending a company event, recounting company folklore, or drawing the organizational chart correctly. This unique orientation process helps people become steeped in company values and culture quickly.

———

At FedEx Corporation, based in Memphis, the most popular column in their newsletter is about the company's competition. At Suburu's Illinois plant, employees requested information about new models the company was planning to market, which helped them serve as ambassadors for the products.

———

Shaheen Mufti, women's manager at an Emporio Armani store in Costa Mesa, CA, shares the following "breakthrough" she had with an employee: "When faced with *again* disciplining an employee whose productivity, attendance, adherence to the dress code, and attitude were all out of line, I was so frustrated I pulled him outside the store and blurted, 'I'm really disappointed in you! I *know* you can do this job, but you're just throwing all your potential away.' To my amazement, he decided to live up to my positive opinion of him—he became the top salesperson in the next accounting period."

———

According to Robert Voyles, vice president for marketing services of Carlson Marketing Group in Minneapolis, "One way of ensuring that people are happier at work is to make sure they have friends at the company." That's one of the reasons behind the company's referral program for new hires. A worker receives a small reward when someone he or she referred is hired, then a larger one when the new person completes several months on the job. "When someone recommends someone else, he or she takes pride in—and feels responsible for—that person's work," Voyles says. "If the new person messes up, it's a reflection on the person who recommended him or her."

———

Studies show that receiving personal attention in a new job increases one's chances of success and helps greatly in the socialization process of getting to know others at work. New employees at Syncrude, one of Canada's largest energy companies, are assigned a mentor to help them with any questions they have as they ease into their new position. Nokia Mobile Phones in San Diego assigns new hires a "buddy" and provides a mug and T-shirt to welcome each one on the first day on the job.

———

> **"**When management shows through actions rather than words that you're a valuable employee, that your input is valued no matter what level you work at, it's very motivating.**"**
>
> —AARON MELICK,
> Circulation and Marketing Administrator,
> Playboy Enterprises

> **❝Continuous, supportive communication from managers, supervisors, and associates is too often underemphasized. It is a major, major motivator.❞**
>
> —JIM MOULTRUP,
> Consultant,
> Management
> Perspectives Group

At the Department of Mental Health and Mental Retardation in Austin, TX, Claudia Smith reports, "We assign a mentor to each new employee who comes on board so that people feel connected right away. The mentor is available for any type of day-to-day questions. At the end of sixty days, there's a follow-up with the mentor, employee, and manager to see how everything's going. It's really made a difference in our retention rate and in how fast people feel 'on board.'"

———

Nissan North America's Smyrna, TN, plant sponsors family orientation programs for new employees that include refreshments and a slide show about the company. Every family is given a set of drinking glasses with "Nissan" printed on them. The day before a new employee comes to work, several people call to welcome him or her to the company. Hewlett Associates invites employees' spouses to attend company orientations and open houses as well.

———

At automobile maker Honda of America Manufacturing in Marysville, OH, workers are encouraged—and empowered—to become active participants in the decision-making process along with their managers. According to associate relations manager Donnie McGhee, "It was mind-boggling for me to come here and see the amount of involvement of the general associate in problems and situations that I viewed only as management-type issues. There is sharing of responsibility. There is the manager, but right alongside that manager you'll find a general associate. They're both out there, getting their hands dirty, problem solving. Often it's difficult to make that separation between who is the manager and who is the general associate."

———

La Quinta Inns sends new hires at the corporate office to one of its inns, where they work every shift and position, even cleaning toilets. When they finish this aspect of their training, they receive a trophy with a toilet on it, which they display proudly.

———

DEI Inc., a Dayton, OH-based architectural and building firm, knows how to fill the house at its nonmandatory brainstorming sessions: it starts them off with a wine-tasting party.

———

Susan Frankel tells of a fun program instituted by an insurance company she once worked for called "Dump a Dog," in which employees who successfully finished a project could pass on to their manager the assignment they least wanted to handle. The program stemmed from a holiday contest, but its potential as a widespread reward for completion of a successful case or for overall outstanding work was quickly realized.

———

> "For six months now, I've been visiting the workplaces of America, administering a simple test. I call it the 'pronoun test.' I ask front-line workers a few general questions about the company. If the answers I get back describe the company in terms like 'they' and 'them,' then I know it's one kind of company. If the answers are put in terms like 'we' or 'us,' I know it's a different kind of company."
>
> —ROBERT REICH, Former U.S. Secretary of Labor

A CASE STUDY IN COMMUNICATION & INVOLVEMENT

In his first two months as general manager of the new copy products group of Eastman Kodak in Rochester, NY, Chuck Trowbridge met with nearly every key person in his group, as well as with people elsewhere at Kodak who could be important to the copier business. Trowbridge set up dozens of venues to emphasize the new direction: weekly meetings with his own twelve direct reports; monthly "copy product forums" in which he met with groups consisting of a different employee from each of his departments; quarterly meetings with all 100 of his supervisors to discuss recent improvements and new projects; and quarterly State of the Department meetings, in which his managers met with everybody in their own departments.

Once a month, Bob Crandall, one of Trowbridge's direct reports and head of the engineering and manufacturing organization, and all those who reported to him, also met with eighty to a hundred people from some area of Trowbridge's organization to discuss topics of their choice. Trowbridge and his managers met with the top management of their biggest supplier over lunch every Thursday. More recently, Trowbridge created a format called "business meetings," in which his managers meet with twelve to twenty people to discuss a specific topic, such as inventory or master scheduling. The goal is to get all of his 1,500 employees into at least one of these focused business meetings each year.

Trowbridge and Crandall also used written communication. A four- to eight-page "Copy Products Journal" was sent to employees once a month. A program called "Dialogue Letters" gave employees the opportunity to ask questions anonymously of Crandall and his top managers, with a guaranteed reply.

The most visible and powerful form of written communication was the charts. In a main hallway near the cafeteria, huge charts vividly reported the quality, cost, and delivery results for each product, measured against difficult targets. A hundred smaller versions of these charts were scattered throughout the manufacturing area, reporting quality levels and costs for specific work groups.

Results of this intensive alignment process appeared within six months and remained evident more than a year later. These successes helped gain support for the new direction. In a four-year period, quality on one of the main product lines increased nearly 100 times. Defects per unit fell from 30 to 0.3. Over a three-year period, costs on another product line decreased nearly 24 percent. Deliveries on schedule increased from 82 percent to 95 percent in two years. Inventory levels dropped by more than 50 percent in four years, even though the volume of products increased. Productivity, measured in units per manufacturing employee, more than doubled in three years.

> **"**To create a competitive edge in today's business world, organizations are trying to do more with fewer employees, so it's imperative that employees are rewarded for using problem-solving and decision-making skills. No activity is more important to an organization.**"**
>
> —DAVID W. SMITH,
> President,
> Action Management
> Associates

> **❝**Productivity and performance improve the most when work is reorganized so that employees have the training, opportunity, and authority to participate effectively in decision making; when they have assurances that they will not be punished for expressing unpopular ideas; when they realize that they will not lose their jobs as a result of contributing their knowledge to improve productivity, and when they know that they will receive a fair share of any performance gains.**❞**
>
> —EILEEN APPELBAUM,
> Research Associate,
> Economic Policy Institute

Employees at Federal Express have a Guaranteed Fair Treatment (GFT) procedure in which employees are encouraged to file grievances if they believe they have not been treated fairly. The procedure was developed from a policy at Marriott International. Managers are also covered by the procedure. In one case, a middle manager filed a GFT because she thought she had been wrongly denied a promotion. A board of review found in her favor and ordered that she receive a comparable promotion. Far from being penalized for using the GFT, she was given a $5,000 award for outstanding service in her new management position two years later.

Autonomy & Authority

Having autonomy and authority is ranked as one of the top motivators for employees. In my research, the following items were ranked as very or extremely important by today's employees: "employee is allowed to decide how best to do work" (89 percent); "employee is given increased job autonomy" (87 percent); "employee is given increased authority in the job" (85 percent); and "employee is given a choice of assignment" (67 percent).

Autonomy and authority create the foundation of trust and respect that today's employees value so highly. It provides them with a sense of independence and the *freedom* to add their own imprint to their work. This freedom fosters employee creativity, resourcefulness, and best efforts, which in turn leads to higher performance and increased employee satisfaction and fulfillment at work. With autonomy and authority, employees feel more confident in taking initiative in their work and more competent that the initiative they take will pay off, leading to better results and an enhanced ability to take on greater assignments and responsibilities.

No one likes to work for a micromanager, although four out of five workers say they have done just that and one out of three workers has even changed jobs because of it. To tap into the wellspring of potential every employee has to offer, you need to give workers more room and encourage them to take responsibility and recognize them when they do.

Granting autonomy necessitates being clear with employees about the results you expect when you delegate an assignment or a responsibility, yet open and flexible about how those results can be achieved, which may be different from your own approach. Authority is granting the power to act on behalf of yourself and the organization, whether it is to committing resources or making a promise to a client. Both autonomy and authority are developmental concepts, that is, they can be nurtured over time with each assignment or decision in your working relationship—not simply turned on all at once, like a switch—allowing both you and your employees time to become more comfortable with your respective roles.

For example, an American Express office in Phoenix, AZ, teaches managers a concept it calls "link and label" when delegating work to employees. Managers "label" what they are doing by talking about the assignment, its importance, and why they think the employee would be a good choice to do the work, and then "link" the assignment to something that they believe is important to the employee. For instance:

"Jerry, we have budgeting coming up and I was thinking about letting you pull together next year's budget for our department. You've helped me in previous years with this and I thought that this year you could be in charge and I'll help you. I feel there would be some great learning for you in doing this, and since budgeting represents a key skill set in our organization, this would help to put you in line for a management position that we've discussed and I know you are interested in. Think it over and let me know if you are interested in taking this on."

> **"Empowerment is the recognition that employees are not as dumb as employers thought they were."**
>
> —DARRYL HARTLEY-LEONARD, President, Hyatt Hotels Corp.

To encourage employees to take personal initiative in their jobs and to take risks without fear of management retribution, Richard Zimmerman, chairman and CEO of Hershey Foods of Hershey, PA, created a special award, the "Exalted Order of the Extended Neck," for individuals who find ways to "go outside of the box." According to Zimmerman, "I wanted to reward people who were willing to buck the system, practice a little entrepreneurship, and be willing to stand the heat for an idea they really believe in."

All sales associates with Parisian's department stores are taught that the only person who can say "no" to a customer is the store manager. This approach helps empower employees to make decisions themselves instead of always deferring to management.

———

Management at AT&T Universal Card Services in Sioux Falls, SD, allows employees to use their own judgment about whether to waive late fees or raise credit limits when talking to customers on the phone. This has not only made customers happier, but has also improved efficiency and given employees a greater sense of control over their jobs. Similarly, at The Container Store, employees are allowed to decide how much to mark down damaged products for customers.

———

Nurses at San Diego's Mercy Hospital have been given the authority to perform numerous patient-related tasks that were formerly reserved for specialized technicians, such as drawing blood and performing EKGs. This change has improved care to patients and has allowed management to cut six or seven layers of supervision down to three or four, and collapse thirty-five separate job descriptions down to only four.

———

The management team of Phelps County Bank in Rolla, MO, has long promoted empowering employees with the responsibility

> **"Until we believe that the expert in any job is the person performing it, we shall forever limit the potential of that person."**
>
> —RENE MCPHERSON, CEO, Dana Corp.

> **❝**You have to have people free to act, or they become dependent. They don't have to be told, they have to be allowed.**❞**
>
> —JOHN R. OPEL,
> Former Chairman,
> IBM

and authority to make decisions. As employees learn how to solve their problems on their own, the Problem Busters Committee—chartered to untangle bottlenecks and deal with employee grievances—has had less and less to do.

———

At Xerox, one customer service center turned decisions about work schedules over to the employees. With employee work teams in charge of scheduling, the company reported higher morale, better customer service, and a 30 percent reduction in absenteeism.

———

Harley-Davidson in Kansas City, MO, doesn't just encourage, but *requires* line workers to speak up in their work groups and make decisions on the job. The company hires by team consensus, and workers learn each other's jobs and engage in joint problem solving.

———

When the supervisor of the membership-development department of the Girl Scouts of Santa Clara County, California, left the organization, chief executive Nancy Fox decided not to fill the vacancy, and handed over responsibility for all department duties to its staff. Now membership-development department employees have the power to set their own work schedules and determine how they will do their jobs.

———

CASE STUDY #1
IN EMPLOYEE AUTONOMY

At Johnsonville Sausage in Kohler, WI, employees make all decisions about schedules, performance standards, assignments, budgets, quality measures, and capital improvements. Performance evaluations are made by the employees themselves. For example, three hundred wage earners fill out forms rating each other on a scale of 1 to 9 in seventeen specific areas grouped into three categories: performance, teamwork, and personal development.

All final scores, with names deleted, are then passed on to a profit-sharing team, which carves out five categories of performance: a small group of superior performers (about 5 percent of the total), a larger group of better-than-average workers (roughly 20 percent), an average group amounting to about 50 percent of the total workforce, a below-average group of 20 percent, and a small group of poor performers who are often in danger of losing their jobs.

The pool of profits to be shared is divided by the number of workers to find an average share, say $1,000. Members of the top group get a check for 125 percent of that amount ($1,250). Members of the next group get 110 percent ($1,100), members of the large middle group get 100 percent ($1,000), and so on down to $900 and $750.

Overall satisfaction with the system is very high, partly because fellow workers invented it, administer it, and constantly revise it in an effort to make it more equitable.

> **"**People want to feel empowered to find better ways to do things and to take responsibility for their own environment. Allowing them to do this has had a big impact on how they do their jobs, as well as on their satisfaction with the company.**"**
>
> —JAMES BERDAHL,
> Vice President
> of Marketing,
> Business Incentives

> **"The mistakes that people will make are of much less importance than the mistake that management makes if it tells them exactly how to do a job."**
>
> —WILLIAM McKNIGHT,
> Former CEO,
> 3M

At 3M, a diversified manufacturer with more than $13 billion in annual sales headquartered in St. Paul, MN, creativity is a highly valued attribute. The company not only allows but encourages its technical employees to devote an average of 15 percent of their time to their own research projects, which has led to the development of many innovative products, such as Post-it Notes. Some spend as much as 50 percent of their time on their own projects. Employees are allowed $100 cash to spend on any innovative idea or process related to their job without further approval. This has been so successful that new products account for 30 percent of each business unit's sales.

At Chaparral Steel in Midlothian, TX, workers are given extraordinary freedom and trust to use company money and resources to improve work processes. Because of freedom, two maintenance workers were able to buy the parts necessary to invent and build a machine for strapping steel rods at a cost of $60,000— almost $200,000 less than the cost of the old machines.

At aerospace manufacturer United Technologies Corporation, headquartered in Hartford, CT, employees are getting involved in their organization in many ways, including:

✔ Teaming up and serving together on problem-solving productivity task forces.

✔ Contacting customers directly to identify and correct quality problems.

✔ Chairing meetings to address issues of quality, productivity, capital equipment plans, and customer relations.

✔ "Stopping production" when quality is not up to standard.

✔ Actively participating in plant tours and customer presentations.

✔ Visiting vendors' facilities to learn more about their manufacturing processes in order to improve the quality of incoming products.

CASE STUDY #2
IN EMPLOYEE AUTONOMY

When Kip Tindell and Garrett Boone founded The Container Store twenty-five years ago, they wanted the philosophies by which they ran their lives to be the same philosophies by which they ran their company. They didn't have any formal business or management training, yet they set out "to create the best retail store in the United States" and to offer their customers the very best products available, while providing incredible customer service and fair pricing.

Their key strategy was their employees, many of whom started out as avid customers. They take great care in hiring employees who are excited about making a difference in their jobs and then give them as much autonomy as

> ❝If you ask people confidentially what they want most in their jobs—if they're paid anything decent at all—they will say that they want a greater sense of self worth ....And I think this giving of responsibility and respect and authority is one of the things that motivates people.❞
>
> —FRITZ MAYTAG,
> President,
> Anchor Brewing Co.

possible. This is true even if the person is a part-time employee, which they refer to as "prime-timers," "because they're here when we most need them."

Guiding the efforts of all employees is the company's culture. Says Barbara Anderson, the company's first employee and director of company culture and education: "Every company has a culture. It may not be working for you, but one does exist. It comes from within and it takes time to create." The Container Store's culture has been perpetuated through consistent application of a few foundation principles—simple yet powerful concepts that help shape the attitudes and daily behaviors of all employees.

For example, "Fill the other guy's basket to the brim. Making money then becomes an easy proposition," a statement attributed to Andrew Carnegie, has become the Golden Rule for their business, shaping relationships with customers, employees, and vendors alike. Another principle, "Man in the Desert," uses an analogy of someone lost in the desert who asks for water when really what they need is much more: transportation, shelter, food, comfort, etc.

"Intuition does not come to an unprepared mind," a quote attributed to Albert Einstein, is another foundation principle. Employees are expected to have an obsession with learning so as to be able and ready to apply what they know to the unique solutions-based approach to helping customers. All full-time employees receive 235 hours of training in their first year alone—and the opportunity to be rewarded with addi-

tional continuing education as they perform well in the organization.

"Create an Air of Excitement" is a foundation principle that places responsibility for the energy of interactions with customers squarely on the shoulders of every employee. And to help sustain that energy, employees have a host of recognition activities and programs such as a "celebration" voice-mail box in each store; the use of symbolic informal recognition awards such as Gumby to represent flexibility; and peer-nominated awards such as the "Colorado Get-Away" in which a dozen employees are selected from over a thousand nominations to spend a week at the founder's cabin in the mountains.

Has Tindell and Boone's approach worked? In addition to financial success and multiple store expansion, The Container Store has been at the top of *Fortune* magazine's "100 Best Companies to Work for in America" since its inception. They have found that truly empowered employees become career employees, resulting in increased dedication, lower turnover, and greater success. (The Container Store boasts a 25 percent employee turnover rate in an industry in which the norm exceeds 100 percent a year.) Clearly, employees are attracted to a company in which they feel special—and customers are routinely astonished as employees probe to understand and then exceed their expectations, fully utilizing their product knowledge, expertise, and sales ability.

> **❝Powerlessness corrupts. Absolute powerlessness corrupts absolutely.❞**
>
> —ROSABETH MOSS KANTER,
> Professor and
> Strategy Consultant,
> Harvard Business School

Flexible Work Hours & Time Off

One reward frequently given in most companies is time off. Whether it is an hour, an afternoon, a three-day weekend, or a six-month sabbatical, this form of recognition is universally valued by employees. In my research, employees have ranked the following as very or extremely important to them: "employee is allowed to leave work early when necessary" (85 percent); "manager allows an employee flexible hours" (79 percent); "manager gives employee time off from work" (76 percent); and "employee is allowed comp time for extra hours worked" (66 percent).

Today's employees don't expect to have to sacrifice their life for their job. In fact, 83 percent of employees say they would like to spend more time with their families and to have their jobs complement their home life. Smart employers know this and try to accommodate employees as much as they can in this regard. Adjust work hours around heavy commute times? Makes sense. Time off to attend to a sick child or a school play? No problem. Change a work schedule to accommodate holiday travel? Let's see what we can do. Of course, if the employee is a high performer, it is easier to accommodate them on such requests.

One employee reported going through a tough personal time when, in the middle of a meeting, her manager looked at her across the conference room table and said, "Mary, I want you to go home, take care of whatever you need to take care of there, and come back when you're ready." She took a few days off to deal with some difficult issues, returned to work grateful and refocused—and has thought about that personal consideration her manager showed her every day for the last seven years!

How valued is time off? In a survey conducted by Hilton Hotels Corporation, reported in *Entrepreneur* magazine, 48 percent of 1,010 workers said they would give up a day's pay for an extra day off each week. (The responses differed somewhat by gender: 54 percent of working women would take a pay cut for extra time, as opposed to 43 percent of men.)

There are three ways you can use time off as a reward, according to Michael LeBoeuf, author of *The Greatest Management Principle in the World:*

1. If the job permits it, simply give people a task and a deadline and specify the quality you expect. If they finish before the deadline, the extra time is their reward.

2. If the job is one where employees must be present all day, specify an amount of work you want done by a certain time. If the work is completed on time and satisfactorily, reward them with an afternoon, day, or week off. Or you can set up a scoring system in which people earn an hour off for maintaining a certain output for a specific period. When they earn four hours, they can have a half day off; eight hours earns a day off, and so on.

3. Award time off for improvements in quality, safety, teamwork, or any other behavior you believe is important.

The Walt Disney Company grants an extra five-minute break (or a candy bar) to the employee who finds the guest who has traveled farthest to come to the park.

———

Workers at Human Dynamics in Research Triangle Park, NC, initiated an office "wacky hour" at 3 P.M. every day, when some of the workers spin in their office chairs for thirty

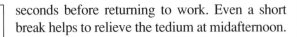

seconds before returning to work. Even a short break helps to relieve the tedium at midafternoon.

———

Crate and Barrel store managers in Houston started a program for their associates involving a "surprise hour off." Once a week, each store manager picks a sales associate and takes his or her shift on the floor for an hour, saying, "You've been working hard, and I appreciate it—take an hour off and come back refreshed and ready to sell some more."

———

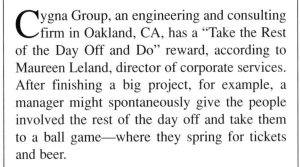

Cygna Group, an engineering and consulting firm in Oakland, CA, has a "Take the Rest of the Day Off and Do" reward, according to Maureen Leland, director of corporate services. After finishing a big project, for example, a manager might spontaneously give the people involved the rest of the day off and take them to a ball game—where they spring for tickets and beer.

———

According to Michelle Gillis, sales manager of Career Track, an organizer of management seminars in Kansas City, MO, the company gives an employee a half day off with pay if he or she recommends a person who is hired and who makes it past the ninety-day probation period.

———

To make it easier for employees to get away for long holiday weekends, employees of

> 66When we create a desirable workplace and find good ways to have work/life balance, we'll attract and we'll retain the best people—and that's our competitive advantage.99
>
> —Lewis Platt,
> Former CEO,
> Hewlett-Packard Co.

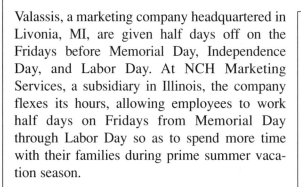

Valassis, a marketing company headquartered in Livonia, MI, are given half days off on the Fridays before Memorial Day, Independence Day, and Labor Day. At NCH Marketing Services, a subsidiary in Illinois, the company flexes its hours, allowing employees to work half days on Fridays from Memorial Day through Labor Day so as to spend more time with their families during prime summer vacation season.

———

Virginia Rego, the vice principal of the North Coast Distance Education School in Terrace, British Columbia, reports: "As a public school, we don't have surplus funds to spend on 'fun' things. One way that we recognize when the staff has had a particularly busy or hectic week is to send them home at afternoon coffee-break time on a Friday while I stay behind to keep the doors open and the phones answered until closing time. This is a staff that regularly works beyond their regular shift when the day is extra-busy, so the one-hour-early home time every few months or so is not a hardship on the school but is a definite winner for our staff!"

———

At BlueCross BlueShield in North Carolina, one department uses a half or full day off to recognize employees for various accomplishments. They receive certificates that they turn in when they want to take time off. And when they finish a degree while working for the organization, they are granted an "Educational Sabbatical"—

> 66Companies that fail to address employees' concerns about home life will only erode their commitment. Companies that are proactive in helping their people make time for their families will be rewarded with greater productivity. Ways to do so include: flexible schedules, company-sponsored employee counseling, job-sharing, and open-door policies where employees can leave at 4 p.m. occasionally for doctors' appointments, kids' athletic games, etc.99
>
> —ROBERT CAREY, *Performance* Magazine

TIME OFF

■ *Provide an extra break.*

■ *Give the person a two-hour lunch and pay for dessert.*

■ *Grant two-hour lunches for one week or for one day a week for one month.*

■ *Give a day off.*

■ *Grant the person a three-day weekend.*

■ *Give spontaneous time off for specific accomplishments.*

■ *Grant the person a week off and arrange to have his or her work done.*

one extra week off for a B.A. and two off for an advanced degree.

———

Jeff White, a Chick-fil-A manager in the Renaissance Tower in Detroit rewards individual team members with a paid day off based on excellent performance.

———

As a result of its commitment to a more balanced work life, employees at clothing outfitter Eddie Bauer can "call in well." The company's Redmond, WA, store has even created Balance Day, an additional day off for all employees.

———

Employees at Polaroid, based in Waltham, MA, get to choose by vote one paid holiday a year in addition to the nine regular ones provided by the company.

———

Integrated Genetics, a biotechnology company in Framingham, MA, hosted a Ferris Bueller's Day Off. All employees were gathered for a business meeting—and then it was announced that instead of a meeting, they were going to have an all-day celebration. Skits were performed, movies shown (including *Ferris Bueller's Day Off*) and refreshments provided, including popcorn. Employees were encouraged to take a day off in the upcoming year to have fun.

———

Valued employees have been granted certificates for bonus days off at Nelson Motivation, Inc., in San Diego to use whenever they wanted throughout the year.

———

Dan Dipert Tours & Travel gives employees two extra days off in December for shopping or holiday preparation. In addition, employees can take more days off at half pay prior to the holidays, as long as there is enough staff to cover the office.

———

At Apple Computer in Cupertino, CA, all employees were granted an extra week's paid vacation when the company had its first $100-million sales quarter.

———

At Johnson & Johnson, absenteeism among workers who made use of flexible work options and family leave policies averaged 50 percent less than for the workforce in general.

———

Rippe & Kingston in Cincinnati offers flexible hours and has found that more and more male employees take advantage to leave early to tend to their children or other family members.

———

Pro Staff Personnel, a chain of temporary help agencies, recently held a drawing for

> **❝Smart companies realize that helping workers, especially around a stressful time, is a very important part of good leadership.❞**
>
> —DR. ANN MCGEE-COOPER, Consultant

> **❝Workers have always known how to work smarter, and when management isn't watching, they do. They then use the time to create a halfway pleasant social experience— discussing last Sunday's football game or Betsy's wedding shower or just working at an easier pace. If companies want people to give that up, they're going to have to offer something valuable in trade—something that meets basic human needs for social interaction and financial well-being.❞**
>
> —JOHN ZALUSKY,
> Economist,
> AFL-CIO

paid time off as part of the company's campaign to recruit and retain employees. All employees who were in good standing were eligible. The winner received two weeks off, and two others received one week off. Jeff Dobbs, president of Pro Staff, explains: "Our research shows that time off is of great value to employees."

———

At pharmaceutical manufacturer Merck Frosst Canada & Company in Kirkland, Quebec, several employees take advantage of flexible work plans involving either telecommuting or job sharing. The company has also provided an on-site dry cleaner, post office, automated bank teller, and day care center, and is studying the feasibility of an on-site fitness center for its 950 employees to help them relieve job stress.

———

Accenture, the consulting firm, has a "7 to 7" travel policy: nobody has to leave home before 7 A.M. Monday, and everyone is encouraged to schedule the return trip so they are home by 7 P.M. Friday.

———

Pilar Dailinger, a single mother of two young children, works in marketing for an Irvine, CA, division of Gandalf Technologies, Inc., a computer networking company, where she is allowed to telecommute from home two to three days a week. "I get up in the morning, check my e-mail, then feed my kids breakfast," Dailinger says. "I work while they are at school, I put them to bed at eight-thirty, and then I go back to work on my Compaq laptop. I'm working longer hours than I did at my previous employer's."

———

Claims adjusters with Farmer's Insurance in San Diego work from home, connected on-line with the district office in Orange County. Adjusters receive case details via phone or e-mail, investigate property damage, and return to their home offices to file the reports. According to Laura Patefield, "It's the perfect mix of client contact and time alone to complete paperwork. No one's interrupting or standing over my shoulder." She adds, "I wouldn't leave Farmer's for more money!"

———

At Reader's Digest in Pleasantville, NY, employees work 35-hour weeks and may choose a flex-time schedule. There are typically twelve paid holidays and an additional five floating personal days.

———

At Deloitte Touche Tohmatsu's West Palm Beach, FL, office, Ann Blanchard has the freedom to move between part-time and full-time schedules as she raises her young children. "I have a lot of opportunity," Blanchard says. Her boss, Susan Peterson, sees such flexibility as the only way to go: "You can't afford to reestablish your professional staff every few years."

———

> **❝An employee with a good family life is healthier and more productive.❞**
>
> —Sylvia Sepielli,
> Incentive Program
> Designer,
> Hyatt Hotels

Employees at Northrop Grumman, the aerospace company, and other government contractors in San Diego work nine hours each workday and have every other Friday off. Employee surveys at the company report that this "9/80" work schedule is more highly valued by many employees even than their health benefits, and plays a key role in helping to retain employees.

Karen Cora, executive vice president at Deland, Gibson Insurance Associates, Inc., in Wellesley Hills, MA, rewards employees with summer hours from Memorial Day to Labor Day. Everyone takes 15 fewer minutes at lunch four days a week and leaves an hour early on Fridays. Deland also offers 15-minute massages during lunch hours, which employees pay for and enjoy immensely. Cora reports that she receives thank-you's almost every time the massage therapist is in the office, which is once every two weeks.

Workman Publishing in New York offers "May Days," allowing employees to take off either a Monday or a Friday each month from May to September, with the approval of their supervisors. This way, they can enjoy three-day weekends during the summer.

Robert W. Baird, a financial services company located in Milwaukee, offers flexible summer schedules and time off on Friday afternoons. Many of their associates also enjoy "flexible work arrangements," which include job sharing, telecommuting, flexible hours, compressed work schedules, and part-time working arrangements, to accommodate family needs. More than 20 percent of the company's associates take advantage of flex-time opportunities.

———

CDA Management Consulting, Inc., shuts down for a week each summer just to give employees time with their families. Company president Carolyn Pizzuto reports that most customers respond positively to the company's voice-mail message and are willing to call again the following week.

———

Linnton Plywood Association in Portland, OR, offers extended personal leaves without pay. A foreperson can approve any leave less than thirty days, and the board of directors approves longer requests. Some workers take off several months a year. No requests have ever been turned down.

———

Employees at The Container Store, based in Copell, TX, get sabbaticals after ten years of service to the company. McDonald's offers a three-month sabbatical after ten years' service.

———

> **"**Like customer service and quality, reward and recognition are highly subjective. Just as they monitor the changing needs of customers, effective leaders constantly try to understand the shifting perceptions and values of everyone in their organization.**"**
>
> —JIM CLEMMER,
> Author and President,
> The Clemmer Group

After seven years at Intel Corporation, the manufacturer of semiconductors, memories, computer systems, and software in Santa Clara, CA, employees become eligible for eight weeks off, with full pay, on top of their regular three-week vacation. They may also apply for six months off, with pay, for public service, teaching, or exceptional educational opportunities.

———

Learning & Career Development

Another highly valued intangible form of recognition is receiving learning and development opportunities. In my research, employees ranked the following as either very or extremely important: "manager supports employee in learning new skills" (90 percent); "manager discusses career options with employee" (81 percent); "employee is allowed a learning activity" (79 percent); and "manager discusses learning after completed projects" (66 percent).

According to another survey, 87 percent of American workers believe that special training is a positive incentive, and that it is deemed most meaningful by employees with postgraduate educations. A reward of additional training serves two purposes: reinforcing desired behavior and helping individuals gain skills to improve their marketability. Since most development occurs on the job, there is ample opportunity to promote learning and development in most work environments.

A promotion or increase in responsibility is a long-term reward used to acknowledge an employee's long-term performance. Apparently, it's underused; only 22 percent of the respondents in one study believed that their organization used performance as the basis for promotion, though this practice was of high motivational importance to the respondents.

Short of promoting them, high achievers' responsibility and visibility can be easily increased. Special assignments can be created for star performers: they can be assigned to train others or sent to an advanced training class. A top performer can also serve as a liaison with home office personnel or as an advisor to other departments. If you have interdepartmental problems, concerns, or projects, consider forming a task force and having your top performers represent you.

Look for every opportunity to publicize your outstanding performers to their peers. By consulting them, assigning them to special duty, or giving them a prized assignment, you're saying you regard them highly. Other employees will notice and aspire to similar recognition.

If you have an in-house publication, encourage one of your top performers to write an article explaining some aspect of the business. Soon your top achievers will understand that if they excel, everyone in the company will know who they are and respect what they've done.

> **❝If you believe that everyone in the organization must perform to his or her fullest potential to make the organization hum, then training—for everyone—is essential.❞**
>
> —GENERAL JOHN M. LOH
> U.S. Air Force

Cunningham Communications, a Palo Alto, CA, public relations firm, has a simple and powerful way of encouraging employees to stay educated: they read trade journals, newspapers, business magazines, or anything related to public relations for at least one hour a day during work.

_____

In a Timberland warehouse in Ontario, CA, Spanish-speaking employees who want to learn English can take classes right at Timberland. Not only that, but all managers are *required* to learn Spanish, also on the premises.

_____

Paychex flies all of its 3,000 to 4,000 new employees every year to its corporate offices for training. Executives participate as well. The company averaged 113 hours of training last year per employee.

_____

Unitel Corporation in New York designed an Employee Certification Program to motivate front-line employees to improve performance and to provide educational development and other services. Employees are eligible to receive salary increases by meeting specific predetermined criteria. The program is especially noteworthy in that it targets employees with an average of a tenth-grade education.

———

Texas A&M University sent teams of student teachers to teach in local schools, where their peers would attend and critique their teaching after each session. This made the student teachers more willing to try new teaching techniques, because feedback and peer support was immediately available.

———

Participants in one of Action Management Associates' problem-solving and decision-making workshops were given certificates commemorating their achievement when they used techniques they had learned in a training program. The programs resulted in a minimum of $20,000 in improvements, cost reduction, and gross profit. Trainers whose combined graduates had saved more than $1 million were named to the Million Dollar Club.

———

Walt Disney World in Orlando offers a three-day seminar for managers from other companies. Colin Service Systems of White Plains, NY, a provider of janitorial services, is one of many companies that have sent managers to the Disney seminar as a reward.

> **❝I think business increasingly recognizes that having a workforce that is trained, that is educated, and that has the right skills is important to maintaining the great competitive steps we've made in the last few years.❞**
>
> —STEVEN RATTNER,
> Managing Director,
> Lazard Freres & Co.

> **"**Education is an essential bridge between awareness and action; it provides employees with specific tools and techniques to achieve goals.**"**
>
> —From the Quality Leadership Guidelines of Baxter International, Inc.

> **"**We have a moral obligation to try to give people the tools to meet tough goals. It's wrong if you don't give employees the tools to succeed, then punish them when they fail.**"**
>
> —STEVEN KERR, Chief Learning Officer, The Goldman Sachs Group, Inc.

Some companies invite groups such as WeightWatchers, Smokenders, Toastmasters, and the Rotary Club to hold meetings on company property, allowing employees to attend easily. San Diego's headquarters for Great American Bank reserved a conference room for its own and neighboring businesses' employees.

Northwestern Mutual in Milwaukee offers dozens of in-house training courses on subjects ranging from raising teenage children to speed-reading. Pitney Bowes, based in Stamford, CT, offers courses in real estate, golf, tailoring, cake decorating, watercolor painting, and photography. And at Bell Labs in Murray Hill, NJ, experts on such diverse topics as bridge-building, bird navigation, and whale songs speak to employees.

New employees take a Dale Carnegie course at Stew Leonard's in Norwalk, CT, that stresses attitude, people skills, and customer relations. All full-time employees have the opportunity to attend a week-long "quality college," conducted in-house, and top performers take a trip to Walt Disney World to attend Disney's "People Management" training program.

At Shimadzu Scientific Instruments in Columbia, MD, outstanding performers are "promoted" to special assistant to the president for two weeks. "It's a great ego trip," reports Louis H. Ratmann, administration manager, "plus the improved understanding of the business is well worth it."

Nissan's Smyrna, TN, plant has a "Pay for Versatility" program: The more jobs a person can perform in his or her area, the more that employee gets paid. The company provides training during work hours for those interested in picking up new skills.

Advanta Corporation financial services in Horsham, PA (formerly based in Atlanta), recognizes skills—and helps develop new skills —by asking top performers to assist in training new hires and temporary employees.

AT&T has a program called Resource Link, which lets employees from diverse backgrounds and with varied management, technical, or professional skills "sell" their abilities to different departments for short-term assignments. It has greatly increased employee retention and satisfaction.

Retired employees of H. B. Fuller Company, a maker of glues, adhesives, and sealants based in St. Paul, MN, have the first shot at part-time openings and special projects.

☑ *Give special assignments to people who have shown initiative.*

☑ *Ask an employee to help you with a project that provides a real challenge.*

☑ *Allow an employee to serve on a task force with the president of the company.*

☑ *Buy the employee a subscription to a journal, magazine, or newsletter.*

☑ *Pay membership dues for a professional organization for your employee.*

The Ford Motor Company awards its version of the Inuksuk (pronounced *ee-nook-shook*), a stone monument created by the Inuits, to individuals who serve as role models for others. Each stone figure is unique, and can be made up of a single rock, several rocks balanced on top of one another, or boulders placed in a pile. The Ford version of the award embodies the essence of what it takes to excel in the marketplace today: people who constantly help others to develop and improve; who are nurturing, honest, enthusiastic, approachable, proactive, and consistent; and who exert a positive influence in the organization.

Anyone can be nominated for this award by anyone else, and can receive it as often as he or she is nominated. For instance, one manager was nominated twice in the same year—first by her vice president and then by her administrative assistant. Additionally, each nominator must tell a story about what the nominee has taught him or her. Through these stories, the awards process not only honors those individuals, but is a vehicle for long-term cultural change as well.

A CASE STUDY IN REWARDING LEARNING

At Johnsonville Sausage in Kohler, WI, the annual across-the-board raise has been replaced with a pay-for-responsibility system. As people take on new duties—budgeting, for instance, or training—they earn additional base income. The previous system rewarded people

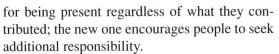

for being present regardless of what they contributed; the new one encourages people to seek additional responsibility.

The company also uses a personal development team to help individual employees plan their career destinations and use the organization to reach their goals. Everyone has an educational allowance to use however they like. In the beginning, some employees took cooking or sewing classes; a few took flying lessons. Over time, however, more employees focused on job-related learning. Today, more than 60 percent of all employees at Johnsonville are involved in some type of formal education.

"Helping human beings fulfill their potential is a moral responsibility, but it's also good business," CEO Ralph Stayer says. "Life is aspiration. Learning, striving people are happy people and good workers. They have initiative and imagination, and the companies they work for are rarely caught napping."

———

Doug Garwood, director of customer service and product management for Collins & Aikman Floorcoverings, carpet manufacturers in Dalton, GA, reports that after eighty employees passed their GEDs (high school equivalency exams), the company hosted a graduate lunch and awarded them class rings.

———

At Tektronix, Inc., employees elect a representative from their work group (one area rep for about every forty employees). Once a

> **❝**Ask people what they want to do. Frequently, when a new assignment comes up, we'll give it to just the wrong person, a person who won't find it stimulating. The cure here is for management to take the time to canvass staff and match chores with interests, to the extent possible. The workplace offers so many opportunities, and when we pair them with the right people, the results are amazing.**❞**
>
> —CHERYL HIGHWARDEN,
> Consultant,
> ODT Inc.

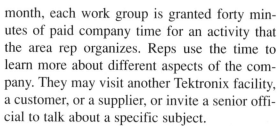

> **❝Always assume each and every person wants to do a better job and grow.❞**
>
> —STEVE FARRAR,
> Sr. Vice President,
> Wendy's International

month, each work group is granted forty minutes of paid company time for an activity that the area rep organizes. Reps use the time to learn more about different aspects of the company. They may visit another Tektronix facility, a customer, or a supplier, or invite a senior official to talk about a specific subject.

Monthly, the approximately 300 area reps get together for a forum on a topic of interest, such as compensation. Employees throughout the company submit questions for their area reps to ask the executives who speak at such forums. Once a year the area rep meeting is addressed by the company president, who delivers a "State of Tektronix" speech. The tougher questions and the president's answers are reported in full in the following issue of the company's weekly newsletter, *Tek-Week*.

———

At Iteris, Inc., the Anaheim, CA, maker of robots and space-borne tape recorders, chairman Joel Slutzky teaches a course called "Industry 101, or How to Start Your Own Business and Grow Gray Hair," which is open to all employees.

———

General Electric employees can complete a master's degree through joint programs with twenty-four universities. In addition, more than 5,000 employees attend classes every year in the company's own management development school.

———

Every year, six to eight United States Shell Oil employees exchange positions with their counterparts in the United Kingdom through an Exchange Scientist program.

————

Au Bon Pain, the Boston-based retail bakery, awards a $500 bonus or $1,000 scholarship toward an employee's education.

————

Burger King pays tuition after three months' steady work. One franchise owner paid for one course at a local college for employees who worked ten to fifteen hours per week, two courses for sixteen to twenty-five hours, and three courses for twenty-six to forty hours.

————

Cumberland Farms, a convenience-store chain in Canton, MA, reimburses its employees for college courses. All part-time and full-time employees at Federal Express are reimbursed for tuition. Steelcase reimburses tuition for job-related courses. Time Warner pays 100 percent of tuition for job-related courses and 75 percent for nonrelated courses at accredited institutions.

————

Part-time employees who have worked at least twenty hours a week for two years at Atlanta-based Chick-fil-A receive a $1,000 scholarship to the colleges of their choice. Four-year scholarships for $10,000 are also given. The company

5 IDEAS FOR EMPLOYEE DEVELOPMENT

1) Encourage employees to work on an advanced degree.

2) Allow employees to select and attend the training courses of their choice.

3) Before employees attend a course, meet with them to discuss what you hope they will learn. After they attend it, meet with them again to see how they will apply their new knowledge.

4) Have employees share what they learned at a seminar or conference with the rest of the group.

5) Create individual development plans for each employee, matching the skills they want to learn with the development opportunities available, including potential job advancement.

has awarded more than $4.5 million since the program began.

———

Nucor Corporation, the steel manufacturer in Charlotte, NC, offers a $1,400-a-year college scholarship to each child of an employee who has been with the company for at least two years. It has offered $2,200 a year toward college tuition, for up to four years, for all children of full-time workers. In addition, spouses of employees can receive $1,100 per year in tuition subsidies for up to two years.

———

Duncan Aviation offers a $5,000 reimbursement for any employee earning a pilot's license and instrument rating.

———

At Mary Kay, Inc., college tuition is reimbursed on a sliding scale: 100 percent if the employee gets an A or a B; 75 percent if he or she receives a C.

———

Polaroid, headquartered in Waltham, MA, places an extraordinary emphasis on continuing education. It picks up 100 percent of the tuition of job-related courses taken by employees and offers more than one hundred courses internally to employees.

———

Reader's Digest in Pleasantville, NY, reimburses employees 100 percent of tuition for degree or certificate programs that enhance on-the-job effectiveness, 75 percent for non-business-related courses and programs at an accredited school, and 50 percent for all other educational, personal-interest classes, from WeightWatchers to cooking. The company also offers wellness education seminars and exercise classes on-site.

RECOGNIZE PERFORMERS WITH TRAINING

■ *Send employees to special seminars, workshops, or meetings outside the company that cover topics they are interested in.*

■ *Have new employees take a Dale Carnegie course that stresses attitude, people skills, and customer relations.*

■ *Grant all full-time employees the opportunity to attend a week-long in-house Quality College.*

■ *Allow top performers to take a trip to Walt Disney World to attend Disney's People Management training program.*

Manager Availability & Time

A final category of intangible recognition is managerial access, ranging from an employee's immediate supervisor, to upper management, to the company CEO. Employees ranked the following items as either very or extremely important to them: "manager is available to address questions/concerns" (90 percent); "manager takes time to get to know employee" (68 percent); "manager spends time with employee" (43 percent); and "manager listens to employee on nonjob issues" (35 percent).

Although most companies have an "open-door" policy where employees are encouraged to approach their managers with questions and suggestions, this policy isn't worth much if managers are not receptive or are too busy to make it a priority. Manager accessibility and time shows employees that they are important to the manager, and thus the organization. It implicitly says, "Of all the things I have to do, none of them is more important than being right here, right now, speaking with you."

> **❝An employee's motivation is a direct result of the sum of interactions with his or her manager.❞**
>
> —Bob Nelson

Sue Copening says she learned an important lesson about listening the hard way several years ago when she was promoted to store manager for a retail chain. She was not taking the time to really pay attention to her staff. When two employees quit within a few weeks, one had the courage to tell her that she was creating an unfriendly work environment. Sue realized that she needed to make time to listen to employee concerns. She now reports: "A manager's job is 95 percent being sensitive to employees and keeping them happy. It's easier to change your own behavior than to expect other people to adjust to you."

———

In order to show employees that senior-level executives are not just top-floor managers at Timberland, they are required to sit with their business units. The proximity makes communication and access to top management easier for employees, making them feel more supported.

———

As part of Chicago-based Hyatt Hotel Corporation's "In Touch Day," all 375-plus headquarter's employees—from the mail room to the executive suite—went to Hyatt properties around the country to provide guest services. Jim Evans, vice president of sales, spent several hours hailing taxis, loading luggage, and collecting tips at the front door of the Hyatt Regency Chicago; Darryl Hartley-Leonard, president of Hyatt, served lunch in the employees' cafeteria, hailed cabs, checked in guests at the front desk, and tended bar. "We're all working toward the same goal, but we corporate people forget what it's like," Hartley-Leonard said. "After a day like this, we know what on-line workers really go through."

———

A former manager at University Associates, now based in Tucson, AZ, often spontaneously took over phone duties for the busy

> 66The most motivating thing one person can do for another is to listen.99
>
> —ROY MOODY,
> President,
> Roy Moody & Associates

receptionist as a way of recognizing her hard work. It served the triple purpose of staying in touch with life on the front lines, hearing customer concerns firsthand, and rewarding the receptionist with some time off.

———

One day a year at Mary Kay, Inc., all white-collar manufacturing employees work on the production lines.

———

To demonstrate trust in their employees, all managers at Quad/Graphics printers in Pewaukee, WI, left the plant for twenty-four hours in the annual Spring Fling and Management Sneak. Normal printing operations continued while the managers held meetings and then went to the Milwaukee Art Museum. The company subsequently expanded the event to a two-day, three-evening affair, including managerial seminars at a local college. During the Fling, none of the managers were allowed to set foot inside the printing plants unless an employee asked for emergency help. As of yet, no manager has ever been called in.

———

Officers of FedEx Freight West make regular visits to operating locations, meeting with employees, and frequently barbecuing for them in recognition of special accomplishments, such as breaking a safety record.

———

What better way to open communication with your employees than to schedule it? At Daired's Salon and Spa Pangéa in Arlington, TX, human resources manager Beverly Debysingh says they help to do this with:

1. Five-minute morning meetings in each department.

2. A five-minute meeting with each employee every week, with each manager giving a checklist to the CEO/owner to show they did this.

3. Recognizing all employees who exemplify each of their seven core values at their quarterly staff meetings.

Awardees for each value category are given $20- to $25-gift certificates to movies, restaurants, etc. They don't limit the number of recipients—employees can be acknowledged for as many virtues as they have! Daired's reports direct results in both morale and productivity as employees feel better informed, involved, and motivated to do their best work every day.

———

Combating and eliminating rumors is a challenging corporate problem, but at The SCOOTER Store, based in New Braunfels, TX, it's all just a game. During company-wide meetings, president and CEO Doug Harrison sometimes takes the stage with his gift bucket to play the Gossip Game. Employees get gifts for telling everyone a rumor they heard around the office. The juiciest rumors receive the best prizes. This

> **"**Having some access to upper management is important in terms of how employees feel about the organization, and how they look at themselves. When employees know that the decision makers are accessible to them, they feel that their ideas are worth more .... Having everyone from the bottom up buying into what we're doing is worth something.**"**
>
> —DARRELL MELL, Vice President of Telemarketing, Covenant House

☑ *Have top managers visit the shop floor, talking informally with individual employees.*

☑ *Once a quarter, choose ten to twelve employees to dine with corporate executives.*

☑ *Have the CEO hold a monthly breakfast or lunch with one person from each department, alternating the employees each month until everyone has had a chance to go.*

☑ *Meet for informal chats with each of your employees at least once a week, finding out what aspects of their jobs they are focused on and how you can better assist them.*

gives Doug an opportunity to personally respond to rumors in a candid, honest, and entertaining manner in front of the entire company.

———

The president of Duncan Aviation makes a point of meeting with all new employees within one week of employment.

———

Jeff Bezos, CEO of Amazon.com, often stocks shelves along with workers in order to hear their problems firsthand.

———

A Motorola manager on the Iridium satellite phone project in Schaumburg, IL, rewarded star performers for a job well-done with special attention. She invited a broad spectrum of engineers, M.B.A.s, salespeople, and customer service staff to brainstorm for an hour at lunch about their most intriguing business problems and solutions. People loved being singled out, and business problems got solved as well.

———

Once a month, Integrated Marketing Services in Princeton, NJ, invites employees to a "Bagels and B.S." meeting, at which management discusses year-to-date performance and plans for the future and then fields questions from the group. Employees are also invited to complain to management about whatever might be on their minds.

———

Executives at Arbitron have an open-door policy and participate in the day-to-day operation of the company. They often hold town hall meetings on specific subjects, serving as panelists; host luncheons with select employees; and visit all the field offices several times a year to get a firsthand look at employee attitudes and needs. They recently completed an executive Q&A, answering questions submitted by employees.

> 66The leader needs to be in touch with the employees and to communicate with them on a daily basis.99
>
> —Donald Petersen,
> President and CEO,
> Ford Motor Company

At Armstrong International in Three Rivers, MI, paychecks are delivered personally to about three hundred workers by the general manager or the controller each week in order to give everyone a chance to be heard. At least once a week, each employee has the opportunity to ask questions, make suggestions, and receive feedback from management.

Tom Thumb president Mark Prestidge and other top managers spend time in the branch stores to support employees during the stressful holiday season. Prestidge has served breakfast to all the company's Dallas headquarters staff prior to Thanksgiving.

Bob Small, former head of Walt Disney Parks & Resorts, used to work "small shifts"—four hours—with all types of workers to experience firsthand the challenges of their jobs. After one frustrating shift trying to fold hundreds of napkins, his shift coworker

> **"**Listen with your full attention, look for the good in others, have a sense of humor, and say thank you for a job well done.**"**
>
> —PAUL SMUCKER,
> Former CEO,
> J.M. Smucker & Co

observed, "It's a good thing you run this place, because you could never make it in this job!"

———

To keep front-liners motivated, WinterSilks, a $35 million silk apparel cataloger in Jacksonville, FL, requires all salaried personnel, including senior management, to take a minimum of fifty phone orders annually. Executives fill in where needed.

———

Rosenbluth International in Philadelphia has an "Associate of the Day" program, allowing any employee to spend a day with the CEO. Twice a year, the company holds an employee focus group to discuss workplace issues. Every new employee spends two days at corporate headquarters, meeting top managers and performing in skits about good service experiences. The firm's officers also serve afternoon tea to new hires. The CEO of the company has an 800-number for employees to call him—he gets seven to eight calls per day.

———

The CEO of FedEx gives his home phone number to all employees to call him if they need to.

———

Executives of Tupperware, based in Orlando, FL, take thirty days on the road each year to spend time with their top 15,000 salespeople.

———

Once a year, the president of H.B. Fuller Company makes himself available to everyone in the company through what's called the President's Hot Line. Anybody can call him on that day at a special toll-free number to make suggestions for improving Fuller's products or to talk about anything else on their minds. The president usually gets forty to fifty calls.

———

At American General Life and Accident Insurance Company in Nashville, TN, a dozen employees are selected at random each month to meet the president and discuss matters of corporate concern.

———

All Knight-Ridder publication offices have "management coffee breaks," during which each publisher meets with twenty to twenty-five rank-and-file employees for an hour and a half over coffee. Employees can send questions in advance. The year-end management meeting is held in a large hall so that all employees can attend.

———

At Hyatt Hotel Corporation, "employees have the obligation, as well as the right, to communicate with managers," says Myrna Hellerman, vice president of human resources. The company holds monthly "Hyatt Talks," at which the general manager sits down with a randomly selected group of hotel staffers to talk informally about operations and procedures.

> **66** You can't know employees as individuals until you're willing to put in the time to talk to them. And you have to talk to them to know what motivates them. **99**
>
> —ARTHUR PELL,
> Author,
> *The Complete Idiot's Guide to Managing People*

Companies Whose Top Management Regularly Meets With Employees

- Dana Corporation
- Electro Scientific
- Federal Express
- Johnson Wax
- Mary Kay, Inc.
- Medtronic Physio-Control Corp
- Pitney Bowes

Employees bring up issues and problems that are important to them, and within a week a member of the hotel's executive committee looks into the issue and responds in writing. "We want people to think of the hotel as 'my hotel,' a place they want to work in," Hellerman says, "and these talks encourage the family feeling we try to have."

———

Advanta Corporation, a financial services firm in Horsham, PA, has its senior managers host a Grill Your Boss cookout, during which the managers dress up as chefs and cook hamburgers and hot dogs for all employees.

———

Nick D'Agostino, owner of the D'Agostino's supermarket chain based in Larchmont, NY, makes rounds of the company's twenty-four stores every week, chatting with workers and observing operations.

———

McDonald's encourages its franchisees to hold quarterly communication sessions. Usually, the store owner sits down with a representative group of employees and listens to suggestions and gripes. "Things like realigning equipment or changing procedures—those get changed all the time due to workers' suggestions," says Dan Gillen, staff director of store employment. McDonald's supplies all its franchise owners with a manual outlining incentive programs they can adapt for their own establishments.

———

PART III

TANGIBLE RECOGNITION & REWARDS

When most people think of recognition or rewards, they think of *items,* such as trophies, plaques, and certificates. Tangible, individual forms of recognition—and others that have monetary value—make up the categories of this section: outstanding employee and achievement awards; cash, cash substitutes, and gift certificates; nominal gifts, merchandise, and food; and special privileges, perks, and employee services.

There are several advantages to using these types of rewards. For one, they provide "trophy value"—a concrete reminder of the achievement. They also offer more value for the money than money alone. According to the "People, Performance, and Pay" study conducted by the American Productivity Center in Houston and World at Work, it generally takes 5 to 8 percent of an employee's salary to change behavior if the reward is cash and approximately 4 percent if it is

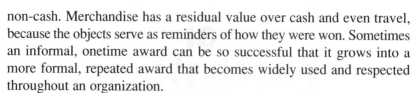

non-cash. Merchandise has a residual value over cash and even travel, because the objects serve as reminders of how they were won. Sometimes an informal, onetime award can be so successful that it grows into a more formal, repeated award that becomes widely used and respected throughout an organization.

Whether it's thank-you cards, tokens, pins, certificates, pass-around trophies, mementos, gag gifts, gift certificates, discount coupons, movie passes, on-the-spot awards, or more substantial merchandise, you need to have some quick-and-easy items to thank and acknowledge people that require minimal administration and evaluation. Such items can be available to all managers or customized to a particular area of the organization, such as the personalized "Applauz" card that is used by the Medical Products Division at Johnson & Johnson or the "Thank You" tokens used with employees at Busch Gardens. Or Chevron Texaco's "Treasure Chest" that supervisors can unlock to allow a performer to select a gift on the spot.

To get the most out of tangible recognition items, try to *personalize* the awards and to provide a *public context* when they are used. Place the person's name on the award—and perhaps the company logo—and take a photo of the presentation when it is given. Have the president of your company meet with those individuals being honored so that you can create a social reinforcement as well. If you are thanking your work group with a gift, consider adding a personal note for every member of the team reflecting each person's contribution to the success of the group effort.

Providing a context is a way of connecting the award to a larger meaning to which more people can relate. Tie the recognition to the organization's values, the company's strategic objectives, or the sense of teamwork you have been trying to build with your team. You might say something like, "We're able to have this great celebration because we once again had a great year and we could not have done it without the dedication and commitment of the people in this room." This will give the award or activity a broader meaning that both reflects on the past as well as looks to the future. Recognition is for the person being honored, but it is for everyone else who is present as well, so take the time to create meaning that everyone can relate to.

Outstanding Employee & Achievement Awards

Traditional forms of recognition typically include outstanding employee and achievement awards, which are often accompanied by recognition items such as trophies, plaques, or certificates. In my research, 54 percent of employees rank a "special achievement award" as very or extremely important to them, and 43 percent cite "certificates of achievement" as having similar importance. Outstanding employee awards are often based on a formal selection process to ensure as much objectivity as possible, and can be given for a single exceptional achievement or employee performance over time. Awards tend to be more meaningful when they have been selected by one's peers, not just by management, and when there is no quota on the number of recipients.

Tom Tate, program manager in the Personnel and Management Training Division of the federal government's Office of Personnel Management in Washington, D.C., tells the story of the Wingspread Award. A beautiful engraved plaque, it was first given to the division's "special performer" by the department head. Later, that person passed it on to another person who, he believed, truly

> **❝**We covet recognition that we earn by dint of our own hard effort.**❞**
>
> —DENNIS LAMOUNTAIN,
> Management Consultant

deserved it. The award came to take on great value and prestige because it came from one's peers. Recipients can keep it until they're ready to pass it on to another "special performer." Each time the award is passed on, a ceremony and lunch is held.

_____

A couple of years ago, Norm Kane, vice president of Synovate, a global market intelligence company based in Chicago, started issuing "Golden Pencil" awards to coworkers who had done exemplary work. The award is quite literally a gold-colored #2 pencil, engraved with the words *Norm Kane's Golden Pencil Award*. It's simple and sincere, and is a token of thanks that Norm and his group can give out fairly often—and they do. Over fifty pencils have been awarded in the past two years alone.

_____

A regional manager for Hallmark created achievement certificates for each member of his team, citing a key attribute that personified each individual, such as: "for consistent follow-through without having to be asked," "for being able to close the really big account," or "for pitching in to help others—and always with a smile." He read them out loud at an end-of-the-year celebration, where employees had to guess whom they referred to. It was a fun team-building experience for everyone.

_____

S am Colin, founder of Colin Service Systems janitorial services in White Plains, NY, used to go around handing out Life Savers to employees. That early tradition has developed into a lasting philosophy of recognition that today includes awards such as "Most Helpful Employee" and "Nicest Employee." Coworkers vote for employees, and executives make the presentations.

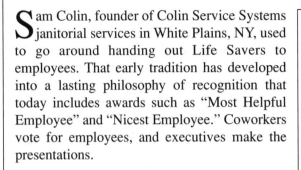

> **"When basic compensation is adequate, it takes something extra and something tangible to motivate people to greater performance."**
>
> —*Incentive*

G eneral John M. Loh, commander of the Tactical Air Command of the U.S. Air Force, says he rewards team members who solve their problems with certificates to hang in their offices.

A t Citibank in Oakland, CA, customers (and other employees) can reward and thank employees with Thumbs-Up certificates, which can be exchanged for merchandise. Early in the program, many workers were so pleased by the recognition that instead of redeeming the certificates immediately, they proudly displayed them on their walls.

L ands' End uses the Big Bean Award to recognize people for using their "beans," such as assisting with a last-minute task, staying late to help with a project, or finding a great employment candidate. Each month, employees attending the employee services divisional meeting get to nominate someone by placing nomination slips in a ballot box. (They can also complete an online nomination form in advance of the meeting.) At the end of the meeting, one name is drawn from the box, and that lucky person gets to play "Bean Machine," otherwise known as Plinko, where he or she gets the chance to win great prizes such as a Lands' End beanbag chair or a gift card to the "Dry Bean"—or some not-so-great prizes, such as pork and beans, kidney beans, or a beanie hat. Everyone nominated is sent a copy of the nomination, along with a special bean prize, and all nominations are displayed for one month on the employee services web site.

———

The *Charlotte Observer* in North Carolina has used FUIEE awards, which stands for Fun-Urgent-Informative-Energetic-and-Essential, for innovative employees, such as a reporter with a great story or a staff member with an idea for cutting costs or improving customer service. The newspaper also gives prizes based on employee nominations. Each week, a rotating committee reviews nominations and announces three winners, who would receive one of the following items: $50 cash, movie tickets, or use of a preferred parking space. All nominations (including those for nonwinners) are e-mailed to employees to read and enjoy.

———

FedEx Freight West has numerous recognition programs, ranging from the EZTDBW (Easy to Do Business With) Award, which is a small gift and a certificate of recognition, to the Extra Mile Award, which is a larger monetary award for exceptional performance. These straightforward award programs allow employees at all levels to recognize one another spontaneously.

To create group rapport and to recognize success, The Phelps Group in Santa Monica, CA, gives out "Atta Boy"/"Atta Girl" awards after weekly staff meetings. The simple plaques, presented with great fanfare, are passed from old to new winners.

Syncrude Canada Ltd., one of Canada's largest energy companies, based north of Edmonton, Alberta, works hard to keep recognition fresh, personal, and meaningful. For example, John Thomas, manager of operations, recently initiated a "Pay It Forward" award, a plaque that is passed from employee to employee for exemplary work. Each recipient is honored twice, both in receiving the award, and in selecting and presenting it to the next winner. Feedback has been very positive.

Employees who go the extra mile at KFC Corporation, headquartered in Louisville, KY, are presented with a "Floppy Chicken Award," a thank-you note, and a $100 gift certificate. Former president and CEO David Novak started the program when he flew into an awardee's city and personally presented him with a rubber chicken that he pulled out of a crumpled brown-paper sack. A photo of the presentation is on permanent display at the "Walk of Leaders," which is a prominent area at corporate headquarters.

———

The most popular award at Synovus is the quarterly Standing Tall Award, for employees who go beyond the scope of their jobs. They are nominated by coworkers, and winners are chosen by a special committee. The awards are presented at a luncheon, by the CEO and other senior officers, and each recipient gets $100, a day of paid vacation, and a tacky pink flamingo with a bow tie, which costs only $3.47. Employees proudly display the flamingos in their cubicles, encouraging others to achieve the award as well.

———

Timberland's John Lewis Award, named in honor of U.S. congressman and longtime civil rights activist John Lewis of Georgia, is given to one outstanding member of the sales team each year. This individual must manifest Timberland's core values—humanity, humility, integrity, and excellence—by making a significant impact on his or her community through advocacy and volunteer service. The award is a $5,000 grant to the nonprofit organization of the winner's choice, a day in Washington, D.C. with Congressman Lewis, and a commemorative plaque. In 2004, John Lewis himself made the award presentation.

———

Employees at Robert W. Baird, a financial services company located in Milwaukee, give fellow associates the Blue Chip Award to show appreciation for good work. Recipients receive a short note from the associate and a small "Baird Blue Chip" with the words *In recognition of a job well done*. These awards are typically presented by the manager during a department meeting so other coworkers can join in applauding the recipients. Many associates display Blue Chips on their desks, and some departments have wall space dedicated to hanging the award notes. The top 2 percent of Blue Chip recipients are recognized each year at the annual meeting for all associates. Baird also has an "Associate of the Month" program, which provides recognition for associates who consistently make superior contributions both to their clients and to the company. Nominations come from coworkers, and the monthly winner receives flowers, $100 in cash, a certificate for dinner for two, an item of Baird clothing, an Associate of the Month certificate, and a traveling trophy to keep on his or her desk for the month. The award is usually presented by a group of fellow associates and human resources personnel, and the winner is featured in an "eBriefs" story in the company's online newsletter.

☑ Create a special award for specific major accomplishments and name it (a Gorilla Award, for example).

☑ Create an ABCD (Above and Beyond the Call of Duty) Award for employees who exceed the requirements of their jobs. Give them a polo shirt emblazoned with "ABCD Award."

☑ Have employees vote for the top Manager, Supervisor, Employee, and Rookie of the Year.

☑ Dedicate the parking space closest to the company entrance to the outstanding Employee of the Month.

The REI store in Ventura, CA, always gives out "appreciation awards" during its store meetings. One day, after it had given out the usual awards, it called attention to two employees who deserved a little more credit than usual.

They were each presented with the Pineapple Award—a fresh pineapple with a healthy crown of leaves.

———

A Tualatin, OR, REI store rewards staff members with the Golden Hanger Award for going above and beyond their responsibilities in providing support to salespeople. It's a plain clothes hanger spray-painted gold; recipients are nominated by peers, and are presented the awards at store meetings. There's an award presentation at each and every meeting. REI also has a peer-nominated and peer-selected formal recognition program called the Anderson Award (named for founders Lloyd and Mary Anderson). Recipients are selected once a year from every department and store, and receive certificates and engraved bricks on a pathway at the headquarters' campus. They are also eligible for the President's Award, which is given to the top ten employees in the company. Those winners are invited (with their partners or spouses) on an adventure-travel trip with REI's president.

———

Emerson Process Management Power and Water Solutions allows employees to give the Rising Star Award to fellow employees for good work. They type up a brief description of the awardee's accomplishments on the Rising Star page on the company intranet, and an award sheet is sent electronically, with the nomination description, to the employee with a copy to his or her supervisor. The employee gets to choose one of a number of $5–$12 prizes, such as movie tickets, car washes, gas or video rental cards, and restaurant or mall certificates; or he or she can receive a Rising Star pin, which many pin to their cubicles or work spaces as badges of honor.

———

Each year, CEDRA, a bioanalytical chemistry company, gives out the "Buttkicker Award" to employees who have the attitude and potential for leadership. They have to have been nominated by existing Buttkickers and approved by management in accordance with strict selection criteria. They each get their names added to a pedestal (in the lobby) with a wooden boot on top, a gold and diamond boot pin or tie tack, and a trip with the company's president to the local western-wear store to pick out a pair of boots.

———

The Legend Award is the highest honor an Alaska Airlines employee can receive. He or she must exhibit a unique blend of spirit, resourcefulness, integrity, professionalism, and caring. Once a year, each new class of honorees (approximately eight to twelve employees) is inducted into the Alaska Airlines Hall of Fame and invited to a luncheon celebration with guests, coworkers, and senior management. In recent years, the award presentation has taken place at the Chateau Ste. Michelle Winery. "Legends" are first flown to Alaska Airlines corporate headquarters to unveil the engraving of their names on marble pillars, and then taken by

> **"What makes employees come to work is a sense of pride, recognition, and achievement. Workers committed to their jobs and recognized for their work will work whatever hours it takes to get the job done."**
>
> —THOMAS KELLEY, Chairman of the Board, Society for Human Resource Development

bus to the Spirit of Washington Dinner Train, which takes them to the chateau. Each "Legend" also receives a hand-painted sphere trophy.

———

Great Plains–Microsoft Business Solutions in Redmond, WA, used to hold a celebration every year called Pioneer Day, where they presented awards to employees who had distinguished themselves in some way: a Jesse James Award for tolerating eccentricity, a Sodbuster Award for innovation, a Heritage Award for customer service, and several awards for excellence in various technical areas. The winners were held up as mentors, and others were encouraged to learn from them.

———

Avis Rent A Car has several recognition programs, such as the Destination Excellence Award, which is given to employees who reflect Avis's values in dealing with customers and who have made some significant, quantifiable impact on the business. The highest award is the Milestone Achievement Award, which is presented by the executive committee to the employee who has made the most significant contribution to the company.

———

Beverly Cronin, a book manager at a Hastings Books, Music, and Entertainment store in Rio Rancho, NM, recalls receiving a "Spark Plug" award in the 1960s, which was a spark plug painted gold and hung on a ribbon, from a department store manager in Akron, OH. In giving it to her, he said, "This is for you, because you add a spark to our workplace." She still keeps the award in her jewelry box to commemorate the first time she was recognized for doing a good job.

———

Ziff Davis, in La Jolla, CA, gives out "Daredevil" awards, a distinction granted to anyone who is caught doing something innovative or helpful beyond the call of duty. Award recipients are regularly announced via e-mail to the entire company.

———

CUNA Mutual Group created the Big Bone Award to play on a theme of "Big Dogs" that it was using for its formal recognition program at the time. A large (four-foot) rawhide dog bone was passed around (à la Stanley Cup) to outstanding members of the leadership team. The winners were chosen by their bosses and the award was presented at one of the three face-to-face meetings held every year. "If you won, you got to sign the bone, bring it home as an airplane carry-on (a lot of people fly to the meeting location), and display it in your work area," explains Eileen Doyle Julien, division manager of administration for the northwest marketing division of CUNA in Latham, NY. "As far as reliving the reception of this award, it was great!" says Eileen. "How can someone who sees this large bone in a business or airport setting not ask about it?!"

———

> **❝Because of our incentive programs, we know that we will be here in the future and that it is because of our hard work now.❞**
>
> —CHARLES GEHL, Coordinator, Frank Implement Company

> **"High achievers love to be measured, when you come down to it, because otherwise they can't prove to themselves that they are achieving."**
>
> —Dr. Robert N. Noyce,
> Cofounder,
> Intel Corporation

BlueCross BlueShield Association in Chicago gives "People Are Tops" awards, which include balloons tied to the person's desk, belly dancers, and a song or message delivered by someone in a gorilla suit. The company also recognizes outstanding employees four times a year with "Superstar" awards. Each Superstar gets a $500 savings bond, a star, and a sweatshirt.

———

At the annual profit-sharing banquet, management at the Angus Barn Restaurant in Raleigh, NC, gives out achievement awards to the top ten all-around employees. The restaurant also recognizes performers with the People's Choice Award, which is given by coworkers.

———

Wal-Mart Stores, Inc., headquartered in Bentonville, AR, offers extensive award programs such as Regional All-Star Teams, the Special Divisions' All-Star Departmental Honor Roll, the VPI (Volume Producing Item) Contest, the Department Sales Honor Roll, and the Shrinkage Incentive Program. Award winners' names and pictures appear in the company newspaper.

———

Nelly Attwater, supervisor for training and development for El Torito Restaurants in Long Beach, CA, reports how the restaurants use the "Be a Star" program. "When a manager or supervisor catches someone doing something right—or above and beyond—that employee is given a 'Star Buck,' which serves as a cash substitute. Each restaurant has a drawing at the end of the month for prizes (cash, TV, etc.), and each region has a drawing for prizes also ($1,000 cash, TV, VCR, etc.). Each employee can have numerous stars for the drawings."

———

Nordstrom, Inc., the Seattle-based department store chain, offers the Pacesetter Award to employees who have exceeded goals by a considerable margin. As a Pacesetter, an employee receives a certificate, a new business card that reads "Pacesetter," and a lavish evening of dining, dancing, and entertainment to share with a guest. For the next year, the Pacesetter enjoys a 33 percent discount on all Nordstrom merchandise, which is 13 percent greater than the standard employee discount.

———

At Ceramics Process Systems Corporation, a technical ceramics manufacturer in Chartley, MA, the Extra Mile Award is given each December to several people who have gone above and beyond. Peter Loconto, president of the company, says, "We were struggling to improve yield and productivity. One person took it upon himself to document all the issues involved and set out the problems so that management could clearly see where the obstacles were." Another person, faced with what management considered overly stringent (even unreasonable) requirements on a particular job from one customer, worked day and night—unasked—to accommodate the client's

> **"When people are treated as the main engine rather than interchangeable parts of a corporate machine, motivation, creativity, quality, and commitment to implementation well up."**
>
> —ROBERT H. WATERMAN,
> Director of
> The Waterman Group,
> Co-author,
> *In Search of Excellence*

wishes. The employee got the job done on time. "When we announced the person's name, everyone in the company stood up and cheered," Loconto says. "That was a true validation of the person's hard work." Winners' names are engraved on a plaque that hangs in the company's lobby, and the chosen employees also receive either cash or equity in the company.

———

At Meloche Monnex, an insurance banking company in Montreal, top performers receive a personal letter from the president, congratulating them on their achievement. They also receive an annual salary increase double the average. A portion of the increase is paid in one lump sum when the employee's salary is in the high range. These employees also get priority in the choice of additional responsibilities and training.

———

CASE STUDY IN RECOGNIZING OUTSTANDING EMPLOYEES

At Stew Leonard's, the ABCD (Above and Beyond the Call of Duty) Award goes to employees who exceed the requirements of their jobs. They receive a polo shirt emblazoned with the words *ABCD Award*. The store also has a "Superstar of the Month" program, in which one person in each department is elected by peers on the basis of different departmental criteria— cleanliness, safety, etc. His or her one month of superstardom commences with considerable fanfare, including a photo for the Avenue of Stars (a

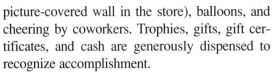

picture-covered wall in the store), balloons, and cheering by coworkers. Trophies, gifts, gift certificates, and cash are generously dispensed to recognize accomplishment.

"We don't just give someone a plaque," says founder Stew Leonard. "We have our costumed animal characters bring balloons to them. Fellow workers gather around, and we present the plaque right on the floor of the store. We take their picture, put it in *Stew's News* [the company newsletter], and mount it on a walnut plaque hung right on the Avenue of the Stars. Everyday you see your picture, and you feel good forever."

Each year, "Stewie" awards recognize the top manager, supervisor, employee, and "rookie of the year"—based on employee ballots. The manager with the lowest turnover also wins an award. Outstanding performance awards are presented yearly to three top employees from among twenty or so nominated by the president and selected by previous winners. Banquets are held to present the honors.

Southwest Airlines allows station managers to reward "Star of the Quarter" employees with celebrations. At one station, the honoree invites a group of people to a lunch or dinner featuring a menu of his or her choice. The station managers do all the shopping, preparation, and serving for the event. Instead of an added hassle, this has become a team-building activity as managers work together to coordinate everything. This is just one reason why it is now harder

> **"All behavior is a function of its consequences."**
>
> —Bob Nelson

66Motivation is based on what you bring to it as an individual. What is motivational to one person isn't motivational to another.**99**

—CRYSTAL JACKSON,
Personnel Manager,
Companion Life
Insurance Co.

(based on the percentage of accepted applicants) to get a job working at Southwest Airlines than it is to get into Harvard University!

———

At *Business First* in Columbus, OH, an employee of the month is recognized at each staff meeting, where the publisher praises his or her achievements. The company also gives out the "Ugly Ben Award," a new $100 bill, which has Benjamin Franklin's picture on it, to the person who "finds a way to meet the monthly sales budget against all odds."

———

At Home Depot, Inc., the home improvement supply center headquartered in Atlanta, each store picks an Employee of the Month: someone who has given time to an area of the store that technically lies outside his or her responsibility. The honoree gets $100, a merit badge (collecting five badges earns an extra $50), and a special badge to wear on his or her apron. In addition, the employee's name is engraved on a plaque at the front of the store.

———

At ICI Pharmaceuticals Group in Wilmington, DE, the Performance Excellence Award is given to employees for any idea that helps the business and to employees who go above and beyond the call of duty. The winner receives $300. Employees can be nominated for this award by anyone in the company.

———

At Gregerson's Foods, a retail grocery chain in Gadsden, AL, outstanding employees are named Associates of the Month at each store location. They receive silver name tags inscribed with that title and with the month and year of the award, to wear as long as they work for the company. The employees' names are also listed on plaques at each store.

———

Managers at D'Agostino's, a supermarket chain based in Larchmont, NY, name employees All-Stars when they go beyond the call of duty. At least one All-Star is chosen each month from each store, up to twenty-four people per year per store.

———

The Carlson-Himmelman Award given by Westin Hotels, headquartered in White Plains, NY, is presented annually for outstanding management achievement. Recipients get a trip around the world.

———

At Valassis, the "Innovator," "Collaborator," "Risk-Taker," and "Employee of the Year" award recipients receive 100 to 200 shares of company stock, crystal trophies, and coveted parking spaces. Recipients are nominated by peers, who simply complete a form, and are selected by a volunteer review and selection committee. In 2003, Valassis's CEO also gave away an "Integrator Award," which was a one-week trip for two aboard the *Queen Mary II,*

66Next to excellence is the appreciation of it.99

—WILLIAM MAKEPEACE
THACKERAY

and in 2004 gave the "Global Thinker Award," which was a trip to the destination of the winner's choice, along with $3,000.

———

Marriott International, Inc., based in Bethesda, MD, honors fifteen to twenty people each year with its J. Willard Marriott Award of Excellence, an engraved medallion bearing Marriott's likeness and words expressing the basic values of the company: dedication, achievement, character, ideals, effort, and perseverance. According to Gerald C. Baumer, vice president of employee communications and creative services, selection is based on remarks made by the nominator and the individual's length of service. Award winners represent a cross section of Marriott's workforce: dishwashers, chefs, housekeepers, and merchandise managers are all included. The Marriott Award is presented at an annual banquet in Washington attended by honorees, spouses, nominators, and top executives. "We want other employees to look up to these people," Baumer says.

———

Cash, Cash Substitutes & Gift Certificates

C ash and cash substitutes, such as gift certificates, rank among the top ten ways employees say they'd like to be recognized when they do good work. Employees ranked the following items as either very or extremely important to them: "employee receives a gift certificate or voucher" (48 percent); "employee receives a nominal cash award" (46 percent); "manager gives the employee dinner out for two" (43 percent); and "employee receives entertainment tickets" (39 percent). This is supported by research showing that 95 percent of respondents considered a cash bonus a positive and meaningful incentive. Almost 15 percent of respondents in a survey by *Workforce Management* give cash awards to their employees and 2 percent give savings bonds as part of their organization's incentive programs.

Most people enjoy getting extra spending money—especially around the holidays or when they have unexpected financial needs. Although cash offers maximum flexibility to an employee in terms of how the money is spent, the problem with giving cash is that it often comes to be expected. If you give a $500 holiday bonus three years in a row, employees will count on receiving it the fourth year as well. The other challenge with using cash is that it has no "trophy value"—no lasting value as a reminder of achievement. Money is often spent on bills and then quickly forgotten.

Cash or cash substitutes (such as gift certificates, coupons, or points that can be traded for products) do, however, possess some trophy value. The products employees choose will help remind them of their achievements. Gift certificates have the joint advantage of quick ful-fillment and flexible dollar amounts and expiration dates, and carry no shipping costs. They can be redeemed in a wide variety of places for a broad range of merchandise, from gourmet food to lawn mowers. Cash substitutes can provide an effective compromise between giving an employee money that is quickly spent and forgotten, and a fixed gift or reward that they perhaps do not want or need.

Lowell G. Rein, chairman of LGR Consultants in McMurray, PA, offers several ideas for rewards that involve relatively small amounts of cash:

- ✔ Offer silver dollars or gold coins for good work, a good safety record, or perfect attendance.
- ✔ Periodically give $20 bills to employees (or groups of employ-ees) who excel.
- ✔ Place small cash awards with personal thank-you notes inside employees' calendars or desk drawers.
- ✔ Choose an outstanding employee to receive a small (but perma-nent) pay raise.
- ✔ Offer unexpected cash bonuses.

> **"Compensation is a right; recognition is a gift."**
> —ROSABETH MOSS KANTER, Professor, Harvard Business School

In Portland, OR, REI employees who come to work on a moment's notice because of under-staffing get $5 gift cards to Starbucks.

———

Rocky Laverty, president of the discount store chain Smart & Final in Commerce, CA, awards "Rocky Dollars" for outstanding performance to employees. The award consists of a silver dollar mounted on a certificate, pre-sented personally by the president with public congratulations.

———

Newell Rubbermaid Inc., based in Atlanta, GA, rewards employees with "rubber bucks" for a job well done, redeemable for company products at a company store.

———

Burger King rewards workers with cash when they recruit management-level employees. Also, for finding entry-level workers, employees receive "burger bucks" redeemable for gift certificates from local stores.

———

At National Office Furniture in Jasper, IN, fake cash is awarded during meetings held to test product knowledge. At the end of the meeting, employees use the money to bid for prizes. Tickets for college football games and the Grand Ole Opry are also given to top performers. When a company-wide slogan contest was held, winning teams received jackets.

———

Kyle Illman, managing director of Messages on Hold in Perth, Australia, shares: "Our client contact is over the phone, so we need our people to impress those clients to overcome the distance factor. I read compliments of employees out loud in team meetings and ask the honorees to pick from a deck of playing cards. For cards 2 through 9, they receive the same amount in dollars. For a 10 or picture card, they receive $10, and for an ace, $20. It's fun, and spurs all the reps to wow the clients."

———

"There's nothing wrong with a cash award, but then it's spent. Seemingly small gestures—a parking spot, a plaque, bulletin boards with pictures of employees—can be as effective as banquets and travel.**"**

—DONALD GAGNON,
Training Coordinator,
Brunswick Mining and
Smelting Corp.

Managers and supervisors at Busch Gardens–Tampa use thank-you tokens labeled "Making Friends Is Our Business" to recognize employees on the spot for behavior that directly relates to the organization's core values, such as service, teamwork, and safety. Employees can redeem the tokens for $10 cash, although most prefer to keep the token instead.

———

The *Dallas Business Journal* keeps a supply of gold-colored tokens in $10 and $20 denominations, redeemable at any store in a local mall. Managers provide the coins to employees for meeting weekly goals or making large sales. The paper also gives out movie passes, small cash bonuses, and certificates for in-office back massages.

———

Pitney Bowes, headquartered in Stamford, CT, awards a $25 savings bond for the best oral and written questions submitted at the annual stockholders' meeting.

———

Sandy Edwards, human resources representative for Great Western Drilling Company in Midland, TX, says the company offers a $25 savings bond to the employee who poses the most challenging question to the president at company communication meetings.

———

Great Western hosts an employee apprecia-tion banquet with a twist: Each employee receives $200 in play money to use at an auc-tion. As part of the auction, managers take bids on services such as washing cars, babysitting, house-sitting, baking a cake, cooking a meal, and doing an employee's job for six hours. Employees also receive two gold pieces and a sit-down dinner.

> 66Economic incen-tives are becoming rights rather than rewards.99
>
> —PETER F. DRUCKER, Author and Management Guru

———

Coupons worth $35 are given to employees at Wells Fargo Bank in San Francisco for "extra effort" and "a job well done." They are redeemable for gifts such as season tickets to a sporting event, a pedigreed puppy, five shares of company stock, Rose Parade tickets, shop-ping sprees, a one-month mortgage payment, and paid days off.

———

Quad/Graphics printing company in Pewaukee, WI, pays employees $30 to attend a seminar devoted to quitting smoking and gives $200 to anyone who quits for a year.

———

At Celestial Seasonings, the packager of herbal teas in Boulder, CO, every employee receives a $25 check on his or her birthday, a $50 check at Thanksgiving, and a $100 check at Christmas.

———

Strengths of Cash Incentive Awards

Desirable

Easy to administer and simple to handle

Understood by everyone

Can provide an extra boost to a long-term program

Employees at the Naval Publications and Forms Center in Philadelphia nominate coworkers for the Wilbur Award, named after a longtime employee, which comes with $25. Workers have the chance to earn a top award of $35,000 for an outstanding suggestion.

———

At Anchor Communications in Lancaster, VA, everyone receives a $50 gift certificate when they meet their quarterly cash flow target. Anchor also asks employees to try to conserve resources. As part of this effort, management puts up posters of the quarterly cash balance target all over the building and updates them daily. Those who guess the current cash balance in a pop quiz are given travel certificates for $1,500.

———

G. S. Schwartz and Company Inc., a public relations firm in New York, holds a Hit Parade contest in which it awards $50 a week to the PR representative who demonstrates the best method of getting coverage of an event or generating a story for a client. Winners receive one point toward a $100 quarterly prize, and runners-up are awarded half a point.

———

Mary Jo Stuesser-Yafchak, president of Accudata in Fort Myers, FL, found a way to encourage her employees to attend monthly after-hours training sessions. She holds a monthly drawing for $50 and enters the names of everyone

who has attended in a drawing for $1,000 of travel credit at year end.

———

Every other year, employees are offered selections from a gift catalog in lieu of a year-end bonus at Hatfield Quality Meats in Hatfield, PA. Every employee receives the same monetary amount and can select an expensive item or several less expensive ones.

———

American Express Company's "Be My Guest" plan treats an incentive-winner to dinner at the company's expense. The employee receives a certificate redeemable for a meal at a participating restaurant. The certificate charges the meal to the gift-giver's account.

———

At Pfeiffer & Company, a publisher now part of John Wiley & Sons, employees were financially rewarded for prolonging their business trips by an extra day or so. For example, a plane ticket with a return on Sunday night might be $150 cheaper than one with a Friday return, so they would give the employee $75 of that saving. "It turned out to be a great way for employees to bond with clients, vendors, or coworkers in the other city when there simply had been no time during the normal work week for social activities," reports Marion Mettler, former CEO of the company.

———

> ## Weaknesses of Cash Incentive Awards
> ———
>
> No trophy (i.e. lasting) value
>
> Not exotic
>
> Can't be enhanced
>
> Tends to become an "expected" reward

A manager at Gap Inc., headquartered in San Francisco, wanted to thank everyone for working madly to meet a big deadline. She gave them gift certificates from a spa for a facial or a massage. "It was a much appreciated treat to help calm down and relax after a tough time," reports Carol Whittaker, another Gap manager.

————

Steve Ettridge, president of Randstad North America LP, a temporary-employment service based in Atlanta, had a problem with young workers who would not admit having done something wrong. "Most of the mistakes could have been fixed or minimized, but I never found out about them until they blew up," Ettridge says. "One day I pulled out five hundred dollars in cash, and I told them about a mistake I'd made that week. I said that whoever could top it would get the money. Of course, they were afraid it was a trick." One employee finally admitted to a data-entry error that had caused a $2 million paycheck to be printed and almost mailed out. He got the $500. Since then the company gives out quarterly $100 awards to employees who admit mistakes they have made on the job. Ettridge says the award is designed to allow people to be human and to encourage risk taking.

————

Victor Kiam, president of Remington Products in Shelton, CT, maintains a $25,000 discretionary fund to give instant cash recognition to workers who have been spotted by their supervisors doing an exceptional job.

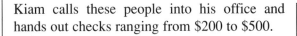

Kiam calls these people into his office and hands out checks ranging from $200 to $500.

A t the Internal Revenue Service, cash awards of at least $100 are given for ideas (some go as high as $4,000). Workers who score well on their performance evaluations get cash bonuses averaging $500.

W hen J. Pierpont Morgan, founder of the JP Morgan Bank, died in 1912, he bequeathed one year's salary to each member of his staff.

A CASE STUDY IN CASH INCENTIVES

S olar Communications, a direct-mail and pack-aging business based in Naperville, IL, has evolved a system of cash bonuses over the years. Initially cash bonuses were casual, even paternal-istic. At the end of most months, founder John F. Hudetz would hand out checks—usually $20 to $60—with everyone getting the same amount.

When the company reached $2 million in sales, the owners wanted to try a more clearly defined program. Employees were assigned to specific machines and divided into work teams of four or five; the more a team produced dur-ing a given month, the bigger the bonus for each member.

The new incentive system had an immedi-ate effect. The packaging machines ran faster

> 66Money is not going to have the same impact with upper level management as it does with lower salaried employees. However, everyone appreciates recogni-tion.99
>
> —Martha Holstein, Associate Director, American Society on Aging

☑ Provide tickets to a sporting, musical, or cultural event, depending on the employee's preference.

☑ At an employee meeting, tape gift certificates to the bottom of chairs in the first three rows.

than ever as employees jockeyed for larger and larger payments. In many cases, production rates doubled. In good months, team members in the top group would see bonuses of about $250, while their counterparts might receive a quarter of that. Because of the pressure to produce, however, other problems occurred, such as machine breakdowns caused by a failure to carry out regular maintenance.

Now the company rewards everyone for bottom-line results according to the clear-cut formula: Every quarter, managers set a target for profitability based on what they think is within reach. Assuming the company meets the goal—and the numbers are openly discussed within the company—25 percent of the incremental earnings goes into a bonus pool. The pool is then divided in relation to a person's earnings during the previous quarter. If, for example, an employee earned 0.5 percent of the total payroll, he or she is entitled to 0.5 percent of the bonus pool, modified by two factors: It takes two years to become fully vested in the program, and unexcused absences or tardiness can shrink a check.

EVOLUTION OF SOLAR PRESS'S CASH INCENTIVE PROGRAM

INTERNAL BONUSES, COMPANY-WIDE, 1977–84

Upside: No promises, easy to administer
Downside: Employees didn't know what they were being rewarded for; no motivational effect

PRODUCTION BONUSES, BY TEAM, 1984–88

Upside: Stimulated output and creativity
Downside: Set off rivalries among departments and individuals; created equipment and quality problems; administrative nightmare

PROFIT-SHARING BONUSES, COMPANY-WIDE, 1987–PRESENT

Upside: Simple to understand; emphasizes teamwork and interdepartmental coordination
Downside: More difficult for individuals to influence

> **"**Greed is still a great motivator.**"**
>
> —TOM STAFFKAMP,
> General Manager for
> Large-Car Operations,
> Chrysler

During especially busy periods, Nucor Corporation, a steel manufacturer in Charlotte, NC, has six-day workweeks, paying bonuses for the sixth day based on time-and-a-half pay.

In Algoma, WI, WS Packaging Group holds monthly bonus meetings called STP (share the profit). The company shares information on every line item of its budget and shares profits beyond their goals with employees. However, if there's a loss, it has to be made up before any additional bonuses can be paid.

The fibers department at E. I. du Pont de Nemours & Company in Wilmington, DE, has an Achievement Sharing Program in which all employees put 6 percent of their salaries at risk and are paid a sliding percentage of that amount based on how close their department comes to its annual goals. Less than 80 percent means no increase; 80 to 100 percent means a 3 to 6 percent increase; 101 to 150 percent means an increase of 7 to 19 percent.

Bagel Works, based in Keene, NH, puts 23 percent of earnings over budget into a bonus pool every four weeks, to be shared by all employees.

At D'Agostino's supermarkets, based in Larchmont, NY, every employee, including part-time workers and delivery staff, is eligible for the gain-sharing program. The concept is simple: Stores that exceed their budgeted profit goals for the quarter share most of the excess with their employees. Gain-sharing funds are allocated by department—so if the meat department pulls in 25 percent of the excess business, its employees receive proportionally more than a department that pulls in less. "This is an incentive to work together to improve performance and also to push each department to its potential," says Roi R. Tucker, vice president of human resources.

———

Wells Fargo Bank employees can make as much as 25 percent of their annual salary in bonuses if they achieve certain performance levels, and about 60 percent of employees receive bonuses each quarter. John Gavin, the divisional head in Fort Worth, says, "We found that a typical bonus was seen as just part of the salary. Now everyone is paid based on performance. The difference in employee behavior is significant."

———

Employees at Jaycraft, a manufacturer of precision components for aerospace applications in Spring Valley, CA, recently rewarded employees for a 50 percent increase in sales with a year-end bonus of 15 percent of salary. Company president Doug Van Vechten explains: "Jaycraft has always held the belief that motivated and productive employees are the key to success."

———

Amsco Steel spends 30 to 40 percent of annual net income on incentives and bonuses for 60 employees, based on three separate financial thresholds.

———

PUT YOUR MONEY WHERE YOUR HEART IS

■ *Offer a cash bonus with taxes prepaid.*

■ *If an employee works overtime, send a $20, $50, or $100 bill to a spouse with a thank-you note for his or her support.*

■ *Give employees who recruit new workers a cash bonus.*

■ *Buy the person a gift certificate.*

■ *Pay for the tutoring of an employee's child.*

■ *Pay an employee's parking or traffic ticket.*

■ *Pay an employee's mortgage for one month.*

■ *Pay for a house-cleaning service for an employee's home.*

Nominal Gifts, Merchandise & Food

A lmost any type of product, merchandise, or food can be used as a form of recognition or reward. Employees reported the following items as being very or extremely important to receive when they do good work: "manager provides food to celebrate success" (39 percent); "employee is given flowers, a gift, or memento;" (39 percent); "manager buys the employee lunch or dinner" (36 percent); "employee gets coupons for food, car wash, movies" (35 percent). In a survey of American workers by *Workforce Management,* 63 percent ranked merchandise incentives as meaningful. More than 50 percent of respondents reported using jewelry and 41 percent use watches as part of their organizations' recognition programs.

There are many advantages to the use of merchandise for recognition. Merchandise incentives are desirable and promotable, since a good selection can appeal to every taste and can be used to reward achievement at various levels and times. The best merchandise for incentive campaigns has lasting value, reflects the quality of the recipient's achievements, inspires pride of ownership, suits the recipient's lifestyle and tastes, projects a positive image of the company, can be fulfilled promptly and without hassle, and is guaranteed and exchangeable.

Fred Maurer, sales manager of special markets at Canon USA in Lake Success, NY, points out that with merchandise, people receive retail values while the company pays discount or wholesale prices. "This fact of life—that we offer people more for their money—is key to the incentive business, and it isn't publicized enough," Maurer says. Maurer's preference in incentive merchandise is "anything to do with home offices, fax machines and home copiers in particular. These items are not only nice to have, but also help make people that much more efficient."

Merchandise also offers trophy value to recipients and can be "drop-shipped" directly from the manufacturer. Items valued up to $400 for safety and length-of-service awards are tax deductible for the company. Finally, redemptions take place at the end of a program, so major costs are incurred after results are in. However, merchandise incentives require detailed administration and are inappropriate for participants who earn low wages.

According to a survey sponsored by Specialty Advertising Association International, the imprintable goods people most appreciate are clothing (T-shirts, jackets, caps), desk or office accessories, writing instruments, glassware and ceramics (including mugs), and calendars. Some of the more interesting items people received were: flyswatters, flower seeds, broom holders, rocks, underwear, athletic supporters, bricks, and a scarf from an Elvis impersonator, demonstrating that—given the right circumstances—anything can serve as a form of recognition!

ChevronTexaco Corporation, headquartered in San Ramon, CA, keeps a large box, secured with a padlock, brimming with all sorts of gifts. An employee being recognized on the spot for some accomplishment is brought to the Treasure Chest by his or her supervisor, who holds the keys. The employee gets to choose an item from the box: a coffee mug, pen-and-pencil set, gift certificate, coupon for lunch or dinner, or movie tickets. Recognition can come from peers as well. At Boardroom Inc. in Stamford, CT, CEO Martin Edelston keeps a closetful of fun recognition items any manager can use to quickly acknowledge a deserving employee.

> **"The way we see it, spending $1 on something clever and unique is better than spending $50 on something ordinary and forgettable."**
>
> —RICHARD FILE,
> Partner,
> Amrigon

Motivating Merchandise

Electronics—Tools help people improve their efficiency: multimedia cell phones, PDAs, fax machines, and wireless laptop computers.

Appliances— Compact appliances save space: combo washer-dryers; under-the-counter can openers, TVs, and radios.

Services—Services help people save time: a housecleaner for a year, babysitting coupons, spa visits, and facials.

Unique gifts— Customized gifts add special meaning: special-edition lithographs, first edition books, antiques, and company-imprinted credit cards.

Managers at Bronson Healthcare Group in Kalamazoo, MI, set up "toolboxes" filled with $150 worth of recognition items suggested by employees, such as movie tickets and coupons for ice cream, time off, valet parking, and restaurants. The items are used to recognize employees when they do a good job, and the toolbox is replenished as needed.

———

One recent January, the snow was really coming down at Valassis's corporate headquarters in Livonia, MI. CEO Al Schultz wanted to thank employees who made the long trek into the office and were hard at work despite the inclement weather outside, so he ordered pizza and soft drinks for everyone at all three Michigan locations and joined employees in the auditorium at corporate headquarters for an impromptu lunch while the snow fell.

———

Dave Baldwin, the manager of management development training for Abbott Laboratories in Abbott Park, IL, tells how he gave a bouquet of flowers held together with a watch to an associate who delayed her vacation and "took the time" to help when needed in the department. The employee wears the watch as a badge of honor to this day. In another instance, his company honored an employee who set up an off-site management meeting by having each senior executive give her a flower at the beginning of the event with a personalized word of thanks. She reported that although she had received flowers before, the personalized thanks by the company's senior executives made this recognition event the most meaningful of all.

———

The Maritz Performance Improvement Company office in Fenton, MO, has a "Thanks a Bunch" program in which a bouquet of flowers is given to an employee in appreciation for special favors or jobs well done. That employee then passes on the reward to someone else, and so on and so forth. Each recipient also gets a thank-you card. At certain intervals, the cards are entered into a drawing for rewards such as binoculars or logoed jackets. The program is used during periods of especially heavy workloads or other stressful times.

———

The Hartford Steam Boiler Inspection and Insurance Company in Hartford, CT, spends up to $50 per year per administrative employee on gifts tailored to various interests, including dinners for two, tickets to movies and sporting events, gift certificates, and coffee for a month. There are four requirements for the award: The employee must be a team player, take initiative to solve problems, provide leadership in supporting company goals, and show an attitude that inspires others to do their best. Spokesperson Karen Block says, "I believe that when the final results are in, the investment will be returned to us many times over."

———

> **"**There's no knowing what any given employee will value as a reward. That's why, with noncash items, we recommend offering employees a wide range of rewards. Let them choose whatever is to their personal liking.**"**
>
> —BARCY FOX,
> Vice President,
> Performance Systems,
> Maritz, Inc.

David Walling, training coordinator for the Natural Resources Conservation Service in Champaign, IL, reports using "spot awards"— specially designed coffee mugs, watches, and pen-and-pencil sets—to recognize good work. He also gives people special framed prints of wildlife or other subjects, depending on the person's preferences.

The Houghton Mifflin Company in Boston, as well as other publishers, customizes books to fit specific occasions. Books can be customized in several ways:

✔ Have the CEO personalize a book with an inscription to commemorate an occasion or achievement.

✔ Incorporate a company's logo on the front or back cover, or on the spine.

✔ Alter a book's title to feature a brand or a company.

✔ Insert product allusions into a book's text.

✔ Feature a letter or brief message from a company on a separate page before the title page.

✔ Excerpt an appropriate chapter from an original work and create an entirely new book.

As an exciting alternative to employees selecting merchandise from a catalog, some companies host shopping sprees, allowing award winners to go on a rampage through a warehouse that stocks appropriate prizes. Carlson Marketing Group has opened its Dayton, OH, distribution center to employees of Mobil, Toyota, and Nabisco.

Carlson marketers fly their employees to Dayton for a prespree party the night before the appointed date. On the day of the event, employees walk the winners through the warehouse, pointing out where the most valuable goods are. The 200,000-square-foot warehouse contains about 4,500 items, including electronics, glassware, golf clubs, and vacuum cleaners.

Carlson recommends that sponsors limit the run-through to two minutes. According to Michael Barga, director of distibution in Dayton, "More than two minutes becomes a struggle for the participant, who's dashing down the aisles and throwing items into a big shopping cart." On average, winners accumulate about $3,500 worth of goods per minute.

———

The Smurfit-Stone Container Corporation in Chicago topped a profitable year in which it gave every employee a television set by giving everyone a VCR (retailing for several hundred dollars at the time) the next year. 24,000 were distributed. To announce the gift, the company made a ten-minute video with two actors impersonating Roger Ebert and the late Gene Siskel. The characters reviewed the company's year, and footage of the various facilities was shown. Chief executive officer Roger Stone then appeared, gave the two-thumbs-up sign, and announced the gift. At the end of the presentation, each employee

❝I don't like cash because the cost-value relationship is one to one; I don't use travel because when dealers win, they have to use their vacation time to take the trip. Incentive travel can be self-defeating if it's a 'must' vacation. Merchandise, on the other hand, has a high perceived value and lots of flexibility. With premiums, there is a very *thick* line between junk and quality.❞

—ROD TAYLOR,
Group Promotion
Manager of
Paper Products,
Procter & Gamble

☑ Find out the person's hobby and give an appropriate gift.

☑ Buy the person something for his or her child.

☑ Give an employee a copy of the latest best-selling management or business book.

☑ Inscribe a favorite book as a gift.

received a certificate resembling a movie ticket, which was used to claim the VCR.

———

Recognition items can be generated around a theme such as summer. Towels, umbrellas, rafts, chairs, and coolers work well as standard promotional beach items. For a barbecue theme, options include grills, cooking utensils, hats, and aprons—even a custom-built barbecue pit and patio furniture. Floats, boats, and inner tubes can also be customized; for larger prizes, companies can use canoes and dinghies. Recent users of such items are Pepsi, Columbo Frozen Yogurt, Sunkist Soda, and Moosehead Beer.

———

In Dresden, Ontario, where winters are harsh, manager Craig Bullen of TD Canada Trust decided to thank his employees in a weather-wise way. A winter storm was in effect, and as the snow accumulated, Craig sent out a note to all of his employees: "To celebrate our year-to-date branch results, I've placed a little treat in each of your vehicles to help keep your path clear and safe. The three items are:

1) A jug of washer fluid to keep your vision clear

2) A snowbrush to help you stay on the journey ahead

3) A lock deicer to provide a warm, comfortable experience."

———

In Mary Kay, Inc.'s Career Apparel Program, sales consultants who reach specific goals become eligible to buy specific outfits. Once someone qualifies to become a director, for example, she is invited to attend Mary Kay's management conference and, while there, is fitted for a director's suit at the expense of the company. The style changes every year. Laura Whittier, manager of incentive merchandising, says, "Our directors love the suits because they are functional and provide a visual symbol of their success. Qualifying to buy the suit indicates high status; wearing it results in a more professional look and instant recognition of success."

FIVE WAYS TO CUSTOMIZE AN APPAREL AWARD

1. Design an eye-catching graphic featuring your company name, logo, or popular product name and place it prominently on the apparel.

2. Opt for a more subtle placement by sewing a tag with your name or logo onto a sleeve or cuff.

3. Create a special label to appear inside the cap or garment.

4. Place a crest with your logo on the pocket of a shirt, using a color slightly darker than that of the shirt.

PERSONALIZE IT

■ Give a personalized company coffee cup or belt buckle.

■ Have a pen-and-pencil set engraved for the person.

■ Personalize the label on a wine bottle with a message of thanks.

■ Have a personalized cartoon made for an employee award. Comic Arts of Wilton, CT, can include the recipient's name, a team pennant, a sports picture, and a customized caption in a cartoon.

**Most Popular
Specialty Items**

- Wearables
- Writing
  instruments
- Desk and office
  accessories
- Glassware and
  ceramics
- Calendars
- Sporting goods
- Buttons, badges,
  and ribbons
- Auto accessories
- Houseware and
  tools

5. For loyal long-term employees, offer a very high-quality brand-name item without your company name or logo, and present it with a special card conveying your sincere appreciation for their hard work and support.

———

"Everyone eats," says Rick Farone, product and program coordinator for Royal Appliance, based in Glenwillow, OH. "When you reward people with food, you know it's something they'll use. Food makes people happy." An almost infinite variety of food gifts can be used to reward employees, including fruit baskets; fruit-of-the-month clubs; home-delivered steak, seafood, or lobster; jelly and jam; and spices.

———

DDB Worldwide Communications Group, an advertising agency located in New York City, gives bottles of champagne to employees who develop great ideas.

———

At the Angus Barn Restaurant in Raleigh, NC, an employee "caught in the act of caring," gets a choice of entree from the restaurant's menu.

———

"When it becomes extremely hot during the summer months, I carry an ice chest full of freezer pops around and give them out to employees who are working in areas that are not air-conditioned," reports Cynthia M.

Wood, team manager at an International Paper office in Eastover, SC. "You should see their faces light up!"

Stew Leonard's in Norwalk, CT, has an "Out-to-Dinner" program, rewarding employees with dinners for two when they do something special, like coming in on their day off or working through a break. Each manager is authorized to award similar items; some walk around with lunch coupons in their pockets so they can hand them out on the spot.

A physical therapist's office instituted a "Margarita Award" for the therapist who had to work with the toughest client that week or month. The awardee is treated by the group to a margarita happy hour.

Employees of Long's Drugs, the drugstore chain, who work late into the night to stock shelves for holiday sales are given certificates for free pizza and soft drinks and time off later the same week so they can be with their families.

MetaSolv Software, based in Plano, TX, uses keg parties to introduce new employees to the rest of the 350-person fast-growth company. The new employee works the tap and gets to meet everyone.

Unusual Specialty Items

- Boxer shorts
- "Mick Jagger" lips alarm clock
- Jalapeño lollipops
- Portable picnic table and benches
- Spanish-speaking calculator
- Desktop toy train
- Coffee cup imprinted with a message that appears—or disappears—when the cup is filled

LET'S DO LUNCH

■ *Buy the person lunch and include three coworkers of his or her choice.*

■ *Bring the person bagged lunches for a week.*

■ *Authorize managers to walk around with lunch coupons so they can hand them out on the spot.*

■ *Arrange for the employee to have lunch with the company president.*

■ *Leave a card for a lunch date at the employee's discretion.*

■ *Have lunch or coffee with an employee or a group of employees you don't normally see.*

Persistence Software in San Mateo, CA, brings in a breakfast tray and places it near a new person's desk on his or her first day and then invites the other 110 employees to meet their colleague. Most people come by to grab a bagel or muffin, introduce themselves, and chat.

———

Liz Claiborne's HR Department celebrates "Bagel Fridays," where employees take turns bringing in bagels and cream cheese for the office. It's a great way for everyone to take off 15–20 minutes each Friday morning, come together in a common meeting area, and chat about work, life, and other issues. What started out as just a bag of bagels and some spreads has exploded into an all-out Food Fest, in which the food shopper of the week thinks about a theme, buys tablecloths, knickknacks, and decorations, and then gets not only bagels, but usually coffee, juice, and other goodies. The themes often coincide with holidays, seasons, such as "Summer Fun in the Sun," or events, like the "Super Super Bowl." Employees assigned a Bagel Friday usually start thinking about it two to three weeks in advance, racking their brains as to how to outdo the person from the week before.

———

One manager at American Express Financial Advisors treats employees to lunch by sending someone to TacoBell or White Castle.

———

Once a week, a different staff member at the Rock and Roll Hall of Fame in Cleveland cooks and serves breakfast for the rest of the staff. This is a great morale booster for everyone and gives people some downtime to discuss the week's business.

———

Oscar Mayer in Northfield, IL, holds an event called "Team Lunch," when researchers have lunch together. They eat Oscar Mayer products, work on problems, and tell stories about each other. People about whom enough stories are told have become company legends.

———

Joan Cawley, director of human resources at Advanta Corporation, a financial services company in Horsham, PA, uses the following forms of recognition: surprising internal service departments such as payroll and switchboard/reception with doughnuts or candy; treating female staff members to a lunchtime manicure during an especially hectic period; buying Teenage Mutant Ninja Turtle decorations for an employee too busy to plan a child's birthday party; presenting a monogrammed canvas briefcase to commemorate a staff member's promotion to management; surprising a department with a picnic at a local park, complete with champagne and strawberry shortcake made by the department head in place of a regular Friday staff meeting; and presenting a Life Saver Award—a dozen packs of Life Saver candies and a gift certificate from a local department

> **"One reason food is a good motivator is that it provides the winner with an experience with family and friends. Food is a social gift."**
>
> —JEFFREY GIBEAULT,
> Sales Manager,
> Business Incentive
> Department,
> Omaha Steaks
> International

> **"Merchandise works, but the challenge is to find the right product for your audience. We have four basic criteria for choosing merchandise awards: (1) The product must be of such high quality that it reflects positively on the company image; (2) it must be something everyone wants, preferably a state-of-the-art item that's on its way up in the consumer buying chain; (3) it must carry a high perceived value in relation to cost; and (4) its brand name must be instantly recognizable in a positive way."**
>
> —MARK WEINBERGER,
> Marketing Service Manager,
> Cathay Pacific
> Airways Limited

store—to recognize an employee's efforts in filling two jobs during a period of transition.

———

At Electronic Data Systems in Plano, TX, managers are encouraged to get to know their employees' tastes, hobbies, and interests, so deserving staff members can be rewarded with appropriate incentives such as tickets to a sports event, the opera, or a dinner for the family at a restaurant. Molly Edwards, EDS's manager of recognition services, says one employee in Dallas was even given a washer and dryer for a particularly good performance. Another employee in Michigan returned from vacation to find that her kitchen had been completely remodeled.

———

Special Privileges, Perks & Employee Services

A final category of tangible recognition that employees value for doing good work involve special privileges and perks. Two items that were cited as very or extremely important to them: "employee is given special privileges or perks" (52 percent); and "employee gets to use a preferred parking space" (25 percent). Special privileges and perks can accompany other forms of recognition, enhancing the honor of those awards and thus their desirability. They can also add fun and excitement to the recognition activity for everyone involved. Ideally, items in this category would be given on a contingent basis for specific behavior or performance, although in this chapter we have also included services and activities that are made available to everyone in the organization.

A VIP Pass allows the recipient free privileges for a certain period (a month or a quarter) at the Management 21 training and consulting firm in Nashville. An honoree might receive free lunches in the cafeteria, free membership in the company's fitness center, or free parking in the parking garage.

> **"Everybody works smarter when there's something in it for them."**
>
> —MICHAEL LEBOEUF,
> Author,
> *The Greatest Management Principle in the World*

Depending on the office location, Robert W. Baird, a financial services company located in Milwaukee, offers discounts for local fitness centers, retail clothing stores, Sam's Club and art museum memberships, theater and sporting event tickets, tourist attractions such as Disney World, and entertainment events such as Milwaukee's Summerfest. In addition, a local vendor provides on-site services at the company's Milwaukee location for shoe shine and repair, dry cleaning, and film processing.

———

There's only one reserved parking spot at Iteris, Inc., the manufacturer of robots and space-borne tape recorders in Anaheim, CA, and that's for the person selected as Associate of the Month.

———

Carla Levy, training specialist for Indianapolis Power & Light Company, recommends paying an employee's parking fees for a month or a year as recognition for a job well done.

———

Corey Wedel, employment services manager for Central Missouri State University, relates how the staff of seven offered to wrap holiday presents for other employees of the university, even providing gift wrap. "We picked up the gifts at people's desks and brought back their wrapped packages," he continues. "People loved it! They enjoyed the hassle-free service and the results, especially one person who has eight children."

At General Mills, headquartered in Minneapolis, new employees can pick a work of art for their office from a large collection. Similarly, those who work in individual offices choose their own furnishings and works of art at Mary Kay, Inc.

———

Production workers at Worthington Industries, the steel processor and plastic products manufacturer in Columbus, OH, can get $2 haircuts on company time at barbershops in the plants. Employees can also fish for bass and bluegill during their off-hours at a stocked pond near corporate headquarters.

———

Shannon Kearns, R.N., in quality management at Jackson Health System in Miami, FL, writes, "We wanted to improve the appearance of our security guards so we started giving those who were dressed appropriately in full uniform their choice of work schedule as an incentive. We were surprised to find that peer pressure is making the biggest difference. At the beginning of each shift, the shift commander has everyone who is in their correct uniform stand up, and the staff members call each other on any slip-ups."

———

Employees at Wilton Connor Packaging, Inc., in Charlotte, NC (now a part of Weyerhaeuser), could take their laundry to work and have it washed, dried, and folded, courtesy of the company. They also had a handyman on staff

RESEARCH THEIR FAMILY

Family Connection traces the history of family names. The information is presented on a 12" x 14" certificate made of parchment-tone paper. "We write up all the key details in the history of a surname, and the information dates back to when it was first recorded in writing," says Martin O'Shea, president of the company. "Aside from telling where the name originates and what it means, we can document famous people who have the same name and provide family coats of arms where available." The company has a computer data base of over 300,000 surnames.

☑ *Offer a deserving employee a change in job title.*

☑ *Give the person a better office: larger, better location, better furnishings, etc . . .*

who did free work for employees, and any hard costs were deducted from paychecks over a period of several months. "We have virtually no turnover, we have no quality problems, we have very few supervisors," Wilton Connor, the company's chief executive once said. "Those are the hard-nosed business reasons for doing these things."

Customer sales representatives at Emerald Publications in San Diego are allowed to wear casual clothing every Friday. Says one employee, "It's often my best sales day, because I don't have to worry about sitting properly or how I look. I wish we had even more latitude on other days." American Airlines now allows employees at company headquarters in Fort Worth, TX, to dress in business casual everyday. The policy applies to about twenty thousand management employees. Jayne Allison, vice president for human relations, explains, "We have heard from our employees that they believe they are more productive in casual dress."

To reduce stress from working long hours, many companies, such as S. C. Johnson & Son in Racine, WI, hire a masseuse for employees. In fact, many massage services specialize in corporate clients, serving a different company each day of the week. Masseuses are also brought in each Valentine's Day at Nelson Motivation, Inc., in San Diego, giving neck and shoulder massages to all employees.

Concierge services at Accenture, the consulting company, arranges for someone to stay at an employee's home when the cable guy comes, or to pick up a car from the repair shop. George Trojack, director of finance for Accenture's Chicago office, uses the service about twice a week for everything from getting subway tokens to waiting for furniture delivery. "When things come up, they're not as stressful as they used to be because the concierge can take care of them," Trojack says.

———

Bronson Healthcare Group offers a host of varied employee services such as concierge, Bronson Bucks (for use in their Snack Shop or Athletic Club), and valet parking for expectant moms. The CEO hosts office hours, "snow day camps" when schools close, and many themed celebrations.

———

Arbitron offers a host of concierge-type services to make life less stressful. They have mechanics who come on-site to perform minor operations, such as brake repairs and oil changes; a day- and elderly-care consulting service; discounts for major retailers, fitness club memberships, and community associations; and a host of community and charitable activities.

———

PepsiCo headquarters in Purchase, NY, has hired a full-time concierge to help its 800

> **"Offering incentives is the most positive way to reward achievement goals, improve service, and develop cost-saving programs."**
>
> —Advertisement for Thomson Consumer Electronics, Inc.

employees save time with personal errands, such as booking restaurant tables and theater seats, arranging events for children, and household repairs. The company started the service after a survey showed that employees had no free time for running such errands. Other time-saving services the company has arranged include a dry cleaner in the headquarters building, a mobile oil-change service in the parking lot twice a month, a shoeshine man roaming the halls twice a week, and the sale of take-home dinners in the cafeteria every day at 4:30 P.M. They recently brought in a shoe repair service and hope to bring in a tailor for employees' use. Employees can also receive financial counseling services for about $20 a month.

———

WRQ, a software company based in Seattle, offers dock space for kayaking commuters, as well as a nap room with futons, on-site massages, and a flextime policy (which 94 percent of employees use).

———

Replacements, Ltd. of Greensboro, NC, a supplier of old and new china, crystal, silver, jewelry, and collectibles, allows its 565 employees to bring their dogs to work every day. The company reports a 10 percent drop in absenteeism. On any given day, about 25 to 30 dogs come to work. Happily, there have been no problems with dog fights or broken inventory.

———

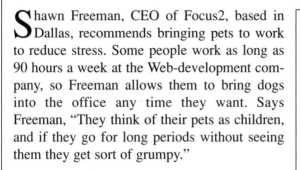

Shawn Freeman, CEO of Focus2, based in Dallas, recommends bringing pets to work to reduce stress. Some people work as long as 90 hours a week at the Web-development company, so Freeman allows them to bring dogs into the office any time they want. Says Freeman, "They think of their pets as children, and if they go for long periods without seeing them they get sort of grumpy."

☑ Volunteer to do another person's least desirable task for a day.

☑ Answer the person's telephone for an afternoon.

☑ Wash the employee's car in the parking lot during lunch.

———

At Parrett Trucking in Scottsboro, AL, Mike Parrett allows drivers to take their pets on the road. But he did have to limit the break room to cats and dogs, after one of his drivers went in with a boa constrictor around his neck, causing some alarm among the office workers.

———

A Xerox Corporation office in Palo Alto, CA, recently had fifty dogs on "Take Your Dog to Work Day," up from thirty the previous year. Systems Engineer Greg Newell says there wasn't a single complaint from the five hundred employees.

———

ADVO, Inc. an advertising and merchandising company based in Windsor, CT, offers pet insurance to all its employees. "It was a no-brainer for us," says Leslie Lenser, director of corporate benefits. "The benefit is completely paid through MetLife, a vendor we already had a relationship with."

———

BUY THEM A STAR

There are several companies that operate a Star Registry that allows you to purchase an unnamed star in someone's honor. They provide a certificate along with a map showing where in the night sky you can find your star.

Levi Strauss & Company, headquartered in San Francisco, has a "quiet room" where employees can take a solitary break to relax, pound on the walls, scream, meditate, or read. Lowney Associates, a Palo Alto, CA, consulting firm, has a nap room at its headquarters where employees can take a break in peace and quiet.

———

Magic Pencil Studios, a creative services company based in Los Angeles, has a "time-out room" complete with children's furniture and toys that any employee is free to use—sometimes with their children, whom they're allowed to bring to work.

———

FedEx Freight West, based in San Jose, CA, provides off-duty rooms for drivers and dockworkers with pool tables, video games, color TVs with VCRs, refrigerators, and vending machines with healthy choices.

———

365 IDEAS FOR INFORMAL RECOGNITION

Following is a list of special perks you can use to recognize employees, developed by Rita Maehling and The Tennant Company in Minneapolis.

Magazine subscription	Paid benefits for a year	Fun tickets
Dinner gift certificate	Well-day off	Savings bond
Cultural event tickets	Event tickets for family	Movie tickets
Overnight at a hotel	Time-at-the-Top Day	Ski trip
Letter with copy to manager	Paid mileage for a week	Raffle tickets
Attendance award	Chocolates	Limo ride to and from work
Social event tickets	Trophies	Corner office for a week
Golf balls	Prime parking spot	
Special chair/throne	Cafeteria theme	Letter from president
Training class	Jackets	Celebrity visit
Sporting event tickets	Certificate of accomplishment	Breakfast
Favorite snack	Plaque	Work at home option
Family day at the office	Supervisor for a day	"Degree"
Athletic team jersey	Calculator	New pair of shoes
Anniversary gift	Coffee mug	"You measure up" ruler
Free postage for a year	Cash for company store	"Expert" status
Paid sabbatical	Trip to customer site	Handshake
Key chains	Service award	Free dessert coupons
Letter with copy to family	Traveling trophy	T-shirt
Weekend at a cabin	Special project clearance	Host party for friends
Free video/DVD rentals	Star pin	Stuffed animals
Golf outing	Article in newsletter	Suspenders
Company car for a year	Stickers	Points toward award
Lunch with president/CEO	Flowers	Day off with pay
Senior managers host a party	Professional membership	Standing ovation
	Free coffee for a month	Hall of Fame picture
		Valet parking
		Pen

Pat on the Back Award

Charm bracelet

Fishing trip

Caribbean vacation

Company products

Dry cleaning for a year

TV appearance

Recent bestseller book

Trade show attendance

Free cell phone
for a month

Porsche for a month

Balloon bouquet

Smile

Bonus

Violinist at your desk

Cross-training

Day at camp

Ice cream sundaes

Hot-air balloon ride

Cash on the spot

Pool party

Grocery store
certificate

Special holiday party

Visit from president

Personalized stationery

Watch

Band serenade

Training seminar

Valentines

Banners

Special name tag

Photo on bulletin board

Group/family photo

Rubber stamps

Gift catalog

Visit to supplier site

CDs

Public announcement

Weekly
acknowledgment

Popcorn party

Poem

Free lunch

Project kick-off party

Free haircut

Birthday card

Barbecue

Fancy trip

Stock

"You're a Winner"
dartboard

Free babysitting

YMCA family night

Statue in front yard

Welcome letter

TV

One month off with pay

Skywriting message

Boat trip

Free soda for a month

Use of company condo

House cleaning service

Ring

Athletic equipment

DVD player

Shopping spree

Pin

Movie night

Cap

Work area upgrade

Free vacation day

Software

Bumper stickers

Health club
membership

Use of company
equipment

Hardware

CD player

Make-your-own
taco party

Spouse's day

Bungee jump

Buttons

Recognition
thermometer

Give-a-hand gloves

Comedy club tickets

Free photo finishing

Passalong note

Snow brushes

Airline tickets

Photo on placard

Office cleaning service

Video of
accomplishment

Trip to favorite TV show

Free snow shoveling

Accomplishment collage

Sit in on management
meeting

Thermos

Breakfast meeting

Internal customer party

Car allowance

Fanny pack

Name on electronic board

Car for a month

Outward Bound trip

Scholarship

Free holiday cards

Party for children

"Lettuce entertain you" visit

Appliance

Dept.-to-dept. recognition

Paid car insurance

Free glasses/contacts

Tools

Comp time

Belt buckle

Pet

Atlas

After-work party

Bigger office

Safety glasses

Visit to headquarters

Escort to event

Six-month car lease

Temp help for a day

Tickets to concert

Gag gift

Headbands

Free car washes

Magnets

Gas

Fish fry

DustBuster

Collectibles

Olympics party

Oil changes

Desk supplies

Job exchange

Display safety record

Coasters

Extended lunch hours

Makeover

Singing telegram

Car seat

Las Vegas Night

Bus pass

Train trip

Off an hour early

Company honor roll

Birthday off

Potluck dinner

Blanket

Flashlight

Entertainment book

Jewelry

Door knocker

Cruise

Blue ribbon

Lakeside party

Pop/beer can holders

Calendar

Sports bottle

Field releases

Necktie

Barrette

Lunch bag

Day at the races

Travel bag/tote

Spa day

Emergency roadside kit

Spouse included in trip

Theme party

Sweatshirt

Umbrella

Letter opener

Tokens for points

Speaker for group

Travel mug

Free checking account

Casino "money"

Job sharing

Disney tickets

Lottery tickets

Group roast

Framed memento

Rotating birthday cake

Retreat

Sandwich board statement

Paperweight

Visit state capital

New office furniture

Wok cooking party

"Qu-owl-ity" owl

Car detailing

Fishing equipment

Bowling party

Gift to charity

Earthquake kit

Car start in winter

Tennis racket

Barometer

Tickets to art exhibit

Notice in newspaper

Society meeting

Turkey

Company blazer

Golf clubs

Cooler

Spring cleanup at home

Assistant for a week

Billboard

Landscaping

Picture on cup

Portfolio

Fire extinguisher

First-aid kit

Golf lessons

Artwork

Massages

Facials

Dance lessons

Frisbee

Afternoon at the mall

Dinner with favorite
    actor

PA announcement

Congeniality award

Chef-prepared meal

Start an hour later

Lawn care

Pony

Travel upgrade

Personal CD player

Valor Award

Attend conference

Plant

Authorship

Socks

Tie tack

Candy

Brag board

Sunglasses

Personalized luggage

Free dog grooming

Newspaper subscription

Costco membership

Coffee shop card

Manicure

Pedicure

Personal trainer

Song composed

Dog training

Dog walking

Personal shopper

Free groceries for week

Satellite TV for 6 months

Internet service

New office chair

Ski lessons

Omaha steaks

Lasik eye surgery

Braces

Day care for a month

New outfit

Bike

Patio furniture

Digital camera

Windows washed

Cooking lessons

Yoga lessons

Tanning sessions

Snowblower

Leaf raking

Cake/pie per month

Red carpet treatment

Car wash by executives

Pick a project

Chair massages

Snowmobile trip

Guest ball game
    announcer

Family oil painting

Bus trip with friends

Astronomy class
    (for stars!)

Horseback-riding
    lessons

Trip to a dude ranch

Meet sports hero

Day with a senator

Conduct an orchestra

Throw out opening
    pitch

Homemade cookies

Sub sandwiches for
    a month

Credit card for a week

. . . or name your own!

PART IV

GROUP RECOGNITION, REWARDS & ACTIVITIES

We know recognition works with individuals, but it can be just as effective with groups. This section discusses forms of effective group recognition, rewards, and activities, from group-based recognition programs to specific team awards to fun activities, games, contests, celebrations, parties, special events, and travel.

As with recognizing the achievements of individuals, some of the best forms of team recognition are informal and intangible, such as a manager thanking group members for their involvement, suggestions, and initiatives, or sending a letter to all team members thanking them for their contributions. Team spirit and group morale can also be bolstered by informal reviews throughout a project or by hosting a lunch celebration with project teams once they've completed interim findings. At the end of the project, let the group celebrate as it chooses.

The task of recognizing teams does present a dilemma, however, in balancing the team's collective effort and acknowledging the individual contributions of its members. You run the risk of slighting those members who contributed most to the group's success and reinforcing other members who might have barely made it to the meetings. "Jelly bean motivation"—giving equal recognition for unequal performance—is detrimental to the group's sustained productivity and morale.

One way to mitigate this dilemma is to be sure the team leader recognizes the contribution of individual members as the team makes progress, and encourages group members to do the same. As the group becomes a team, its productivity and morale is shaped by specific behaviors of any member of the group, not just the designated group leader. To develop a team that functions well, it's important for members to feed off each other's success; to support each other in various, explicit ways such as acknowledging productive contributions, new ideas, or suggestions by others; and to create positive interventions, such as volunteering for a group assignment or assisting another member of the group with his or her assignment.

Managers must also learn to couple individual performance with group output. Research by Deborah Crown of the University of Alabama shows that a combination of individual goals coupled with overall group goals results in team performance 36 percent greater than what would happen otherwise. "It might be as simple as changing to rewarding people for the percentage of goals to which they contribute," says Crown. "You're more likely to have success if you give people a goal and direct their action where you want it directed, rather than hoping over time they'll try to do the right thing because they identify with the group."

Eight Ways to Praise Teams

1. Have an upper manager stop in at the first meeting of a special project team and express his or her appreciation of the members' involvement.

2. When individuals present an idea or suggestion, thank them for their initiative and contribution. Encourage involvement in the group's goal-setting process, problem-solving, brainstorming, etc.

3. Celebrate progress, interim findings, and final results, letting team members decide how to celebrate.

4. Open the floor for team members to praise anyone at the beginning or end of the meeting. Provide a "praising barrage" by the team for one or more of its members.

5. Have members of the team create awards for each other. Invest in team mementos and symbols of a team's work together, such as T-shirts or coffee cups with a team motto or company logo.

6. Conduct team-building activities and field trips such as bowling, laser tag, a visit to a state fair, a "popcorn lunch," or a team challenge or contest against a group goal or another team.

7. Invite upper management to attend a meeting with the team during which individuals ask questions and the group is thanked for its efforts.

8. Send letters or e-mails to every team member at the conclusion of a project, thanking them for their contribution. Consider thanking the team members' families, as well, if the team effort was significant.

Group Recognition & Rewards

The important thing to remember about group recognition is that the entire team needs to be recognized. If only the manager or highest performer of a group is recognized, the group may lose motivation.

> **❝What's important to me is getting together with all the others who achieved that same goal, and the pride I take in satisfying a goal the company has set.❞**
>
> —BARION MILLS, JR.,
> Agency Manager,
> State Farm Insurance

At MicroAge Computer in Tempe, AZ, managers fine individuals who come late to company meetings and pass the money out to people who arrive on time.

———

When Randy Dorr was a supervisor at MCI, he motivated a team of low-performing telemarketers by calling their mothers to tell them how great they were every time they met their performance goals. As a result, the group became the top-performing team in the company.

———

At Advanced Micro Devices in Sunnyvale, CA, photos of work teams often appear in company publications.

———

Terry Horn, human resources director at Household Automotive Finance in San

Diego, reports: "I recently wanted to thank all the employees in my department for their great work in meeting financial goals. The group is all women, except for one man, who is very health conscious and eats a banana at break daily. I gave each of the women a bunch of flowers and the guy a bunch of bananas. They all really appreciated the gesture. It was fun!"

———

To energize their teams, laboratory managers at a Kaiser Permanente office in Pasadena, CA, collaborated to convert a little-used conference room into a Strategy Center, purchasing furniture and equipment and decorating the room to make it conducive to creative thinking and brainstorming sessions.

———

Montefiore Nursing Home in Beachwood, OH, a 500-employee nonprofit facility, started a "Keys to Our Commitment" program, in which teams promise to uphold certain values, such as helping one another, serving patient needs, or being helpful to relatives. Basically, workers are challenged never to say, "I don't know." Staff members who embody a value are awarded paper keys by fellow staff members. They can then trade them for pins, from bronze to gold; for instance, ten paper keys equal one bronze pin. The program has helped employees to work more cooperatively, share information with management, and feel more supported. Turnover has been cut in half.

———

> **"**Our main employee incentive program has raised the average level of performance considerably. Teamwork and interdepartmental relationships have been enhanced.**"**
>
> —DANIEL J. WILDERMUTH,
> Director of Marketing,
> Mirassou Vineyards

> **"Nothing, not even the most advanced technology, is as formidable as people working together enthusiastically toward a shared goal. Whether as a nation, an army, or a corporation—people become unstoppable when they are moved by a common vision, and have the power and tools to achieve it."**
>
> —United Technologies Corporate Brochure

Every four or five years, new store managers of J. C. Penney Corporation, headquartered in Plano, TX, are "affirmed" in a ceremony held at more than a dozen locations across the country. A pledge is made to the founding principles of the company, and at the conclusion each newly affirmed associate receives an HCSC pin, standing for Honor, Confidence, Service, and Cooperation.

At Delta Airlines, based in Atlanta, employees fill out Team Recognition Cards to give to teams that they feel have gone "above and beyond." Cards are entered in a drawing for a prize of $500, to be donated to a charity or civic organization of the team's choice.

At the West Union Good Samaritan Center nursing home in West Union, IA, teams are recognized for the compliments they receive from patients, relatives, and administrators. Comment cards are read out loud and posted on the central bulletin board, and administrators bring baked goods or flowers to recognize the team with the most favorable comments.

Grinnell College, located in the heart of Iowa, recently held a recognition initiative entitled "Above & Beyond" for departments and individuals who demonstrated positive attitude, innovation, and outstanding service to others. A traveling trophy was passed from one deserving office to another, departments formed teams to compete onstage in "Family Feud: Customer Service," and Excellence Award forms were widely distributed around campus so that staff, faculty, students, and college visitors could share memorable campus service experiences. Those recognized were also featured prominently in each issue of the college's employee newsletter.

BlueCross BlueShield of North Carolina uses several forms of group recognition:

✔ One department has three teams working on different projects, each with specific deadlines. To motivate the employees, they allow teams to wear jeans for a week if they meet the previous week's goals. Everyone pushes to make sure they are not wearing business casual when another team is wearing jeans.

✔ A team composed of Project Managers and Business Analysts (PMBA) recognizes accomplishments each month by awarding a stuffed "Pumbaa" (from Disney's *The Lion King*) to the team member with the most significant accomplishments.

✔ A team manager reports: "For one project, I awarded each team member various items to represent their contribution to the project: a giant bottle of glue for the team member who held us together with sales, a jar of jam for the team member who 'hand jammed' (a.k.a. manually entered) enrollment data, a set of pom-poms for our always positive cheerleader, etc."

TIPS FOR BUILDING AN EFFECTIVE TEAM

■ *When hiring, look for people who work well with others. You want employees who can handle the collective process.*

■ *Set a good example for your staff. For instance, leave at a reasonable hour so that they know it's OK to do the same.*

■ *Encourage one-to-one discussions between staff rather than structured meetings. Personal relationships build trust.*

■ *Hold informal retreats to foster communication and set goals.*

■ *Reward collective accomplishment whenever possible, even if the reward is only juice and bagels.*

> **"**If you have to have a program to do recognition, you've missed the point. In our culture, someone is thanked or recognized every two minutes. It's part of who we are and the sincere mutual respect, caring, and empowerment we have for one another.**"**
>
> —AUDREY ROBERTSON,
> Director,
> Public Relations,
> The Container Store

✔ One special projects group is involved in a major, multiyear, enterprise-wide effort that crosses multiple divisions within the company. Participants are eligible for the "Most Valuable Ant" recognition award. The award is a 6-inch-high custom-painted ant figurine and is a personalized certificate is attached.

✔ In the I.S. department, any member can nominate any other member for a "Golden Graeme" award. The awards are given for going the extra mile in ensuring the success of the department, putting in long hours to get the work done against a tight deadline, improving processes to better ensure success and/or quality, improving a business relationship, taking on a stretch assignment and delivering on it, etc. The award is given out quarterly at an all-hands meeting.

✔ In another division, the senior vice president, nicknamed "Bob," presents pins for "Bending Over Backwards" at quarterly departmental meetings. Employees nominate coworkers who have "bent over backwards" to achieve department goals. Photos of the presentation are posted on bulletin boards in the department.

———

James Allchin, head software guru at the Microsoft Corporation in Redmond, WA, rewarded programmers for meeting a key milestone on a project code-named "Cairo" by bringing a camel into the office. The camel was an immediate hit with the Cairo team, who petted it and had their pictures taken with it.

———

Team members get pins when they complete a project at the Naval Publications and Forms Center in Philadelphia. Employees also received a $500 bonus when the agency won the government's quality improvement award.

———

A CASE STUDY IN GROUP RECOGNITION

Elsie Tamayo explained how she improved the morale, pride, and productivity of the training department when she was training director of the City of San Diego's Department of Social Services.

When Tamayo started, employee morale was low and the group's identity in the organization was weak. Tamayo met with the thirteen employees in her department and asked how they wanted to be perceived by the organization. The group created its own identity, designed a logo, and painted it on the exterior and in the lobby of their building. For the first time, everyone got business cards that showed the new logo.

At each department meeting, Tamayo solicited the help of one employee to come up with a fun way of rewarding another member of the group. To announce one employee's promotion, the group staged a parade through the building; another employee was presented with an Energizer Bunny "because he kept going and going and going, helping others when needed"; and someone who

> **❝**Each employee has to be asked, 'What should we hold you accountable for?' What information do you need?' and, in turn, 'What information do you owe the rest of us?' This means that each worker has to be a participant in decisions as to what equipment is needed; how the work should be scheduled; indeed, what the basic policy of the entire company should be.**❞**
>
> —PETER F. DRUCKER,
> Author,
> *Post-Capitalist Society*

> **"**Treating your staff better will make your business perform better. It's that simple.**"**
>
> —JULIAN RICHER,
> Founder,
> Richer Sounds

worked even faster received a toy Roadrunner. Tamayo started each department meeting by reading letters praising the department or the people in it. At all times, she gave the group the latest information she had about developments in the organization.

Tamayo used numbers as recognition to increase the visibility of the group's achievements. The number of employees trained each month was tracked, as were cost-saving ideas, and progress was communicated throughout the organization. In the department, flip charts were hung tracking progress toward goals, and "master's degrees" were awarded to trainers and managers who trained 1,000 hours.

Tamayo also used extensive spontaneous rewards, such as a quick handwritten note or a note on a flip chart that read, "You really handled the meeting well yesterday," including specific remarks on why the activity was important, and posting the flip chart on the person's door. She often let group members come in late the day after finishing a training session.

Once a week, every person met with Tamayo for an hour to talk about anything they wanted. Initially many of the meetings lasted less than ten minutes, but over time everyone came to use the full hour. An employee might discuss the results of a training session and how he or she could improve, problems with other employees, or ways to improve skills and career potential.

Tamayo then announced that the group would spend a half day per month as a Reward and Recognition (R&R) Day, and that the group would come up with things they wanted to do together. They took the train to Los Angeles to visit a museum, went shopping in Tijuana, and went to the zoo. They had no budget for these activities, so the employees paid expenses.

Tamayo hosted a make-believe marathon for all project members. T-shirts and "records"—old LPs with specially designed album covers—were handed out during a mock marathon celebration to recognize individuals' achievements. Tamayo bartered her services with other training companies to get slots for her group members or facilities for an off-site retreat. She also started a self-development library and used it as a reward.

All these activities cost little or no money, and employees still knew they had to put in the hours needed to get their jobs done. But within several months, the morale, pride, and energy of the department skyrocketed, and the group was held in higher esteem by the rest of the organization.

———

Merck & Company's Wilson, NC, plant has a rewards program called "Reasons to Celebrate" and a unit incentive program called "Pay for Performance." Teams can nominate fellow teams or team members for gift certificates of up to $300 for individuals and $500 for teams.

———

At *Business First,* in Columbus, OH, team members receive $500 each if the team reaches a certain goal; if it reaches a higher goal, they receive $1,000 each. To be eligible

The Ten Best Ways to Reward Good Work

Reward # 1:
Money

Reward # 2:
Recognition

Reward # 3:
Time off

Reward # 4:
A piece of the action

Reward # 5:
Favorite work

Reward # 6:
Advancement

Reward # 7:
Freedom

Reward # 8:
Personal growth

Reward # 9:
Fun

Reward # 10:
Prizes

—Michael LeBoeuf,
Author,
*The Greatest Management
Principle in the World*

for team bonuses, members must make at least 90 percent of their individual goals.

———

At Great Plains Software in Fargo, ND, where projects could last as long as nine months, project leaders celebrated along the way with dinners, picnics, and other forms of informal recognition as they reached preset goals. The company used a two-part bonus program to spur on its project teams. Team members received half the bonus when they hit the product's target release date, and the other half ninety days after the release, based on the performance of the product. At the conclusion of projects, the teams created a "Friends List" to recognize non–team members who supported them along the way. Friends received gift certificates and thank-you letters.

———

In the team program at Cal Snap & Tab in City of Industry, CA, everyone can win, but one team wins big. "We're using a combination spoilage/attendance program," says marketing manager Richard S. Calhoun. "[One year] put forty thousand dollars into a special fund, and every time a mistake was made, we deducted from the forty thousand dollars. We ended up giving out about seven thousand dollars." The next year the thirty-six employees were divided into four teams, with a prize kitty of 1.25 percent of shipments. One-quarter of a percent is credited to each team, and spoilage by any team member is deducted. At the end of the program, the team with the lowest spoilage also gets the leftover .25 percent. A Chicago hospital took the same approach, creating a $100,000 cash pool that was used to satisfy billing or customer service complaints. Whatever was left in the pool at the end of the year was distributed to employees.

> **"Knowing that what you do is important and appreciated is the best reward."**
>
> —JOHN BALL,
> Service Training Manager,
> American Honda
> Motor Company

A CASE STUDY IN GROUP MOTIVATION

When Richard Nicolosi became the head of the paper products division of Procter & Gamble, headquartered in Cincinnati, competition had taken its toll. The company's market share for disposable diapers had eroded from 75 percent to 52 percent in less than ten years. Nicolosi found a highly bureaucratic and centralized organization that was overly preoccupied with internal functional goals and projects. Almost all information about customers came through highly quantitative market research. Moreover, the technical people were rewarded for cost savings; the commercial people focused on volume and share; and the two groups nearly always worked in opposition.

Nicolosi immediately began to stress the need for the division to become more creative and market-driven instead of just trying to be a low-cost producer. "I had to make it very clear," he later reported, "that the rules of the game had changed."

The new direction included much greater stress on teamwork and multiple leaders. Nicolosi pushed a strategy of using groups to manage the division and its specific products. Two months later, he and his team designated themselves the paper division's "board" and began meeting first monthly and then weekly. The next month they established "category teams" to manage their major brand groups (diapers, tissues, towels) and started pushing responsibility down to these teams.

He asked the marketing manager of diapers to report directly to him, eliminating a layer in the hierarchy. He also talked more to the people who were working on new products.

A month after that, Nicolosi's board announced a new organizational structure that included not only category teams but also new-brand business teams. Within four months, the board was ready to plan an important motivational event to communicate the new paper products vision to as many people as possible. All the Cincinnati-based personnel in the paper division, as well as district management and paper plant managers—several thousand people in all—met in the local Masonic temple. Nicolosi and other board members described their vision of an organization in which "each of us is a leader." The event was videotaped, and an edited tape was sent to all sales offices and plants.

All these events helped create an entrepreneurial environment in which large numbers of people were motivated to realize the new vision. Most innovations came from people dealing with new products, but other employee initiatives were oriented more toward a functional area, and some even came from the bottom of the hierarchy. For example, a few of the division's secretaries developed a Secretaries' Network, which established subcommittees on training, rewards and recognition, and the "secretary of the future." Echoing the sentiments of many of her peers, one paper products secretary said, "I don't see why we too can't contribute to the division's new direction."

Within four years, revenues at the paper products division were up 40 percent and profits were up 66 percent—while the company's competition continued to get tougher.

Anita Nimtz at Iowa State University in Ames, IA, celebrated Administrative Assistants' Week with a variety of freebies, including potted plants on Monday, lotto tickets on Tuesday, boxes of Band-Aids on Wednesday, and Crunch 'n Munch snacks on Thursday. Her staff loved it and still calls her the "greatest" manager. Mary Kay, Inc., also celebrates this week by giving its secretaries flowers.

The Carmel Clay Public Library in Carmel, IN, celebrated Staff Appreciation Week with the following activities, all planned and executed by the library's twelve-member management team. None of the details were divulged in advance, so each day brought surprises!

Monday
   ✔ An appreciation display consisting of a banner, balloons, and photographs of staff members at work was set up in the lobby and remained throughout the week so that patrons could help celebrate and say "thank you" to the employees.

> **❝The best thing you can say to your workers is: 'You are valuable, you are my most important asset.'❞**
>
> —PHYLLIS EISEN,
> Senior Policy Director,
> National Association
> of Manufacturers

✔ Upon arrival at work, each staff member received either an electronic thank-you card or a handwritten note from a manager from another department.

Tuesday

✔ Each staff member was given a commemorative bookplate with his or her name, and invited to insert it into a favorite title at the library. This allowed the person to be remembered and appreciated each time a patron checked out their books.

Wednesday

✔ The library published a 4-by-5-inch ad in the local newspaper inviting the public to join the management team "in recognizing the 135 CCPL staff members who serve our community with professionalism and dedication on a daily basis."

✔ The independent coffee shop in the library gave a 20 percent discount to all library employees for the entire day.

Thursday

✔ Managers baked or purchased cookies, brownies, muffins, fruit, chips, and other treats and delivered them to each department via a snack cart in the morning and again in the afternoon.

Friday

✔ Employees were given a bonus casual dress day (usually limited to the last working day of the month).

✔ Each employee received rolls of Life Savers labeled "We Appreciate You."

"We received extremely favorable feedback on our efforts," reports Cindy Wenz, human resources manager for the library. "With the exception of the $150 ad, which was paid for with funds provided by the Friends of the Carmel Clay Public Library, all of the items were no-cost or low-cost, with the latter absorbed by the members of the management team."

> ❝If you show people you don't care, they'll return the favor. Show them you care about them, they'll reciprocate.❞
>
> —LEE G. BOLMAN and TERRENCE E. DEAL, Authors, *Leading with Soul: An Uncommon Journey of Spirit*

Fun, Games & Contests

Fun is a great motivator, making work go faster and creating a buffer to stress. Increasingly important, given that 40 percent of today's employees say their jobs are very or extremely stressful and 25 percent view their jobs as the number one stressor in their lives today, according to the National Institute for Occupational Safety & Health. Having fun can also lead directly to increased productivity. At the Colorado Health Sciences Center in Denver, employees who viewed humorous training films and attended fun workshops showed a 25 percent decrease in downtime and a 60 percent increase in job satisfaction.

Fun can also achieve more serious objectives, such as communicating critical information or encouraging desired behaviors or performance. A good way to do this is to couch those goals in a game or contest. The relevant information or behavior becomes highlighted in the process, and a general sense of excitement is created along the way. Keys to a successful employee contest include:

✔ Promoting the program and its purpose

✔ Setting realistic, achievable, and measurable goals

✔ Limiting the contest to a short period

✔ Keeping contest rules uncomplicated

✔ Ensuring that prizes are desirable to employees

✔ Linking rewards directly to performance

✔ Giving rewards and recognition promptly

If you systematically do things that encourage a fun work environment, the morale of your group will directly benefit. Being thoughtful about planning activities that are fun for your group can also serve as a powerful source of team building.

EASY OFFICE MORALE BOOSTERS

1. Designate a bulletin board for employees to post favorite jokes, cartoons, etc.

2. Attach cartoons or humorous anecdotes to the more mundane memos that need to be circulated.

3. Schedule a staff meeting off-site in a congenial atmosphere; if possible, follow up with a casual social event.

4. Schedule an Ugly Tie (or Crazy Sweater or Silly Socks) Day with a joke prize for the winner.

5. Hold betting pools for high-profile events like the Super Bowl, Kentucky Derby, Oscars, Emmys, and World Series.

6. Take a daily humor break; designate someone to share a joke or funny story with the rest of the staff.

7. During a lunch break, screen a funny film or television show in a conference room or large office.

8. Bring a Polaroid camera to work. Take candid shots of employees and post them throughout the office.

9. Give everyone an opportunity to arrive an hour late or leave an hour early one day a week.

10. Never take anything too seriously. Keep reminding yourself, "This isn't brain surgery." (Unless, of course, it *is* brain surgery.)

> **❝** I think it's important to have fun at work—and not just at holiday time. **❞**
>
> —ELLEN JACKOFSKY,
> Assistant Professor,
> Southern Methodist
> University

Accounting software developer SBT Corporation (now owned by ACCPAC International) in Sausalito, CA, gave receptionists petty cash to stock the front desk with yo-yos, candy, and toys. They knew that laughter and fun are infectious, and that if their receptionists were relaxed and happy, then their clients would be in good spirits as well.

———

Schwartz Communications, a public relations firm in Waltham, MA, feels like a big family, with employees' kids—and a company dog— on-site most days. The company has a game room, creativity training, sports teams, and four well-stocked kitchens. It also doles out cash on the spot for special accomplishments and shares profits with employees. When clients renew contracts, the team that services the contract receives a percentage of the annual retainer fee. Says Paula Mae Schwartz, cofounder, "People are motivated to perform every day because they know we'll reward them emotionally, educationally, or monetarily. I don't think people give their all unless you give yours to them."

———

During the summer, Rich Willis of Paychex's Cherry Hill, NJ, office buys tubs of ice cream, puts them on a cart, and wheels them around so employees can help themselves.

———

Once a month, employees who play musical instruments at KFC Corporation in Louisville,

KY, are asked to bring them to work. This motley crew of musicians is then given a list of the month's top performers and asked to serenade those individuals. The recognition activity has been so successful that the company has initiated a second musical serenade, performed by a string quartet.

———

To lighten the atmosphere, one California company gave different Page-A-Day calendars to staff members and encouraged them to share their daily cartoons or jokes with others. Calendars included Dilbert cartoons, crossword puzzles, vocabulary words, and gardening tips.

———

In Georgia, the Augusta Technical Institute wanted to create a highly interactive and fun exercise to help team members get to know one another. Participants had to answer questions such as "What is the name of a person you'd like to meet?" and "What is the most exciting place you've ever visited?" Answers were written on colored paper and hung as a mosaic in the hallway.

———

At OOP!, a specialty store in Providence, RI, employees are allowed to celebrate offbeat "holidays" from Chase's Calendar of Events, such as National Hug Week and Willie Nelson's birthday, dressing to suit the occasion. It costs the store nothing and actually attract customers as well.

———

> **"**People are going to be most creative and productive when they're doing something they're really interested in. So having fun isn't an outrageous idea at all. It's a very sensible one.**"**
>
> —JOHN SCULLEY,
> Former Chairman,
> Apple Computer

> **"A business has to be involving, it has to be fun, and it has to exercise your creative instincts."**
>
> —RICHARD BRANSON,
> Founder,
> Virgin Music Group and
> Virgin Atlantic Airways

Charleston Memorial Hospital in Fall River, MA, asked employees to bring in pictures of their pets and had them posted on a lunchroom bulletin board. Everyone had a lot of fun trying to guess which employees the pets belonged to. Jossey-Bass Publishers in San Francisco used a similar idea to help new employees become acquainted with the staff: they asked existing employees to post family pictures, along with cute captions, in the work areas.

Ben & Jerry's has a permanent committee for planning fun activities, known as the "Joy Gang." Over the years, various people have assumed the title of "Grand Poo-bah," as they led the committee in generating fun ideas for the workplace. Perkins Coie LLP has a "Happiness Committee" that consists of five anonymous employees who can initiate fun activities for the organization.

Employees at a Capital One Services office in Tampa, FL, created a fun environment by forming "scream teams" to recognize peers and celebrate important occasions like birthdays and holidays. The team also developed theme days for people to dress up and bring food, and sponsors a quarterly picnic and the "Wacky Olympics" competitions.

Employees at Silicon Valley's Berkeley Systems (now part of Sierra Entertainment

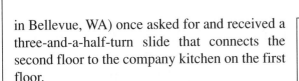

in Bellevue, WA) once asked for and received a three-and-a-half-turn slide that connects the second floor to the company kitchen on the first floor.

———

One night during the Christmas holidays, the Walt Disney Company opens Disneyland to employees and their families only. Concessions and rides are run by upper managers who dress in costumes. Besides being a lot of fun, this event allows employees to see the theme park from the customer's perspective. A multitude of other programs builds a sense of camaraderie and identification with the Disney organization, including peer recognition programs and informal root-beer-float parties. Employee and customer satisfaction with Disney is among the highest in the industry and is the cornerstone of the company's success.

———

Employees at Pacific Power in Portland, OR, use Frisbees to deliver memos on "Frisbee Memo Day."

———

Rebecca Rogers at University Health Care System in Augusta, GA, does a fun activity she calls "communal captions." She posts photos from newspapers and magazines over the copy machine and invites staff members to write funny captions for them, making copy-making time more interesting.

———

> ❝Small things work, even seemingly corny things like putting cartoons above your desk or having everyone bring in pictures of themselves from the sixties. You don't have to be a comedian to display a light touch.❞
>
> —MALCOLM KUSHNER,
> President,
> Malcolm Kushner
> and Associates

One of the greatest honors employees can receive at Microsoft is a sodded office: While they are away, fellow employees remove all the furniture and lay down a wall-to-wall layer of sod. This became such a popular prank that a memo was distributed: "Whoever wants to sod someone's office, call this number and we'll do it." Legitimizing the prank, however, made it less fun, so the sodding was soon replaced by other high jinks, such as filling offices with Styrofoam peanuts or popcorn. In one memorable case, a manager returned from a business trip to find his office door removed and the space Sheetrocked over and painted to perfectly match the corridor wall.

Suzy Armstrong of State Farm Insurance in Tulsa, OK, watches a video filled with cute songs and silly exercises with her employees, and leads the fifteen-member team of underwriters in aerobics exercises in the common area.

❝For eight minutes every afternoon, I have department heads lead their employees in stretching exercises at their desks," says Pam Wiseman, training coordinator for Designer Checks in Colorado Springs, CO. "It's a little silly, but it's fun, and it gives everyone a break. I think we're more productive because of it and we feel better, too."

Merle Norman Cosmetics in Los Angeles buys its female employees makeovers. The company also sponsors an Employee Night every other Saturday at the San Sylmar container manufacturing facility located in the San Fernando Valley outside Los Angeles. First-run movies are shown for employees, who may bring as many as six friends. After the movie, employees and their guests can make their own free ice-cream sundaes.

Linda L. Miles, president of L. L. Miles & Associates, a seminar-planning firm in Virginia Beach, VA, treated her staff of six women to a pedicure in a reward that came to be called "Happy Feet Day."

The Bank of America offices in San Francisco have a "Laugh-A-Day Challenge" for one month. Each employee tries to make coworkers laugh the whole day with cartoons and jokes. Winners receive T-shirts and books containing the best jokes and cartoons.

Matt Weinstein of Playfair, a Berkeley, CA, company that offers humor seminars, has several suggestions for keeping the work environment fun. He recommends giving "joy breaks," during which employees can look at cartoons or listen to tapes. He also suggests getting everyone together on the floor for childhood

> **❝Take your work seriously and yourself lightly.❞**
>
> —Bob Nelson

☑ *Create humorous awards or certificates related to each achievement and a special outfit or hat to wear when they are presented.*

games like marbles and penny-pitching. Other ideas from Matt:

✔ Give your employees a casual dress day such as Hawaiian Day or Suspender Friday.

✔ Plan a surprise picnic for your employees in the parking garage or lot.

✔ Make campaign buttons out of employees' baby pictures. Have them wear one another's buttons and try to figure out who's who.

✔ Put rubber fish in the water cooler.

✔ Staple Kleenex tissues to potentially stressful memos.

✔ Glue chocolate kisses to boring memos.

Ritch Davidson, "senior vice emperor" at the company, adds:

✔ Designate days when anyone who makes a negative comment forks over a small sum of money—25 or 50 cents—and use the money to start a Fun Committee fund.

✔ Instead of giving out holiday bonuses in checks, give out cash, close a few hours early, and take everyone to a shopping mall. After the spree, stage a show-and-tell.

✔ Hold fun contests—Nerf basketball, volleyball, or bubble-blowing competitions—or play cooperative games such as charades and treasure hunts.

✔ Have a party for no reason at all.

During a recent canning season, overtime had climbed so high at the Dole Food Company plant in Springfield, OH, that workers wondered if they were going to go crazy. As one technician said, "I couldn't look at another bag of lettuce!" To prevent burnout, manager Donna Lynn Johnson started a kazoo band. At first, the 325 plant employees were skeptical, but they soon got into the spirit of things and started smiling more.

———

At Eastman Kodak in Rochester, NY, an executive formed a Humor Task Force to gather Monty Python videos, Woody Allen books, plastic chattering teeth, and other props for a "Humor Room."

———

Children's Hospital/King's Daughters Corporation in Norfolk, VA, hosts a stress-relief fair for employees with booths (dunk tank, Velcro dartboards, massages) and food.

———

IBM, Coca-Cola, Ford, Monsanto, and Nikon all purchase gold-sealed Star Certificates declaring employees' ownership of actual stars, with a star album containing a sky chart and star verification record. Star certificates are available for $45 from the International Star Registry in Ingleside, IL.

———

> **"**In my experience, there are two great motivators in life. One is fear. The other is love. You can manage an organization by fear, but if you do you will ensure that people don't perform up to their real capabilities. People are not willing to take risks when they feel afraid or threatened. But if you manage people by love—that is, if you show them respect and trust—they start to perform up to their real capabilities. Because, in that kind of atmosphere, they dare to take risks.**"**
>
> —JAN CARLZON,
> CEO,
> SAS

Iteris, Inc., based in Anaheim, CA, has its own Fun Committee, which launched Project Girth. For every pound an employee lost, a dollar would be sent to his or her favorite charity. Iteris also sponsored a "Guess the Stock Price on March 31" contest in which the winner got a free lunch at the Hoagie Bar in Santa Ana. Finally, the plant's conference room has an exact replica of the space shuttle *Columbia* made out of Budweiser beer cans.

MCI, based in Ashburn, VA, had top management work together to shoot a movie. Famous scenes from movies such as *Raiders of the Lost Ark* were filmed, using team members in the roles of the actors and actresses. The project was a great team-building experience. The completed movie was shown to all employees at a company meeting.

Small teams of food service executives received a Kodak K12 camera and a list of captions at a recent Society for Foodservice Management conference in San Francisco. After a twenty-minute lesson covering the basic points of photography, they had two hours to snap pictures of their teams to match captions such as "to boldly go" and "team spirit." Claudia O'Mahoney, executive vice president of the association, says, "The cameras made the meeting successful because they allowed people to be their most creative."

William Pickens, owner of Pool Covers, Inc., in Richmond, CA, often hangs a number on the wall and rewards employees who know how it is related to the business. For example, 22.5 is the average miles per gallon of the delivery truck fleet, and those who knew that received a $10 prize. Pickens says this game gets employees to think about the business and also creates camaraderie.

> **"The most important thing I learned from big companies is that creativity gets stifled when everyone's got to follow the rules."**
>
> —DAVID M. KELLEY,
> Founder,
> IDEO Product
> Development

At Mid-States Technical Staffing Services (now owned by AccuStaff), in Davenport, IA, teams of employees competed to produce the most accurate time sheets (which originally had a 38 percent error rate). Within three weeks, time sheets were 100 percent accurate. The teams only competed for ten weeks, but time sheets were still 99.6 percent accurate at year-end.

Robert Marn of the Chilcote Company in Cleveland, OH, used a bingo game to teach workers proper procedures, to lower injury rates, and to cut compensation claims against the company. Accidents decreased by 56 percent the following year, with a savings of $21,000.

At Valassis, a marketing company headquartered in Livonia, MI, employees were given cards and stampers to play bingo at work. Numbers were called out over the PA system each hour in the morning until about two in the

> **"If you want to thrive and remain competitive in a world that is changing radically and relentlessly, you need the fluidity and flexibility of humor."**
>
> —C.W. METCALF,
> President,
> Metcalf & Associates

afternoon, with a break for lunch. Winning cards were placed in a drawing for one of five prizes, which were tied into a theme such as Fourth of July, movie night, summer, or winter.

———

Teams of employees at Tower Records headquarters in Sacramento, CA, dress up as game pieces and assemble on a giant board every two weeks to learn about sticky hiring situations. Contestants are asked questions about specific scenarios and advance one step whenever they answer correctly.

———

During staff meetings at the *Phoenix Business Journal,* an employee is chosen to read the mission statement; then the publisher quizzes people on what it means for them. Token prizes are handed out for correct answers.

———

Memtron Input Components in Frankenmuth, MI, created its own version of Monopoly, called "Memtronopoly." Managers supply caricatures of themselves to serve as game pieces and submit lists of problems that are made into "Process" and "Systems" cards. Players roll a die, draw a card, and discuss problems or hand out employee recognition as they progress around the board.

———

One health services company in Oakland, CA, holds bowling games during Friday afternoon breaks. They set up the pins in a long hallway and award prizes for the winners. It ends the week on a lighter note.

☑ *Hold a raffle for members of an outstanding work group, giving away a night on the town, a resort weekend, or a home computer.*

———

As a break for busy assembly or warehouse workers who are meeting quota or ahead of schedule, some firms in Silicon Valley call for a surprise 15-minute basketball break, although Ping-Pong or pool works as well. At Microsoft, it's not uncommon for employees to take a break to throw a Frisbee.

———

A CASE STUDY IN FUN & GAMES

Fun and games are an important aspect of work at Robert W. Baird, a financial services company located in Milwaukee. Some departments have "humor rooms" where associates can unwind with puzzles and games.

At one branch, sales associates were told to reserve time on their schedules for a mandatory compliance meeting, where they were to watch a compliance video. When they arrived, they were treated to a comedy movie and junk food instead, while brokers covered their phones. Everyone appreciated the opportunity to drop what they were doing, relax, laugh, and enjoy the afternoon.

Another branch celebrates Christmas in July. One year, families were invited to a bowling alley, where the branch manager showed up in a summertime Santa suit complete with red shirt, suspenders, red gym shorts, red high-top Converses, white hair and a beard.

> **❝**You've got to give people a voice in their jobs. You've got to give them a piece of the action and a chance to excel. You've got to give them the freedom to have fun.**❞**
>
> —MIKE CUDAHY,
> President,
> Marquette Electronics, Inc.

The company also hosts numerous contests. The public finance group held a "Talk Like a Pirate Week" during which associates wore pirate hats to work and were judged on their performance. The information technology department held a three-legged race where the winning team was allowed to leave early. And in celebration of a record month, one branch closed the office early and held a putt-putt match. Teams played on a makeshift golf course built from 2x4's, toy windmills, and bridges, which snaked in and out of offices and cubicles. After nine holes, everyone wanted to play another nine.

———

The U.S. Postal Service sponsored a national contest to sell the greatest number of First Class Phone Cards in one month. The winner of the $1,000 prize was the Rio Linda, CA, post office, with average sales of $25.58 per employee per day—well above the $22 figure achieved by the runner-up. Employees planned to use the money to buy a refrigerator to store their lunches and refreshments.

———

Remington Products, Inc., the personal care products maker based in Shelton, CT, held a company contest tied to the theme "What Makes Remington Good." Prizes included a trip to Acapulco, won by an employee who submitted a poem about the company.

———

Southwest Airlines, based in Dallas, runs a Halloween costume contest, a Thanksgiving poem contest, and a design contest for the December newsletter. The firm also has an annual chili cook-off.

> **"Laughter is the shortest distance between two people."**
>
> —VICTOR BORGE, Musical Humorist

———

Truck drivers with FedEx Freight West in San Jose, CA, participate in truck-driving championships, competing in events such as maneuvering a tractor trailer through a barrel course. State winners receive special recognition, a trip to "boot camp" to prepare them for the national championships, and a trip to the national championships itself. The Chairman's Challenge gives national winners a number of opportunities, including a choice of several vacation options, including a seven-day, all-expenses-paid cruise in the Caribbean or a trip to a major sporting event, such as the NFL Pro Bowl in Hawaii.

———

Hardee's Food Systems, the fast-food chain headquartered in St. Louis, held a Competition for Excellence, in which three-person teams from each of more than 2,000 restaurants competed against other Hardees in their districts. The teams were judged by regional managers on the three basic qualifications for fast-food employees—service, product makeup, and work area cleanliness—as well as on how well they worked together.

Winning teams advanced to the regional competition, and seven finalists were flown to the company's headquarters. Cash awards were given at each level, with the winners of the national competition receiving $1,500 each. All the national finalists flew in on the company jet, were whisked around the city by limousine, and were generally treated like VIPs.

In a more recent competition called "Bonus Bucks," employees "caught in the act of doing something right" were awarded bonus points. At the end of each quarter, each district (five to seven restaurants) held a party where workers used their collected points to bid on items like T-shirts, televisions, and VCRs.

———

For every job listing a graduate passes on to the Career Planning and Placement office at Fordham University in New York, a piece of paper bearing his or her name is entered in a lottery. A random drawing, held every three months starting in October, selects a winner who is featured in the *Fordham* magazine. Prizes consist of season tickets to Fordham sports events, dinners at local restaurants, and vacations to spots like historic Tarrytown, NY.

———

QuizMaster Productions, a quiz show company focused on team training based in Roswell, GA, holds contests modeled after TV game shows such as *Jeopardy, Wheel of Fortune,* and *Win, Lose, or Draw.* Contestants play in teams, answering questions about their company's products and operations.

———

To promote product knowledge, BI Performance, a Minneapolis-based perform-ance improvement company, has foreign and domestic car salespeople call an 800-number and take a product knowledge test over the phone. During the test, a computer randomly chooses 15 to 20 questions out of a pool of about 200. Salespeople who answer 80 percent of the questions correctly win instant merchandise.

> **❝I want people to get what's in their heads into our share-holders' pocketbooks and have a good time doing it.❞**
>
> —Lou Noto,
> President and CEO,
> Mobil Oil Company

Teams of custodians at Texas A&M University in College Station hold their own annual "Olympics" to test their proficiency with every-thing from dust mops to floor waxers. Just as in the real Olympics, participants hold preliminary meets, in key events such as the "Peanut Push" and the "Obstacle Course."

Domino's, Inc., based in Ann Arbor, MI, holds an annual company-wide "Olympics" in which it promotes events ranging from accounting to dough making, vegetable slicing, truck loading, dough catching, and tray scraping. The Domino's Olympics awards $4,000 to national champions in each of sixteen categories. The team leader who supervises the most "gold medalists" wins a free vacation.

The Hotel Association of New York City hosted a "Hotel Olympics" to recognize employees. Chefs had to prepare a Caesar salad and an appetizer of their choice; bartenders

> **❝Unusual sweep-stakes prizes draw an unusual degree of interest.❞**
>
> —*Incentive*

were asked to make a Manhattan and an original drink recipe; maids were timed for bed-making speed as well as tautness of the sheets; and waiters and waitresses had four minutes to carry a tray of champagne-filled glasses 800 feet, spilling as little as possible. All entrants received cash prizes, tote bags, and soft drinks. In addition, first-place winners won cameras and trips to Las Vegas and California, second-place winners received color TVs, and third-place winners got his-and-hers Bulova watches.

CUNO, a maker of water filtration and purification systems in Meriden, CT, knew wholesalers would not sell its products if they knew nothing about them. To change this, managers mailed 5,000 training guides about water-quality problems with a fifty-question multiple-choice test. Wholesalers were asked to review the manual, dial a toll-free number, and answer ten randomly asked questions from the list of fifty. A wholesaler who scored 80 percent or better received a customized baseball cap, a mug, a bumper sticker, and a certificate naming him or her as a water filtration specialist. A total of 1,900 wholesalers enrolled, and 1,000 earned certificates.

To encourage participation, distributors who returned their enrollment cards were entered in a sweepstake that offered eighty-two prizes, including RCA TVs and VCRs, radios, and pen-and-pencil sets. The company also tracked those who did not call and encouraged them to read the manual and take the test. Once certified, wholesalers could qualify for a second-level award.

Anyone who sold fifteen of the company's products in forty-five days won a nylon jacket imprinted with his or her name and the company's logo; 140 jackets were distributed.

Finally, the company placed fifteen "mystery" calls during the promotional period to ask distributors to name the water purification system they carried. All fifteen wholesalers answered correctly and won $100 each.

☑ Let employees take a Dream Day to go to the beach and contemplate work, life, and their futures. Ask them to report insights when they return.

Tupperware, based in Orlando, FL, holds four-month contests and two-to-three-week challenges throughout the year. Both reward high sales or recruiting efforts through points that can be redeemed for catalog merchandise. Meeting or exceeding sales quotas can earn dealers a week for two in Puerto Vallarta, Mexico, or a seven-day cruise.

To combat high turnover among its approximately 90,000 dealers, the company developed an incentive recruiting program. Dealers who recruit at least one new dealer in September—when turnover reaches a peak—receive a porcelain doll. Tupperware gained some 3,000 more dealers than expected through such efforts.

Hostesses whose parties generate a minimum of $61 in party sales qualify for gifts or merchandise from the Tupperware collection. Managers who reach sales quotas or a combination of sales and dealer recruiting goals qualify for the use of a car, which can be turned in for a new model every two years, or cash.

> **❝Now and then it's good to pause in our pursuit of happiness and just be happy.❞**
>
> —GUILLAUME APOLLINAIRE
> French Poet and Critic

Don Lundberg, vice president and cashier of Peoples National Bank of Kewanee, IL, describes a contest for the marketing of new MasterCard and Visa cards in which employees receive gifts tied to the number of new accounts they open. For each of the first four accounts, they receive a flower; for every five additional accounts, they win the following items in succession: a $5 gift certificate for Dairy Queen, a waiver for card fees, a $15 gift certificate at a local restaurant, a $50 savings bond, a day off with pay, a riverboat ticket, and $25.

First Capital Life held an offbeat sales contest called "Murder in Montreux," in which marketers got monthly clues to try to determine who of eight possible suspects was guilty of "murder." To entice marketers to play along, a special grand-prize drawing was held in Switzerland for those who solved the mystery.

US Motivation, an incentives firm in Atlanta, persuaded the king and queen of Sweden to sponsor a sales contest for a group of American employees of a Swedish-owned vinyl manufacturer. During the contest, the king and queen sent the employees letters concerning royal etiquette, autographed pictures, and gifts like Swedish crystal to those who were meeting their goals. At an awards dinner outside Stockholm, the king and queen presented the awards, and the ceremony was videotaped.

Celebrations, Parties & Special Events

C elebrations, parties, and special events are more organized forms of public recognition. While it is often traditional for companies to host holiday or year-end celebrations, group celebrations are more effective when they are linked to the *performance* of the group or organization. With a little forethought and planning, you can make any group event a meaningful form of recognition.

E mployees at The SCOOTER Store throw spontaneous celebrations for colleagues who do something exceptional. This typically involves giving them pats on the back, throwing confetti, and making lots of racket with horns and noisemakers. The guests of honor feel great about their jobs and company, and the "combusters" (the individuals offering the "spontaneous combustion") appreciate the opportunity to play around. The store's Insurance Verification Department also held a contest in which, if it achieved a certain record, the male manager would come to work in a dress picked out by the supervisors, and one of the team members would do his makeup. Not only did they meet the goal, but they exceeded it.

> 66 Celebrate what you want to see more of. 99
>
> —Tom Peters,
> Author and
> Management Consultant

> **"Having a good time is the best motivator there is. When people feel good about a company, they produce more."**
>
> —DAVE LONGABERGER, CEO, The Longaberger Co.

BlueCross BlueShield of North Carolina hosted a "parking lot lunch" with a tent and barbecue to thank staff for their hard work on a major corporate-wide initiative.

———

Jennifer Wallick, a computer software manager working for a subsidiary of Hewlett-Packard in San Diego, rewarded her work group after finishing a demanding project by giving them a "popcorn lunch"—that is, taking them to see a movie over lunch hour. As she explains, "It meant a slightly longer lunch hour, but it was a great break and a lot of fun!

———

To recognize the accomplishment of a team goal, Nancy Lauterbach, owner of Five Star Speakers & Trainers in Overland Park, KS, closed down the office for half a day and took the entire staff to the movies and a restaurant for coffee afterward. At the movie, everyone received money for snacks. On other occasions, the company offered employees a casual dress day to reward extra effort.

———

Jon Holmes at the Anderson Mall & Clemson Boulevard Chick-fil-A restaurant in Anderson, SC, throws an annual banquet for his team, during which he gives each person a present. He believes the key to employee retention is to show you care by attending team functions, ball games, and cheerleading competitions.

———

Firmani & Associates, a public relations firm in Seattle, closes one day per quarter so employees can go to a movie. Besides being a fun stress reducer, the outing promotes camaraderie. Owner Mark Firmani also tries to create a fun atmosphere with perks such as a casual dress code, weekly staff lunches, and supplies of juice, soda, and candy.

The morning after a product passed a crucial test at Iteris, Inc., a maker of robots and space-borne tape recorders, a mariachi band paraded through the plant, followed by clerks from the local Baskin-Robbins offering free ice cream. The company also rents the South Coast Repertory Theater—the largest performance space in Orange County, CA—each year for employee productions.

At the Fayetteville, AR, Crabtree Mall, manager Charlie Kerr throws midnight bowling parties to recognize his entire Chick-fil-A team for meeting performance goals.

Radio rating surveyor Arbitron celebrates the achievement of significant milestones with appropriate dinners and parties. When the company completed a phase of its Mexico project, there was a taco bar, music, and sombreros. Additionally, their finance department gets together every year to recognize individuals with the "Top Dollar Award": they get a fun gift

> **"Employees make the best product when they like where they work."**
>
> —GARY HOLLISTER,
> CEO,
> Xango

> ☑ *Have an apprecia-*
> *tion and welcome party*
> *whenever an employee*
> *leaves or joins your*
> *work unit.*

that changes from year to year, and their names engraved on a plaque. Work groups and departments often use recognition as an icebreaker or welcome break from meetings.

———

L one Star Park in Grand Prairie, TX, threw a party for 400 full-time employees and their families. Children were given small gifts, and employees drew tickets in a raffle for gifts from the park's gift shops as well as larger electronic items such as TV sets.

———

P arties are always breaking out at Time Warner in New York. For example, when *Money* magazine moved from the twenty-ninth to the thirty-third floor of the Time-Life Building in Rockefeller Center, the staff held a block party. Reportedly, the best employee parties are held at Time Warner, Advanced Micro Devices, Apple Computer, Leo Burnett Worldwide, Hewlett-Packard, and Iteris, Inc.

———

M cDonald's has different motivational activities for different groups of workers, such as teenagers and older workers. "Thirty years ago, having an employee softball team was enough to satisfy workers," says Dan Gillen, staff director of store employment. "Today we have to tailor our incentives to the specific nature of our workforce."

A district might hold a "senior prom," a chance for its older employees to meet and socialize outside work, or stage a potluck supper in the restaurant or at a manager's home.

For its teenage workers, the company has established a flexible scheduling policy to accommodate student classes, exams, and papers. "When I was captain of my soccer team and working during high school, I took a month off work during the busiest part of the soccer season," Gillen says. On the day of the high school prom, workers are brought in from other areas to cover for students who go to the prom.

———

Software developer McAfee, Inc., transformed a hotel ballroom into a winter wonderland, complete with 6,100 tiny white lights strung on 49 white birch and fir trees, giant ice sculptures, cotton snowdrifts, and a dance floor made to look like an ice-skating rink.

———

Alaska Airlines has an annual Children's Holiday Party in one of its airplane hangars. Employees transform it into a winter wonderland filled with decorations, pizza, cookies, cotton candy, popcorn, inflatable toys, face painters, and clowns. The best part, however, is when the hangar doors open and one of the planes (with the nose repainted as a reindeer) rolls up. An employee dressed as Santa jumps out with all of his elves (the kids think the plane just flew in from the North Pole), and the crowd of 2,500 employees and family members goes crazy.

———

> **❝I prefer things that are spontaneous. Things I hate the most are the routine, expected things like an annual company picnic. I think it's important for there to be an element of humor, laughter. It adds to the company. It's one more thing that makes you want to get up in the morning and go to work.❞**
>
> —JOEL SLUTZKY,
> Chairman,
> Iteris, Inc.

> ☑ *Invite employees to your home for a special celebration, and recognize them in front of their colleagues and spouses.*

Since Robert W. Baird's headquarters is located in sometimes frigid Milwaukee, one department held a post-holiday ice-skating party for associates and their families. A mock skating "code of etiquette" was circulated, with requirements such as "absolutely no laughing at someone else's fall until you're sure nothing is broken." At the end of the night, surprise trophies were presented in the following categories:

- ✔ Skating as a Weapon of Mass Destruction
- ✔ Most Artistic Fall
- ✔ Ugliest Technique
- ✔ Most Vertically Challenged
- ✔ Most Original Style

Each year, Baird associates and family members also enjoy exclusive access to the Milwaukee Zoo for an evening that includes dinner, refreshments, entertainment, and special animal shows. Approximately 3,000 people attend.

Advertising giant DDB's Sydney, Australia, office throws terrific holiday parties, complete with truckloads of decorations, live bands, theme cocktails, and gourmet finger food. Senior media group head Greg Tremain adds, "We announce the Agency Person of the Year and have a joke award ceremony and a video of all the commercials made throughout the year. It's a big morale builder."

Accounting giant Arthur Andersen's Fort Worth, TX, office rented an IMAX movie theater and threw a holiday party with a Grand Prix racing theme (to match the film then playing at the theater) for its employees.

———

Guests at a corporate Christmas party at Wembley's Conference and Exhibition Center in London were treated to a Cinderella Ball, complete with costumed characters, waltzing, and a Christmas feast.

———

Kaiser Permanente's corporate offices in Oakland, CA, join together for a team-building activity every December, building gingerbread hospitals one year. This type of activity not only reinforces the roles people play at work, but gives everyone a chance to sit down together for a treat after they're finished.

———

A CASE STUDY IN CELEBRATIONS

Lands' End, the Wisconsin-based clothing and merchandise retailer, defines the standard for zany and fun celebrations. Here's a snapshot of some of the activities in a recent year:

Going For the Gold: The company has used the theme of "Going for the Gold" throughout the year in events and activities ranging from company meetings, a fortieth anniversary celebration, the Lands' End Summer Olympics, "Golden"

> **"**He is doing it on his own. Now, that is the sort of thing that makes you feel appreciated, and he really does notice that we do good work. He didn't have to do that.**"**
>
> —An employee of Publix Super Markets, whose manager threw a store Christmas party

Customer Service Week, and "Golden" Service Stories (customer letters).

World's Largest Pillow Fight: On September 29, 2004, 2,776 employees and their families, retirees, community members, and local students joined Lands' End for the "World's Largest Pillow Fight." Following the fight, pillows and pillowcases embroidered with "Sweet Dreams from Lands' End," worth a total of almost $100,000, were donated to the Association of Hole in the Wall Camps. Coverage of the event spanned from New York to California, including MSNBC and a national spot on NBC's *Early Today* show.

Summer Olympics Golden Games: The Lands' End "Summer Olympics" was hosted July 13–August 21, and featured events such as marshmallow golf, a beach ball throw, the plank walk, a free throw contest, and the gurney push. The top team for each event was awarded a traveling trophy and the honor, fame, and status that goes with being an "Olympic" champion. The event included opening and closing ceremonies, and all finalists were honored at the company picnic, which featured games, rides, bingo, and entertainment for all ages, including a game show, the Lands' End Alumni Band "Kids from Wisconsin," and an award-winning entertainer, Neal McCoy!

Torch Sightings: No Olympics is complete without a torch. So "torches" were sent to various departments in the company, and each department had to submit a photo of its torch in a unique location. It ended up in Rome, Japan, the Lands' End swimming pool, a roof, a tractor, and many other places. The division that most creatively displayed its torch received extra credit toward the Lands' End Olympics. (Incidentally, the torch picture did end up swaying the Lands' End Olympics results, allowing a merchandising team to win by a hair.)

☑ *Give the employee a round of golf.*

☑ *Rent a sports car for the employee for a week.*

☑ *Rent a billboard and put up a message featuring the employee's picture and name.*

The Portland, OR, REI displayed its employees' artwork one year by showing it in conjunction with the Portland Pearl District's First Thursday Art Walk event.

Hewlett-Packard Company in Palo Alto, CA, uses informal beer busts in the afternoons to mark special events.

At Dow Chemical Company in Midland, MI, management hosted an ice-cream social where they made and served sundaes to their employees to generously thank them for their accomplishments.

The Texas Rangers Baseball Club treated 150 employees to a serenade by the Hamilton Park Men's Choir.

Lucian LaBarba, president of American FoodService, said he wanted to hold an

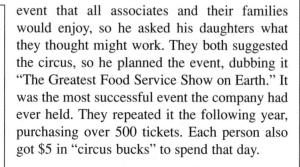

> **66**Pay geared to performance is important, but so is 'rah-rah.'**99**
>
> —DANIEL FINKELMAN,
> Principal,
> McKinsey & Company

event that all associates and their families would enjoy, so he asked his daughters what they thought might work. They both suggested the circus, so he planned the event, dubbing it "The Greatest Food Service Show on Earth." It was the most successful event the company had ever held. They repeated it the following year, purchasing over 500 tickets. Each person also got $5 in "circus bucks" to spend that day.

ACCESS Destination Services in Long Beach, CA, offers many unique themed events. For example, Safaris, Inc. re-creates Hollywood's golden age at the former home of mogul Darryl F. Zanuck. A Hollywood marquee emblazoned with the company's name greets guests; floral arrangements and candles float in the pool, and Chinese lanterns hang outside the poolhouse-turned-casino. Five hundred people dine, play croquet and no-stakes casino games, and dance to a jazz trio at the lavish estate.

The company also arranges Indian-Western barbecues at Indian Canyon, a desert oasis with towering palms in the foothills of the Santa Rosa Mountains near Palm Springs. Authentic Cahuilla Indian dancers and singers perform at the barbecue while potters, weavers, and silversmiths demonstrate their crafts at an Indian marketplace where participants can shop. Stuntmen stage a gunfight, and guests—who wear cowboy hats and bandannas—two-step to a country-and-western band.

The company sometimes arranges other events, like a "Field of Dreams" evening at

Dodger Stadium, where retired ballplayers in vintage uniforms play ball with participants.

———

Recently, Mana, Allison & Associates temporarily took over Napa's Inglenook winery and staged a Renaissance Fair, barbecue, and winery tours for 850 people. Mimes, jugglers, and musicians entertained the group.

———

Viacom in New York City has its own version of the Academy Awards in various categories, such as customer service, leadership, innovation, and teamwork. Nominations can come from employees at any level.

———

☑ *Ask a friend of the employee to suggest a gift or activity the employee might enjoy.*

☑ *Plan a roast of the person at a company meeting.*

☑ *Give employees Post-it notepads with sayings appropriate to their personalities.*

Field Trips & Travel

In a recent survey of American workers, 77 percent ranked a trip to a desirable destination with a spouse or guest as a positive incentive. Travel incentive rewards have a number of advantages: they are extremely desirable and promotable; they provide an exclusive venue for fostering team spirit and education; and they have "bragging value." There are, however, disadvantages: they are too costly for many applications; travelers are out of the office during the trip; it takes extensive effort and experience to create a high-quality travel program; and typically only a few employees can get the reward.

> **66**One of the most important reasons for a company to have an incentive trip is to foster loyalty and good feeling toward the company.**99**
>
> —JENNIFER JUERGENS,
> Former Editor-in-Chief,
> *Incentive*

At Stew Leonard's, proceeds from vending machines in the employee lunchroom are used to subsidize trips and outings for employees.

———

Tina Berres Filipski, editor and director of publications for Meeting Planners International in Dallas, took her staff of eight to the Texas State Fair one Friday afternoon, paying for their admission.

———

Jeff Alexander, a dentist in Oakland, CA, took his staff on a field trip to a shopping mall and gave each an envelope with $200 (all in ones!), stipulating that they buy at least five things and that he would take back any money they had left after two hours. At their next staff meeting, employees had a show-and-tell.

———

Shane Benson, manager at the University Place Town Center Chick-fil-A restaurant in Charlotte, NC, takes team members on a ski trip each year. On the bus, they hold "rolling award" banquets during which awardees walk the aisle to receive prizes.

———

At monthly P&L review meetings, employees at PSS World Medical in Jacksonville, FL, go off-site to amusement parks, bowling alleys, miniature golf courses, or play a business version of *Family Feud*.

———

Panache took a group of several hundred people to the Hacienda Winery in Sonoma and staged an "I Love Lucy" grape-stomping competition, followed by lunch.

———

Incentives To Intrigue, a firm based in San Francisco, provides a staff of writers, producers, and actors who come up with a script for a murder mystery or treasure hunt. One such event was staged for a group of employees during a dinner on the Napa Valley Wine Train. The costumes, decoration of the train cars, and events took participants back to the First International Wine Tasting during World War I. Another murder mystery weekend took sixty-six employees

☑ *Send the person to a health spa for a day or weekend.*

☑ *Pay all expenses for a weekend, including child care.*

Top Incentive Travel Destinations
(ranked in order of popularity)

WESTERN HEMISPHERE

1. Hawaii
2. Caribbean Islands
3. California
4. Florida
5. Mexico
6. Nevada
7. Arizona
8. New York
9. Canada, Bermuda
10. Puerto Rico, Chicago

of Ford Motor Company through Chinatown, Union Square, and the financial district to solve the mystery.

———

Kaiser Permanente in Oakland, CA, encourages work groups to use their cash rewards as a group. Winning groups have purchased box seats at a baseball game and taken a train trip to Napa Valley's wine country, both on workdays.

———

Brier & Dunn stages jungle theme dinners at the lions' den of the San Francisco Zoo, with lots of plants and jungle music. The company also arranges private yacht-club dinners, preceded by a regatta or cocktail cruise, and black-tie dinners in historic mansions; and it offers the Great American Rolling Treasure Hunt, which has teams exploring the city's neighborhoods by streetcar to discover local landmarks.

———

Dick Eaton, owner of Leapfrog Innovations, based in Medford, MA, knows how to structure fun. Eaton hosts scavenger hunts in the city for corporate clients, designed to promote teamwork and build morale. Mercer Inc., headquartered in New York City, also uses a scavenger hunt to orient team members who travel to new cities. They are asked to visit client offices, large hotels, and the convention center when they arrive, bringing back "proof" of their visits to each location.

———

Warren R. Doane, senior vice president of Founders Title Company in Salt Lake City, suggests a wide variety of recognition rewards, including limousine rides to lunch and dinner, a stay at a bed-and-breakfast, a weekend at Lake Tahoe, a cruise on San Francisco Bay, a train ride to Reno, a baseball night for all employees, and an employees' lunch served by tux-clad managers.

———

When Nelson Motivation, Inc., in San Diego achieved quarterly revenue goals they packed everyone into a limo driven by an Elvis impersonator and drove to Disneyland for the day. On other occasions, the company sent employees horseback riding on the beach, gave them a day at a spa, and flew all staff and spouses or significant others to New York City to celebrate for a week.

———

SCA Packaging North America, based in New Brighton, PA, has a novel way of rewarding senior managers who demonstrate successful leadership. They win a trip to the company's manufacturing plant in Bowling Green, KY, to spend a day with line workers there. Likewise, plant workers who are especially productive or offer innovative, money-saving ideas win a trip to any of the company's sales offices in the United States or Canada. Those who have taken part in the exchange have gone back totally pumped.

———

Top Incentive Travel Destinations
(ranked in order of popularity)

———

OVERSEAS

1. France
2. Spain, England, Germany, Italy
3. Australia
4. Portugal, Monaco, Austria, Switzerland, Hong Kong
5. Ireland, Singapore, Bali, Thailand, Israel

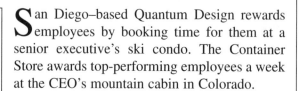

San Diego–based Quantum Design rewards employees by booking time for them at a senior executive's ski condo. The Container Store awards top-performing employees a week at the CEO's mountain cabin in Colorado.

———

PricewaterhouseCoopers, the consulting company, rewards its top ten professional and administrative employees with monetary awards and five-day trips to New York City.

———

Every dollar that marketing staffers save on airfare, hotel bills, and meals while on the road earns them points toward a resort vacation for two at the Dr. Pepper/Seven-Up Companies, based in Plano, TX. The two people who collect the most points by year's end win the weeklong vacations. Travelers save money from their travel allotments by taking connecting rather than nonstop flights, flying on weekends, staying in more modest hotels, and dining in less swanky restaurants.

———

Molson Breweries USA took 325 people from more than eighty of its distributorships across the country on a houseboat excursion. Winners attended an informal dinner with coworkers at a resort, where they were given a brief introduction to houseboat safety and handling. Then everyone headed for the houseboats, which slept from six to ten people. The next five or six days were spent meandering on

a lake; optional activities, such as tours of nearby parks and group rafting, were also worked into the schedule. The last day included a Farewell Fish Fry, after which winners were shuttled back to the airport. The price for the excursion was about $300 a week per person.

Since every distributor "won" a houseboat, each decided whom to send—a salesperson and his or her family (up to six people) or a group of salespeople. Rick Clay, vice president of sales for Molson Breweries USA says, "Houseboating's a great form of relaxation because it's one of the few places where there aren't any telephones. This type of setup really allows you the opportunity to talk and listen to each other."

> ☑ *White-water rafting is popular across the country, especially in Pennsylvania, northern New York, Idaho, California, Oregon, and Alaska. Give a one-day experience, a weekend camping trip, or a weekend stay at a lodge or hotel.*

Dogsled treks across marked, groomed trails are available in different parts of the American snow belt. Lewis Elin, president of the Topps Company, Inc., the maker of baseball cards in New York, has been mushing with friends, customers, and suppliers for the past five years. "It gives you a totally different perspective on winter and the great outdoors," Elin reports, "while offering a really challenging experience as well."

The Travelers Corporation, now a part of the St. Paul Travelers Companies, headquartered in St. Paul, sent winning agents to the Masters golf tournament each year. They were flown on the company jet and wined and dined at the event. Each agent received a bag of customized merchandise—from cookbooks to visors and sun-tan oil. They mailed a Masters scratch-off game card to other key brokers, who have to follow the tournament to win. Prizes ranged from a trip to London to imprinted visors. Richard Brown, second vice president for advertising marketing services for the insurance company, reported a 23 percent response rate on the card. For nonsales employees, a putting contest was held one week prior to the Masters. For three days, the home office set up a golf turf and challenged its employees to make a hole in one. Golf shirts and balls were awarded to winners, who were also entered in a drawing for eight golf-related prizes ranging from warm-up suits to windbreakers.

———

For a truly unique experience—especially for car lovers—there is racing school. At Road Atlanta, a two-and-a-half-mile Grand Prix track in Braselton, GA, individuals can attend a one-day racing school to learn handling techniques such as braking, skid padding, and heel-toe downshifting. They then spend another day racing around the track. The Valvoline Company organized this incentive trip for six buyers from distributorships around the country.

———

At the Space Camp in Cannes, France, employees can train much the way astronauts do, learning about satellite deployment, aerodynamics, and astronomy as well as working in simulated weightlessness and training in other space environments such as hypergravity.

The program culminates in a simulated space flight. French operations of both Microsoft and Aerospatiale, a manufacturer of airplanes, satellites, and missiles, sent their employees to Space Camp.

———

All managers at Quad/Graphics, Inc., printers in Pewaukee, WI, are entitled to a free trip to New York City. The company picks up the airfare for two and lets them use its apartment on Fifty-seventh Street. About twenty managers a year take advantage of this opportunity.

———

When Leo Burnett Worldwide reached $1 billion in advertising revenues, every employee in the New York and Hollywood offices was flown first-class to the Chicago headquarters for the company's annual breakfast celebration.

———

☑ *For a thrilling adventure, give a skydiving package that includes a six-hour introductory course, complete with a written test and first jump. Such packages can be found all across the country at smaller airports, particularly in warmer areas such as California, Texas, and southern Florida.*

☑ *Sailplane or glider rides also appeal to the adventuresome, as does hot-air ballooning. These trips usually begin in the early morning and last about an hour.*

PART V

REWARDS FOR SPECIFIC ACHIEVEMENTS

While everything discussed so far can be used to drive a wide range of behavior, this section looks at examples that were used to elicit *specific* types of perform-ance: sales revenues, customer service, employee sug-gestions, productivity and quality, and attendance and safety. Many of the examples contain multiple aspects or performance goals, and tend to be part of a formal program.

As stated earlier, formal programs have several advantages. They tap into the power of public recognition, which is a significant motiva-tor to many employees. They tend to be ongoing, offering a stability that employees can come to rely upon. If the programs have clear, objective criteria, they can avoid elements of subjectivity and favoritism that sometimes mar more informal forms of recognition.

The downside of formal programs is that they tend to become stale, predictable, and boring over time, unless they are kept fresh and relevant

through periodic changes and improvements—or an influx of new people with new energy and ideas running the programs. Because formal programs are so public, there is greater damage when something goes wrong, such as when a deserving person or group is left out, promised rewards are not delivered or are delivered too late, or upper management is not actively involved with or supportive of the programs.

In an article in *Workforce Management,* Philip C. Grant stresses that corporate reward systems need constant attention. The mere existence of such programs does not guarantee that they will be valued or that they will have any impact on employee motivation and satisfaction. Therefore, managers must manage them. There are several ways to do this:

- ✔ Tie rewards to needs. Because each employee has different needs, reward systems must be flexible. If feasible, rewards should be adapted to each employee.

- ✔ Ensure the rewards' fairness. Every employee must be satisfied that, in relation to the demands of the job and to what workers in similar jobs outside the company are receiving, the rewards they receive are just.

- ✔ Make sure timing is proper. It's best to schedule frequent presentations of rewards so that employees receive them shortly after the achievement being recognized.

- ✔ Present rewards in a public forum. Rewards are not meant to be presented in the privacy of an employee's office. Schedule a special meeting for the occasion, and don't camouflage the rewards. They must stand out and be highlighted; don't squeeze praise among a dozen other topics of conversation.

- ✔ Talk up the value of rewards. If managers show enthusiasm for a reward at the time it's presented, they add to its perceived value. However, be sure not to oversell them. Constant talk about how great a reward is can start to make it sound ridiculous.

Sales Revenue

O ne of the more easily quantifiable achievements in most companies is the attainment of sales goals, and it's no secret that salespeople tend to be highly motivated by recognition as well as
money. For that reason, sales reinforcers are fairly commonplace. But
how you reinforce sales success can vary greatly.

> 66Incentive programs
> can make a difference,
> providing visible
> rewards that build
> up confidence and
> knowledge.99
>
> —Tom Mott,
> National Practice
> Leader for Sales
> Compensation Services,
> Hewitt Associates

H ewlett-Packard marketers send pistachio
nuts to salespeople who excel or who close
an important sale.

C hilton Ellett, a telemarketing consultant
based in Chapin, SC, suggests giving a
penny for every three deals a telephone sales
representative closes. The penny is then
dropped into a gumball machine, and the individual is paid different amounts depending on
the color of the gumball: 25 cents for a white
gumball, $3 for red, and $10 for blue.

P aul Levine, general manager of Miller
Nissan in Van Nuys, CA, awards $5 to the
first and second salespeople to sell cars on a
given day—then gives them $5 for every car
sold by any other salesperson that day. The first
person to make a sale can win $100 in a day just

for selling one car, and as much as $200 or $300 if he or she sells more cars.

———

At St. Louis–based Nestlé Purina PetCare Company, members of sales teams that exceed annual goals in at least two of three categories receive trophies featuring a bronze dog and cat sitting on a company logo.

———

When John Gurden made his monthly target of $125,000 in automated voice-processing system sales, David Woo, CEO of Automatic Answer (now owned by the Amanda Company) in San Juan Capistrano, CA, asked him what he would like as a reward. His response: designate a "John Day." Soon, John Day banners were plastered throughout the offices, and receptionists answered the phone with, "It is a good morning at Automatic Answer, where we are celebrating John Day." Woo also let Gurden use his office that entire day and gave him a special John Day photo album at a lunch in his honor.

———

Whenever they exceed a monthly goal, Turbo Management Systems celebrates on Friday afternoons by taking the entire sales team on an outing, such as miniature golf, go-carting, or paint ball. They always take pictures to display later on a bulletin board.

———

> ❝Informal day-to-day acknowledgements mean a lot. Especially welcome are the spontaneous calls from upper management congratulating me when I exceed a sales goal. Without the personal touch, this job would just be money, and money can only motivate you so much. Recognition gives me personal pride and means something.❞
>
> —IRENE ELLIOTT,
> Account Executive,
> United Postal Savings
> Associates

> **"Though I'm self-motivated to a great extent, some motivation does come from outside. Recognition is great—and if the end result is a promotion, if I can further my career by being recognized as a top seller, that's great too."**
>
> —Susan Charboneau,
> Senior Sales
> Representative,
> United Services
> Automobile Association

There is nothing like a good challenge to stimulate a team of workers. At a pizza party to celebrate a record sales month, Michael Phillips, director of sales for Seattle-based Korry Electronics, told his sales force that if they beat their new record, he'd shave his head. Phillips reports: "Everybody got involved in trying to break the record, even the customers. Returns people were even booking extra rework and warranty sales." When it looked like the record-breaking was imminent, Phillips jokingly put up signs on computer monitors saying it couldn't be done because the computers were down. "That really fueled the fire," he says. To celebrate the "unbelievable" month, he brought in his own "Hair Terminator," who shaved his scalp in front of 565 employees at a rooftop party that celebrated Korry's sixtieth year in business. Reps who had contributed the most sales got first snips. Key customers and sales reps from around the world were also present.

———

Manish Mehta, CEO of ELetter in Portland, OR, said he would wear high heels to work for a day if his company met an ambitious sales target. He had to keep the promise, and now employees have suggested that he wear a dress if ELetter meets another milestone. Mehta explains, "You can match other companies' offers, but to make employees stay, you have to make work fun."

———

A former Paychex manager in Seattle created a sales lead contest in which payroll specialists would receive raffle tickets for each referral they received. At the end of each week, he held a drawing for prizes, which were usually solicited from current clients, such as a free manicure from someone's beauty salon or a small TV. Employees whose names were called during the drawing got to spin the prize wheel, which was colorfully decorated and about five feet in diameter. It was always funny when a male specialist won a free manicure.

> **"There's nothing like a good contest to get sales cranking."**
>
> —Tom Webb,
> Chief Economist,
> National Automobile
> Dealers Association

Recently, The SCOOTER Store held a month-long program to recognize the top nine sales employees on a daily basis. These "Overachievers" took turns "stealing" an executive's chair for the day, in a program called "The Executive Chair Swap." The executives attended the ceremonies and took pictures with the Overachievers, which were then displayed on the company's Star Network. For the company's fourth and goal quarter, employees were featured in a mock-up *SCOOTER Illustrated* magazine cover when they scored personal touchdowns. Many of the covers still hang over their desks.

For salespeople at Valassis, a marketing company located in Livonia, MI, that produces inserts for newspapers worldwide, entry into the company's Hall of Fame is the most prestigious award. The honor is based on sales and leadership, and winners are selected by existing Hall of Fame members. Once selected, their photographs are hung in the Hall of Fame, which is at Valassis's global headquarters. The awards are presented at the annual Sales and Vision Awards, which attracts about 600 employees each year.

To respond to a complaint from customer service clerks that they are unappreciated (compared to salespeople), Bruce Smith, CEO of Safety Vision, a mobile camera business located in Houston, TX, gives each salesperson a blue poker chip every month to award to someone for their effort in closing a sale or satisfying a customer. Each awardee gets to pull a prize—ranging from inexpensive dinners to Mont Blanc pens—out of a hat. Smith says, "It gets people a little more excited about what they do and provides some special recognition."

At the *Phoenix Business Journal,* the sales team gets lattes or bagels in the morning when it sells twice the daily goal. At the *Milwaukee Business Journal,* everyone on the sales team receives a $25 gift certificate to a local store or restaurant when the team meets its goals for the week. If it makes 10 percent more, they get two certificates, and if it makes 20 percent more, they get three certificates. Employees create banners showing how much more is needed to meet the goals.

Patrick Dickerson of the Chick-fil-A Queensborough branch in Mt. Pleasant, SC, posts total drive-through sales each hour. When a record is broken, the entire shift receives "Doodle Dollars" that can be exchanged for Chick-fil-A merchandise.

———

Michigan-based Talking Book World collects daily sales tallies from its various stores and circulates the results to all franchisees. The stores at the top of the list get called by the other stores and share their success stories with them, while everyone else tries to move up the list and be recognized as the number-one store in the upcoming week.

———

Gail Herenda of Supercuts in Fort Lee, NJ, divided her staff into teams competing to sell hair-care products. Each product sold is represented by an ant-shaped sticker, which is placed on the team banner. The team with the most ants at the end of the week wins a free lunch from Gail. Sale of hair-care products is up.

———

At the *Atlanta Business Chronicle,* sales reps get quotas for each of four departments, and receive a $250 bonus if they meet all four. This helps them to focus on all aspects of the publication, rather than simply the total volume of ads sold.

———

The *Cincinnati Business Courier* offers various incentives to salespeople for achieving individual or group sales goals. Some examples from the past include: an afternoon off for a movie or baseball game; maid service at home for the following month; and cash for an afternoon shopping spree with a show-and-tell at the end of the day.

———

As a sales manager for Westinghouse in Los Angeles, Robert Partain threw a barbecue lunch for his sales staff the first time they made their team goal. He promised to do it each time they made their goal again. Seventeen months later, he had given sixteen barbecues, missing only the month of the Northridge earthquake.

———

GreenPages, in Kittery, ME, has each sales team pick a support person of the month and each support team pick a salesperson of the month. Then each team says a few words about the person they have selected at a monthly meeting.

———

At Coronet/MTI Film and Video in Deerfield, IL, Mary Jo Scarpelli, sales director, brings the sales team bagels and cream cheese on the last Friday of each month.

———

For meeting team goals at WFAN-FM in New York, the entire sales staff is treated to trips such as a daylong yacht cruise around Manhattan or a day in Atlantic City.

———

Richard Meyerson, president of Traveltrust Corporation in Encinitas, CA, offered to remodel a nursery in a sales manager's home to accommodate a newborn child if the manager made her sales goals. While the remodeling was taking place, she lived in a house owned by the corporation. On another occasion, the company rewarded a male employee with a fully paid paternity leave.

———

"I try to put myself in their place," says Jennifer Hurwitz, who designs incentive programs for employees of LensCrafters, the one-hour eyewear stores based in Mason, OH. "I remember my retail store experience of working hard for thirteen hours a day on my feet, and I try to design something that will make it a new and interesting day for our people each time they come to work." For example, newly opened stores with expectations of more than $100,000 in sales during their grand opening week are targeted for special attention to help them reach that goal. The whole company watches the daily figures as they are transmitted to every location by computer. On the final day, if the store is nearing its goal, Hurwitz says, "the president and key people from the home office are flown in on a company plane for the last few hours to cheer them on and help them out, and then everyone is

> "My main motivation is the recognition. It's very competitive and tough to move ahead here, so going to the awards luncheons and meeting the VPs is a good way of gaining visibility. My main purpose is to move ahead in my job, not to win a prize. If being a top performer helps me get promoted, it's a means to an end."
>
> —Sara Navarro,
> Senior Sales
> Representative,
> United Services
> Automobile Association

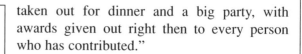

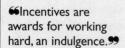

> **❝Incentives are awards for working hard, an indulgence.❞**
>
> —VICKI PRITCHARD,
> Sales Agent,
> Carlson Marketing Group

taken out for dinner and a big party, with awards given out right then to every person who has contributed."

———

Advanced Micro Devices, a manufacturer and marketer of complex monolithic circuits in Sunnyvale, CA, launched an "American Dream" sales campaign as an incentive for reaching $200 million in sales. The reward was nothing less than a house. Every employee's name went into a hat for a drawing in case the goal was reached. Jerry Sanders, president and founder, had local reporters accompany him on his unannounced visit to the home of the winner, Jocelyn Lleno, an AMD factory line worker. Lleno was handed a check for $1,000 and was to receive the same amount every month for the next twenty years to buy her house. Two other employees received Cadillac Sevilles.

———

A spectacular method for recognizing and motivating outstanding employees was created for Pitney Bowes, based in Stamford, CT, by Multi Image Productions, Inc., of San Diego, which produces shows incorporating slides, film, video, music, dancing, and spectacular lighting displays. Pitney Bowes's top sales producers were recognized during the show, produced and staged in Kona, Hawaii. "Our goal was to give them a type of business theater in which they would feel entertained as well as motivated to reach their goals for next year,"

says Multi Image Productions president and CEO Fredric W. Ashman. Budgets for these productions range from $10,000 to $1.5 million.

———

Mary Kay, Inc., awards pink Cadillacs, mink coats, and diamond rings to leading independent sellers.

———

The life insurance industry uses an elite club, the Million Dollar Roundtable, to recognize and give status and special privileges to top salespeople.

———

When Levi Strauss & Co., headquartered in San Francisco, reached $1 billion in sales, its executives gave out more than $2 million in stock and cash to employees as rewards. When it passed the $2 billion level in 1979, employees once again received significant cash awards.

———

Paychex payroll services company in Rochester, NY, awards gold rings to sales reps when they've signed a career total of 300 new clients. The reps receive a diamond for the ring at 500 clients and win additional diamonds after 1,000 and 2,000 clients. Gene Polisseni, vice president for marketing, says the program rewards those who may not win annual sales contests but who consistently perform well.

———

> **"**Travel to exotic and/or foreign destinations is the single most sought-after prize by my sales force of 60. It gives them an escape from their normally hectic schedule and seems to make them feel that the effort they spent to get there was all worthwhile.**"**
>
> —JOHN FRANZ,
> President,
> Brasseler USA Inc.

☑ *Host employee-of-the-month awards for highest productivity, quality, or sales; most improvement; least absenteeism; or whatever you designate as most important. Display a photo of the employee in a prominent place, and honor him or her throughout the month at a series of lunches or other events.*

If an operator of Chick-fil-A, the Atlanta-based restaurant chain, increases sales by 40 percent over the previous year's sales, he or she earns the right to drive a Lincoln Continental for one year. If the increase is repeated the following year, the operator gets the car for good. More than one hundred operators have won Lincoln Continentals.

———

Security systems manufacturer Checkpoint Systems in Thorofare, NJ, names its top eight salespeople to its President's Club. Club members act as an advisory council to the company's top executives and get a five-day group trip to places like Bermuda and Acapulco.

———

Professional Salon Concepts, which sells hair care products and services in Joliet, IL, awards $200 gift certificates from Nordstrom to the two sellers who "touched the biggest number of current and prospective clients" in a month. That includes customer classes, cold calls, appointments, and visits.

———

IBM gets employees to help generate demand for new products by awarding medals for sales leads. Any employee who steers fifteen potential customers to an IBM dealership for a demonstration of a new operating system software wins a bronze medal; additional leads earn silver and gold medals.

———

Chuck Piola, executive vice president of sales at NCO Financial Systems in Horsham, PA, tells how he started a new reward at his company for junior salespeople. "This guy was a year out of college, and one month he finally broke through—so I took him out and bought him a new suit." Piola also lends salespeople his Mercedes for a weekend so they can see how it feels to be a top salesperson at NCO.

———

Rexair in Troy, MI, offered running suits with the company logo to domestic distributors and salespeople who gave a predetermined number of in-home demonstrations of the company's cleaning system over a two-week period.

———

ACCO Brands, Inc., a Lincolnshire, IL, manufacturer of office products and supplies, recognizes outstanding salespeople through the President's Inner Circle, which is open to anyone who has completed one year in a commercial territory as a full-time direct company employee and reached a minimum dollar increase of 15 percent based on commissionable sales figures for the given fiscal year. The reward is a diamond-studded Inner Circle ring.

———

The Boise Office Products Division, headquartered in Boise, ID, annually recognizes its top thirty sales representatives with a sales executive's ring and a two-night, three-day, all-expense-paid trip to a meeting in a resort area.

Recent meetings have been held in Palm Springs, San Antonio, Orlando, and New Orleans.

———

During a recent cross-selling promotion at United Commercial Bank in San Francisco, customer service and customer relations representatives were given "Hula Bucks" for every $100 in traveler's checks they cross-sold. At the end of the promotion a rally and auction was held so they could bid on prizes, including a trip to Hawaii.

———

The United Insurance Company of America's sales incentive program provides a management-by-objectives guide, says Richard L. Lauderdale, director of marketing sales support for the Chicago-based firm. "Every salesperson, no matter what level of performance, can select a goal to strive for within the program. The single greatest result of the program is the growth of the people who strive to achieve it."

———

At Nelson Motivation, Inc., one sales consultant was 187 percent to goal in just seven months. I noticed that he often played with little sports cars when he was on the phone. So one day, I called him and said, "Write down this phone number—I just rented you a Porsche Boxer for a week." Initially, the sales consultant replied, "Oh, Bob, that's very nice. You don't need to do that." But within twenty minutes he called back and almost screamed, "This is the nicest thing anybody has ever done for me in my entire life!" Coworkers took a photo of him in the car, which he ended up using as a screen-saver for his computer monitor. On another occasion, I bought this same consultant a suit to thank him for exceeding his goals.

> **❝Incentives offer that extra 'thank you' for sustaining high performance.❞**
>
> —CHARLES GEHL, Coordinator, Frank Implement Company

Resort Condominiums International, based in Parsippany, NJ, annually stages the RCI 500, a mock Indy 500 race in which agents compete to confirm as many time-share exchanges, subscription renewals to the company's magazine, and space reservation services as possible. With each transaction, the representatives' paper race cars are pushed up a certain number of spaces on an oval track drawn on a bedsheet tacked on a wall. Representatives dress as race car drivers, officials, or fans, and the office is decorated with streamers and checkered flags. The top producer is recognized, as are the highest-finishing Rookie of the Year, the Most Improved Driver, and the three Best-Dressed Drivers.

Xerox Corporation, headquartered in Stamford, CT, used a sports car theme for its Fast Track sales motivation program, which also involved technical support employees and their managers. Everyone accrued points that were redeemable either for merchandise or cash rewards ranging from $10 to $10,000. Also distributed were battery-powered Ferraris and spark plugs "to spark new ideas."

Pentel of America in Torrance, CA, uses the Samurai Award to motivate salespeople to (1) increase sales over the previous year; (2) perform a certain amount of "end-user work," (contact and sales with the final user of the company's pens); and (3) submit sales and marketing reports (SAMs) on new techniques for promoting the company's products. Samurai winners receive a cash award, a Sales Master ring, a genuine Samurai sword, and a weeklong first-class trip for two to Japan, which includes a tour of the Pentel factory as well as a ceremonial luncheon with several Japanese managers. The regional sales manager whose territory performs best in all three areas also wins a cash award, ring, and trip to Japan.

At KXKT-FM, a Top 40 station in Omaha, cash, merchandise, and travel are offered to sales employees. Says Cathy Roach, general sales manager, "We've also done fun things, like have a wheel with cash ranging from ten dollars to one thousand dollars. For every piece of new business they bring in, they spin the wheel and win something. We've also blown up balloons containing cash and had people throw darts at them."

A CASE STUDY IN SALES RECOGNITION

The "FasTrack" program at Morris Savings Bank (now a part of Wachovia Bank, headquartered in Charlotte, NC), rewards workers for landing new business, as well as for cross-selling to new and existing customers. Each salesperson has a quarterly quota of forty-five cross-sale points, earning a point for each additional service they sell to a customer. Tellers have a quarterly quota of fifteen referrals; when customers agree to one of their suggestions, the tellers send them over to the sales desk with a referral card. Each salesperson also gets a $2 commission for every cross-sale, and each teller receives $2 per referral. A sales coordinator tracks each person's progress on a poster in the lunchroom.

Other awards are given out at quarterly meetings. The top salesperson of the quarter and the teller with the highest number of referrals each gets $300, an extra vacation day, and an engraved pewter mug. The manager of the branch with the highest deposit level gets a trophy and an engraved Cross pen, and that branch is treated to a party by the sales department.

Branch managers are eligible for bonuses as well. If 90 percent of the staff meets the quota, the managers get the same bonus as the employees. They get double that amount if all the employees attain the quota and if the branch is awarded a certain number of "mystery shopper" points from the mystery shoppers who visit each branch at least once every quarter.

In the Gold Coin Club, employees are given ten gold coins when they meet their individual quarterly quotas; the top salesperson in each branch gets an additional five coins; everyone gets five coins if the entire branch meets the quota, twenty-five coins for reaching the quota in all four quarters, and three coins for having a sales tip published in the newsletter. Coins are

> **❝**Involving both customers and employees in a sales promotion makes a powerful statement about the importance of everyone in an organization.**❞**
>
> —BRUCE BOLGER,
> *Incentive*

> **❝Keep the right goal in mind: don't look for money, look for applause. If you create something of value, the sales will come.❞**
>
> —ROBERT RONSTADT, CEO, Lord Publishing, Inc.

displayed on the salesperson's desk in a clear acrylic box with his or her name on it. At an awards banquet, employees use their coins to bid on prizes—including televisions and a trip to the Bahamas. The banquet features an awards ceremony modeled after the Oscars. Award categories include Salesperson, Teller, and Branch Manager of the Year. Winners receive SARAs (Sales and Recognition Awards), which are statuettes of *Winged Victory.*

One employee who has twice been a top teller says the program helped her. "I pay more attention to customers, and I try to offer more service, which can be more important than the product," says June Barbee, head teller at the Mendham Village branch. "And when I won the top teller award, that was really motivating."

———

The Miami Lakes, FL, cosmetics company Elizabeth Arden implemented a sales program in which staffers who increased their sales by at least 25 percent over those of the same five-month period in the previous year earned a weeklong Caribbean cruise for two. Besides increasing sales, the program reduced turnover. Cynthia Bloom, resident makeup artist at Bloomingdale's in New York, says, "I've been offered jobs for more money with other companies, but I didn't take them. I'm loyal to this company—Arden's been good to me, so I'm good to them."

———

Customer Service

I t is said that it costs five times more to win a new customer than to keep an existing one. So satisfying customers is a goal most companies want to constantly recognize and reinforce. Here are some great reinforcers that companies have used to foster exceptional customer service.

R on Smith, now at the City of Sacramento Department of Public Works, says that years ago, when he owned a deli, he would ask all the servers to greet each customer as if that person were a favorite aunt or uncle. He promised that if they did, he would make up the difference if they received less than $75 per day in tips. He only had to do so once in ten years.

S everal guests at the Walt Disney World Dolphin Hotel in Orlando were so impressed with one of their servers that when they returned to the hospital where they worked in Indiana, they named the "Jason Chestnut Customer Service Award" after him to recognize superior customer service in their own organization.

A t Busch Gardens–Tampa, employees who offer exceptional service to guests receive a scratch-off card. These cards are issued on the

> 66 You have to treat your employees like your customers. When you treat them right, they will treat your outside customers right. 99
>
> —HERB KELLEHER,
> Chairman,
> Southwest Airlines

spot by the management staff and can be redeemed for a variety of rewards.

———

One manager of a cable installation company in North Carolina holds a weekly lottery for installers who were praised in customer letters. The winner gets to grab as many quarters as possible out of a fishbowl, with the average grab about $30.

———

When John Kapp was general manager and president of Del Taco in Atlanta, he wanted to improve service by focusing on positive stories about customer service. So he asked his seven regional managers, and received 12. He then wrote a note to each employee praised in the stories. These stories were photocopied and put in the break areas in every store. One month later, he asked his managers for stories again, and this time, he received 65; the following month produced even more. By the fourth month, the group produced 125 pages of stories, and copies were distributed to all the stores—each with a note of thanks from John. Not only did good service skyrocket, but turnover of managers and assistant managers improved over 300 percent!

———

Doug Barnett, manager at Chick-fil-A in Perry, GA, runs a DOTS program (Delivering Outrageous and Tremendous Service). Team members accumulate dots on index cards for excellent performance in areas such as high check average and low deletions. The dots can be cashed in for meals or merchandise from local businesses.

———

The Eagle Award is used at SKF USA Inc., in Norristown, PA. Each employee is given two Eagle Award coins to give to other employees for outstanding customer service, along with a certificate briefly describing the service. Employees who receive five or more Eagle Awards are given a decorative display holder. Ten Eagle Awards can be exchanged for a $50 American Express Be My Guest certificate. The employee who receives the most Eagle Awards in a six-month period is recognized with a trophy and a $250 American Express gift certificate at the president's semiannual State of the Company meeting. Jeff Minkoff, corporate quality assurance manager, reports that more than 1,500 Eagle Awards were given out in the first one and a half years of the program alone.

———

Every year, Robert W. Baird celebrates Client Service Week to demonstrate its "clients come first" principle. Baird president and CEO Paul Purcell and managers at all levels work on the front lines as help-desk representatives, receptionists, client services representatives, mail and office services staff, and graphic designers in order to interact with clients. Baird also gives the G. Frederick Kasten, Jr., Award, named after Baird chairman

HOLD A SERVICE LOTTERY

■ *Award a silver pin or similar prize for positive customer comments.*

■ *Whenever a service employee receives a letter of praise from a customer, enter his or her name in a weekly drawing. Offer a fun prize.*

Fred Kasten, to associates who provide outstanding service to their clients and continually strive to improve customer service. A winner is selected from each business unit, based on nominations by fellow associates, and awards are presented at the Annual Meeting for All Associates. Each winner receives a one-week, all-expenses-paid vacation to anywhere in the United States.

Employees can give one another "PEOPLE" awards at Parkview Health, a hospital system in Indiana, for providing exceptional customer service. PEOPLE stands for *P*atients and families; *E*mployees, physicians, and volunteers; *O*ur communities; *P*artnerships; *L*eadership; and *E*mpowerment. Anyone, whether inside or outside the organization, can nominate employees for awards. One copy of the small piece of paper is presented to the awardee, one to his or her manager, and one is sent to the PEOPLE Award department in HR. Accumulated awards can be traded for merchandise: 5 awards = a sticker for name badges, 10 awards = an umbrella, 25 awards = a duffel bag or blanket, 50 awards = a windbreaker or sweater, and 100 awards = a jacket. Yet another award is presented for every 50 awards accumulated beyond 100.

Doug Barnett of the Sam Nunn Boulevard Chick-fil-A in Perry, GA, gives POSSE (Positively Outrageous Service) buttons to team members when they receive positive customer

comments on feedback cards. They're encouraged to wear them at all times and to uphold high standards, as members of an elite group.

———

Donna Friedman, an employee at a Home Depot in Ft. Lauderdale, FL, received special recognition for returning a $3,000 bracelet to a customer. The customer gave her a pure silver bracelet, and the company gave her a special letter of praise for her personnel file and a watch of her choice.

———

Pioneer Eclipse, a manufacturer of floor-care machines based in Sparta, NC, takes customers to meet line workers who have worked on their products. Employees love to tell customers about their ideas and to listen to their suggestions.

———

Broward County Government in Fort Lauderdale, FL, has a program called SUNsational Service to promote the way internal and external customers should be treated. Employees are nominated for embodying the organization's 10 Standards of Customer Service Excellence. Winners are chosen on a bimonthly basis by a group of employees called the "Prize Patrol," with music, dancing, and fanfare. Each recipient gets a basket containing a variety of prizes from the County store. The organization also hosts a customer service week, including an energy profile seminar, a customer service movie day, stress massages, and fun contests, such as an ugly tie contest, customer service *Jeopardy,* customer service quizzes, and word search puzzles.

> **"Once people trust management, know they're responsible, and are given the training, it's astonishing what they can do for customers and ultimately for the stakeholders."**
>
> —JAMES HENDERSON,
> CEO,
> Cummins Engine
> Company, Inc.

Rhonda Lowe, publisher of the *Los Banos Enterprise* newspaper, found a way to thank loyal advertisers by creating "Thanks A Million" bouquets. Using a computer program that makes currency, she designed some $1 million bills. She then wrapped them around 25-cent suckers to look like petals on a flower. She bought some inexpensive potted plants and inserted the "flowers" into the potted plant, then added a bow and a sign that read, "Thanks A Million For Being Our Customer." Sales representatives signed their names and personally delivered the award to their top accounts. It gave them the chance to be real heroes and to create a buzz—and clients prominently displayed the awards.

Whenever a cashier thanks a customer by name, the customer drops a coupon with the cashier's name into a big box at Stew Leonard's. Known as "The Name Game," the three cashiers who have thanked the most customers each week get $30 each. Employees also display "Ladder of Success" charts, mounted at cash registers, for customers to see each employee's progress. At Hecht's department stores, based in Arlington, VA, employees win points toward a shopping spree if managers hear them calling customers by name.

———

In "Todays Way Giveaway" at Dallas-based Todays Staffing, every time a temporary employee exceeds a client's expectations, he or she is entered in an annual drawing for prizes. Clients rate them on evaluation cards, which are then submitted to the company. Approximately 950 prizes have been awarded over three years.

———

McDonald's owner/operators are given jewelry bearing the company's "Golden Arches" logo to distribute to employees who provide superior service.

———

Every month at the Nordstrom department store chain, based in Seattle, every store manager meets to pick a Customer Service All-Star—the person who has made the most striking contribution for that period. Managers draw from their own observations, customer comment sheets placed near every cash register, reports by "mystery shoppers," and letters from customers. The winner gets $100, "Customer Service All-Star" stamped on his or her business card, and a larger employee discount on store merchandise. A Customer Service All-Star store is also picked each month, with headquarters providing money for a storewide barbecue or pizza party.

———

> **"The highest achievable level of service comes from the heart, so the company that reaches its people's heart will provide the very best service."**
>
> —HAL ROSENBLUTH,
> CEO,
> Rosenbluth Travel

> **❝**It's vital that you motivate your people—customers and employees—anyone who can contribute to the company's success.**❞**
>
> —ROBERT EVANS,
> Director,
> Promotional Services,
> Gillette Company

The Omni Service Champions program of Omni Hotels recognizes employees who go out of their way to deliver extraordinary service with medals, ribbon pins for their uniforms, cash, dinner, recognition in the company's newspaper and on posters in each hotel, and, finally, a three-day celebration at an Omni hotel chosen by company executives. At the end of the year, the three employees from each hotel who receive the most commendations are awarded medals (gold, silver, and bronze) and cash ($1,000 for gold and $500 each for silver and bronze), and all attend a gala.

In New Jersey Transit's Customer Service Awards program, employees who serve the public directly earn awards for exemplary customer service, while internal workers such as secretaries, maintenance people, and accountants receive awards for service to other employees. Two months before the awards are announced at the end of each year, posters with ballots are placed in train stations and at bus stops. Both riders and employees can make nominations for the awards, as can vendors who sell supplies to the agency.

In a recent year, the agency received 300 nominations and chose 10 winners. The number of ballots a person receives is taken into account, but the quality of the nomination is more important. "If we have one nomination for a person, but it's outstanding, that person might win." A nominating committee made up of managers selects the winners. Among the criteria are

exceptional customer service, especially to correct something that has gone wrong; demonstrated creativity or resourcefulness in assisting a customer; and development of new ways to solve problems.

The type of award varies each year. Past winners received savings bonds and a two-day trip to Atlantic City, and each recipient gets a plaque or trophy. Awards are given out at an annual company-wide meeting held at a conference center.

———

The Good Samaritan Hospital in Cincinnati instituted a recognition and reward program to improve customer service that incorporates monthly drawings and internal publicity, but also uses continuing training to reinforce a list of ten performance standards on which the program is based. To make sure goals, criteria, and progress are being communicated constantly, all 3,200 employees attend a one-hour training session every other month.

———

Delta Airlines has a "Feather in Your Cap Award" for customer service above and beyond the call of duty, such as that provided by the flight attendant who drove a passenger from Houston to Beaumont, TX, for a funeral she would otherwise have been unable to attend because she missed her connecting flight.

———

☑ *Create a Praising Board—a white board (or flip chart) where you post letters of appreciation from customers.*

☑ *When paychecks go out, write a note on the envelope recognizing an employee's accomplishment.*

☑ *Write five or more Post-it notes thanking the person for superior customer service and hide them among the work on his or her desk.*

> 66We will move mountains to let our employees and customers know we care. I've traveled 4,000 miles to spend five minutes with a customer, to let her know how important her business is to us. Caring is contagious, and we try to spread it around.99
>
> —HARVEY MACKAY,
> President,
> Mackay Envelope Corp.

At Andersons Management Corporation retail stores in Maumee, OH, store managers were given a certain number of silver dollars to give out when they observed or received comments about good customer service. Employees who received silver dollars were enrolled in the Silver Dollar Club and became eligible for monthly prize drawings.

———

At FMC Lithium Division (a subsidiary of FMC Corporation) in Bessemer City, NC, managers take deserving employees on trips to visit customers or vendors. This not only recognizes operators for their efforts, but also educates them and builds a sense of ownership of their work and the company's products. The additional cost is more than repaid in increased motivation and overall business understanding.

———

LensCrafters optical stores, headquartered in Mason, OH, granted $100 bonus checks for outstanding customer service, with the top nine people getting $1,000 and a crystal memento.

———

American Airlines gives "You're Someone Special" notes to its top frequent fliers to give to American employees when they receive exceptional service. The employees receive credit toward their own travel, and customer comments are printed in the company newsletter. Continental Airlines mailed "Pride in Performance" certificates to its top 50,000 frequent fliers and asked them to pass them out to particularly helpful employees. Continental workers could redeem the certificates for dinners, luggage, hotel stays, flight passes, and other merchandise.

———

For its Service Excellence Award, Citibank in New York rewards employees at all levels, except senior management, who demonstrate outstanding customer service. An employee is nominated by his or her manager, then reviewed by management within the employee's division. Award winners usually get a gift certificate for up to $500 in merchandise.

———

The Service Leader Award program at the American Hospital Association in Chicago offers winners a $100 check, a certificate, and an engraved plaque at the monthly manager's meeting. A Service Leader of the Year is selected from the twelve monthly leaders. That person receives a $100 check and an engraved plaque.

———

In the Most Valuable Player program at St. Louis's Busch Stadium, ten randomly selected fans are given two small MVP cards, which they can give any two employees who show them some courtesy—defined as "a smile, a welcome, a way of handling a question or problem," says Vicki Hutchison, manager of special projects for the Civic Center Corporation.

> **❝Our business is about technology, yes. But it's also about operations and customer relationships.❞**
>
> —MICHAEL DELL,
> President and Founder,
> Dell Computers

Employees then turn over the cards to supervisors; if the group of workers collects at least fifteen of the twenty cards during the game, a drawing is held and the winner gets a $100 bill.

A monthly Outstanding Teamworker program encourages workers to nominate fellow All-Stars, who receive recognition in the form of a pregame, on-the-field ceremony, a lapel pin, their choice of merchandise from a catalog, and brunch in their honor.

———

At Park Lane Hotels International, based in San Francisco, guests are asked to nominate hotel workers who provided outstanding service. The company rewarded all nominees with Sony personal electronics and held a grand-prize drawing for a TV; the guest who nominated the grand-prize winner received two free nights at the hotel.

———

MCI, based in Ashburn, VA, used picnic baskets from Harry and David in Medford, OR, to reward fifty of its customer service reps. "MCI wanted to recognize employees who saw a problem and stepped right in to solve it," says Jon Silver, a sales rep for Harry and David. A note of appreciation was tucked inside each basket.

———

Indianapolis-based Cellular One has a bonus plan that awards employees $10 for every customer compliment they get (mostly on customer comments cards) and deducts $10 every time a customer complains about service. Customer compliments have tripled since the company began the reward program.

———

The San Diego Convention and Visitors Bureau awards the title "Cab Driver of the Year" to the driver who exemplifies outstanding hospitality. The winner is feted at the city's Annual Cab Driver Appreciation Day, and receives 500 business cards, an engraved dashboard plaque, and a magnetic sign for the cab that announces the award. One recent winner, Montag Plank, says he provides riders with extras such as newspapers and information about local attractions. "No matter what your job is, if you're courteous and do the job right, people will respect you for it," he says.

———

When Dick Radell, vice president of human resources for The Marcus Corporation in Milwaukee, receives exceptional service at one of the company's restaurants, he writes a short note on the back of his business card and gives it to the server immediately.

———

Joan Cawley, director of human resources for Advanta Corporation, the financial services firm in Horsham, PA, describes the GEM (Going the Extra Mile) Award for customer service representatives. Each month peers and managers select an employee whose specific

> **❝From the beginning I was empowered to take responsibility to deal with clients directly. It adds a lot of satisfaction to the job and, compared to what my peers tell me about their work, this is an oasis.❞**
>
> —IAN HARRIS,
> Actuarial Consultant,
> Hewitt Associates

performance went beyond the call of duty for a customer. Each winner's name is added to an engraved brass plaque, and he or she enjoys a rotating crystal desktop plaque for the month. Photos are taken at the award presentation (held at a staff meeting) and made into a colorful collage that decorates the department wall. At the end of each program year, the names of the twelve winners are put into a hat for a prize drawing. The grand prize is a cruise for two.

A CASE STUDY IN CUSTOMER SERVICE

❝We share the dream to be recognized as the very best company when it comes to delivering value to customers, employees, shareholders, and communities," says Kent B. Foster, president of GTE Telephone Operations (now owned by Verizon Communications), headquartered in Stamford, CT. To help reach that dream, the President's Quality Awards program recognizes employees in four categories: area and region, individual employees, teams, and vendors.

The company's four areas and fourteen regions compete each year for Quality Champion Cups. Award recipients are selected directly by customers who are surveyed annually. The most improved region is also recognized with a trophy.

Individual employees are rewarded at three levels of achievement: The top ten employees receive $2,500 along with a personalized award and a letter of commendation from the division president. The thirty finalists receive $750 and a

personalized award, and the forty semifinalists receive $500 and a personalized award. One individual who has demonstrated exemplary commitment to quality is chosen for the Individual Quality Champions to receive the President's Distinctive Commendation. He or she receives a monetary award, a special medallion, and a letter of commendation from the president.

Team awards are given to two first-place Gold Award winners (one for external and one for internal customer service), two second-place Silver Award winners, and three Bronze Award winners for external efforts. Members of each team receive cash, a personalized award, and a letter of commendation from the president.

> **"Good treatment of workers results in similar treatment of customers."**
>
> —TODD ENGLANDER,
> *Incentive*

Employee Suggestions

Only 41 percent of employees believe the average company listens to their ideas. No wonder, then, that the average American worker makes 1.1 suggestions per year—one of the lowest among industrialized nations. Compare that with the 167 suggestions per employee in Japan, and you can see the untapped potential.

> **"Companies don't need management stars or heroes to thrive. What they absolutely do need is an effective system for getting and implementing ideas from the people who do the work."**
>
> —MARTIN EDELSTON, CEO, Boardroom, Inc.

Radio Shack, based in Fort Worth, uses a four-foot stuffed gorilla to recognize initiative and innovation. The gorilla goes to an employee with a useful idea until another one comes along. The person who has the most ideas in a given quarter receives yet another prize.

During a downturn in business, Rosenbluth International, a Philadelphia-based corporate travel agency, ran a program called "Operation Brainstorm," asking employees to think of ideas to cut costs. More than 400 were submitted, and the company was able to avoid laying off employees.

When Vic Anapolle was operations manager for a chemical specialties group at W. R. Grace in Atlanta, he set out to motivate employees to increase the number and quality of their suggestions: using "Starperks" scratch-off lottery tickets from the Bill Sims Company, he was able to obtain an average of twelve to fourteen suggestions per employee, leading to cost savings of $175,000 per year. Each lottery ticket gave employees the chance to win various prizes and all tickets (winners' and losers') were used for an overall drawing for a trip.

> "The deepest principle in human nature is the craving to be appreciated."
>
> —WILLIAM JAMES, Philosopher and Psychologist

The SCOOTER Store crowns employees "Superheroes," if they "come to the rescue" with revenue-generating ideas or implement cost-cutting programs and procedures. They are donned with red tablecloths closely resembling superhero caps.

Each year at FedEx Kinko's, the employee who submits the best suggestion wins an all-expense-paid trip to Disney World for his or her entire store. While they're away, top brass fill in.

Peavey Electronics Corporation in Meridian, MS, rewards hourly workers for their suggestions by paying them 8 percent of estimated first-year savings based on those suggestions. Melia Peavy says this system generates more excitement than the old system of simply rewarding suggestions with a flat amount.

———

The Office of Human Resources and Administration at the U.S. Department of Energy in Washington, D.C., sponsored an "Ideas Day" for employees to think of ways to improve the way they worked. They collected 2,134 ideas, 68 percent of which were implemented.

———

At Kodak's Image Loops and Sundries Department in Rochester, NY, production is shut down when operators reach their weekly goals for each type of loop, so that they can work on other projects. Employees have used the extra time to develop ideas, which has resulted in improvements and great camaraderie.

———

Arthur Hogling, executive director of the Developmental Disabilities Resource Center in Lakewood, CO, reports: "Employees who aggressively cut costs receive baseballs, signed by our management team, at monthly meetings. They have become a source of pride on people's desks."

———

A Deere & Company office in Dubuque, IA, doubled employee participation in an employee suggestion program by providing all participants with pocket protectors, magnetic calendars, and notepads with the slogan: "Got an idea? Write it down!" Employees whose suggestions were implemented received awards.

———

Urban Bianchi, a machinist with Cleveland-based Parker Hannifin Corporation, has turned in more than 800 cost-cutting proposals that his bosses have approved—so many that the *Los Angeles Times* has dubbed him "the undisputed king of the suggestion box." The company has rewarded him with a flood of microwave ovens, coupons for free dinners, tools, and other gifts, with an estimated value of $17,000 in a four-year period. "I've got so much stuff, it's unbelievable," Bianchi says. While he adds that for him doing a job well is what's motivating, he also admits that he gets a kick out of sharing his riches with family members. "When I gave them radios, they loved it," he says. "It meant more to them that I got a radio doing a good job, working hard, than if I'd bought it at a store."

———

Ben & Jerry's distributes grants to departments at corporate headquarters if they come up with creative suggestions. They can use them to purchase merchandise such as popcorn makers or hot chocolate machines.

———

At Stew Leonard's, a suggestion program rewards employee ideas with retail gift certificates worth up to $500. The company's

> **"**An idea is a fragile thing. Turning it off is much easier than keeping it lit. Ideas shine because somebody had them and somebody helped them and nobody turned them off. Companies have to reward people for being creative, for coming up with new ideas.**"**
>
> —Tom Peters,
> Author and
> Management Consultant

INCREASING EMPLOYEE SUGGESTIONS

■ *For most people, simply using their suggestion is recognition enough.*

■ *When an employee presents an idea or suggestion, thank the person for his or her concern and initiative.*

■ *Make sure you respond to and actually try to use as many suggestions as possible.*

■ *Widely publicize suggestions used, along with a description of their positive impact on the organization.*

bimonthly newspaper reports on the ideas that are adopted.

_____

Two county employees in San Diego have been awarded $10,000 each for suggestions that saved the county government more than $1.1 million. Ken Buccellato and Renee Sherrill received the bonuses through the Do-It-Better-By-Suggestion Program, which rewards employees for ideas that save money, improve safety, or increase efficiency.

_____

A CASE STUDY IN EMPLOYEE SUGGESTIONS

Boardroom Inc., a newsletter and book publisher based in Stamford, CT, expects every employee—from receptionist to chairman—to submit at least two ideas each week for improvements. The program, "I Power," is credited with a five-fold increase in revenue as well as an invaluable benefit to the morale, energy, and retention of employees. The suggestions are evaluated each week by an employee volunteer, and usually go back to the owners with "What a great idea!"—which is an implicit "go-ahead" to implement the idea.

As Martin Edelston, chairman and CEO of Boardroom, says, "Sometimes the best idea can come from the newest, least experienced person on your staff." For example, an hourly paid shipping clerk suggested that the company trim the paper size of one of its books in order to get under the 4-pound rate and save some postage. Boardroom made the change and ended up saving half a million dollars each year. Martin explains, "I had been working in mail order for over twenty years and never realized there was a four-pound shipping rate. But the person who was doing the job knew it and knew how his work could be improved, as do most employees."

In the first year of the "I Power" program, suggestions were limited to employees' own jobs, until they got the idea that the intention was less about complaining about things than trying to think of how to improve them. The company still holds group meetings just to brainstorm and share ideas about specific issues and functions.

And the benefits of the suggestions are not limited to saving money. Antoinette Baugh, director of personnel, explains: "People love working here because they know they can be a part of a system where they can make a contribution." Adds Lisa Castonguay, renewals and billing manager, "My first couple of weeks I was kind of taken aback because everyone was smiling and everyone was open." On her first day of work, she was pulled into a group meeting and within 30 minutes was asked, "What do you think we should do about this problem?"

Lisa almost collapsed on the floor, because she had worked for eight years at a company where no one had ever asked for her opinion. Once she got over the shock, it felt good to have her opinions and ideas sought after and valued by those she worked with. As a result, it was easy for her to think of additional ways to help the company.

The impact is both positive and contagious. "People became agents of their own change," says Martin. "There's so much inside of all of us and we don't even know it's there until someone asks about it. And in the process, it just builds and builds." Adds Brian Kurtz, vice president of marketing, "It's a constant flow of communication. People are not sitting in a cubicle, totally isolated from one another."

In San Diego, seventy-one county employees came up with ideas that generated nearly $400,000 in savings. They were honored at a year-end ceremony, and received cash awards ranging from $25 to nearly $5,000.

In three months, the American Achievers program at American Airlines inspired nearly 3,500 seven-person teams to come up with more than 1,600 ideas that were adopted, resulting in more than $20 million in cost-saving or revenue-generating improvements. Employees reaped $4.7 million in merchandise prizes, each prize based on the cash value of the idea implemented. More importantly, employees wholeheartedly supported the changes because they had designed them. That success has led to a continuing system called AAchievers that includes instant points-for-merchandise rewards for good work by individuals and groups.

The focus of the American Achievers program has since expanded to recognize employees for doing anything special, or for consistently

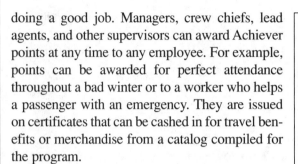

doing a good job. Managers, crew chiefs, lead agents, and other supervisors can award Achiever points at any time to any employee. For example, points can be awarded for perfect attendance throughout a bad winter or to a worker who helps a passenger with an emergency. They are issued on certificates that can be cashed in for travel benefits or merchandise from a catalog compiled for the program.

___

66Everyone Counts" is a program at Black & Decker, headquartered in Towson, MD, that uses teams to brainstorm and develop ideas about training, communication, administration, and rewards. People from different departments are grouped into thirty-nine teams, and two evaluation committees for managerial personnel receive ideas and judge their merit. The evaluation teams also note leadership potential in some employees when they make their presentations. A total of two hundred ideas have been submitted and fifty-nine approved, one of which was worth $700,000 in cost savings. The twelve ideas that have already been implemented deal mostly with improved operations that result in cost savings. One $700,000 idea concerned the substitution of a new material in one of the company's product lines. The program has also improved the company's vertical lines of communication.

___

The pharmaceuticals company Cyanamid Canada has a "Key to Innovation" campaign that encourages workers to contribute ideas and

> **66**One of the stepping stones to a world-class operation is to tap into the creative and intellectual power of each and every employee.**99**
>
> —Harold A. Poling, Former Chairman and CEO, Ford Motor Company

> **❝**We believe that most people have capabilities beyond those they are called on to demonstrate in their jobs.**❞**
>
> —From a statement of philosophy printed by Hewitt Associates

become "Frequent Innovators." For productivity-enhancing ideas, employees receive 40 to 1,000 points, redeemable in an award catalog for such prizes as glassware, radios, televisions, and weekend trips for two.

———

At Eastman Kodak in Rochester, NY, an employee whose suggestion is implemented receives 15 percent of the out-of-pocket savings achieved in the first two years. If a suggestion results in a new product, he or she gets 3 percent of first year sales achieved. Kodak has given rewards—averaging $3 million annually—to more than 30,000 people.

———

Fel-Pro, a gasket manufacturer based in Southfield, MI, holds a $1,000 drawing once a year for all employees who participated in the firm's suggestion program.

———

At Levi Strauss & Company, based in San Francisco, employees nominate one another for the firm's Koshland Award for showing initiative, taking risks, generating cost-saving measures, coming up with creative ideas for promoting products at the retail level—anything that puts the company at a competitive advantage. Winners receive a plaque and a cash prize at an annual awards ceremony.

———

A CASE STUDY IN RECOGNIZING EMPLOYEE SUGGESTIONS

IBM's suggestion program awards $50 to $150,000 for money-saving ideas or suggestions with benefits like enhanced health, safety, or customer service. The amount of the reward for an idea that leads to measurable savings is based on 25 percent of the first year's net material and labor savings. For awards of more than $200, the suggester also receives 25 percent of projected net savings for the second year, up to $150,000.

Awards for suggestions that yield intangible benefits depend on such factors as the seriousness of the problem and the creativity and effectiveness of the solution. These awards usually range from $50 to $100, although the $150,000 maximum applies as well. The program is open to all employees. In a recent year, IBM gave out eight $150,000 rewards, out of 153,000 ideas submitted by its 223,000 U.S. employees. Other programs include:

Invention Achievement Award Plan These awards recognize a significant record of invention. The first patent application the employee files under the provisions of the plan earns $1,500. Employees receive points for patent applications and other qualifying inventions that are published. At each twelve-point plateau, the employee gets a certificate and $3,600. The first plateau also earns jewelry.

> **"If workers cannot inform managers— and managers cannot learn and respond— workers' insights have no credibility, and the notion of their partnerships with management becomes empty verbiage."**
>
> —DR. MITCHELL RABKIN, President, Beth Israel Hospital

> **If managers ask people to give of their creative talents and commitment and to take apparent risks by doing such things as proposing labor-saving ideas, those people should share handsomely in any profit that results.**
>
> —TOM PETERS,
> Author and
> Management Consultant

IBM Division Award Plan This award recognizes and rewards achievements that have "outstanding value" to the company in terms of cost savings and the impact on the major mission of a specific division. Awards range from $1,500 to $25,000.

———

At the 10,000-person Honda of America factory in Marysville, OH, employees receive $100 for each accepted suggestion, but they also get anywhere from 1 to 12 V.I.P. points for each one. If they make a presentation to a quality circle meeting, they get an extra 50 points. When they accumulate 300 points, they get a plaque; 1,000 points nets $800. Higher-level prizes are a Honda Civic for 2,500 points, and an Accord, two extra weeks of vacation, and four weeks' pay for 5,000 points. The company received more than 10,000 suggestions in a recent year, resulting in savings of $5 million.

———

Productivity & Quality

In America, the current use of rewards to encourage productivity and production is unfortunately underused and ineffective. According to one study, only 40 percent of employees believe the average American company offers meaningful incentives to maximize quality and productivity. In Japan, on the other hand, 93 percent of workers felt certain they would benefit. Let's look at some other discouraging statistics about the American workplace:

✔ 93 percent of employees say American products could compete better against Japanese products if American management involved workers in continual efforts to improve quality.

✔ 89 percent of American workers think their companies would perform better if employees were given meaningful incentives to improve quality and productivity.

✔ 81 percent of workers believe they will not receive rewards for any increase in productivity.

✔ 60 percent of managers believe their compensation will not increase if their performance improves.

> **❝What the American worker is telling us is that the answer to increased productivity and motivation can be found inside their own companies and that meaningful rewards need to be offered to workers at every level in the organization.❞**
>
> —Patrick Delaney,
> President,
> Society of Incentive Travel
> Executives (SITE)

At Worzalla Publishing Company in Stevens Point, WI, the quality services department exceeded its goal of 99.85% accuracy in customer specifications for five years in a row. Bill Downs, the quality supervisor and continuous improvement manager, wanted to celebrate, but he was limited to a budget of $20 per person. So he took the department to lunch and gave each member of the team a certificate of appreciation and a gift card for a movie rental and pizza. The group enjoyed the lunch and gift cards, but seemed to take even more pride in displaying the certificates in their offices and explaining their achievement to anyone who cared to listen.

When Jennifer Wallick was software development manager at Four Pi Systems, a developer of manufacturing test equipment in San Diego (now a part of Hewlett-Packard), she found that programmers did not like to bring up errors. To keep employees from getting frustrated when they found a bug in a new software product, she started the "Find a Bug, Win a Prize" program that awarded a candy bar to anyone who found a bug in the new software product. Jennifer says, "It certainly changed people's attitudes. It also improved the quality of the software because more bugs were reported and fixed sooner."

At Ryder System truck rental and leasing, based in Miami, employees in quality action teams (work groups put together to come up with quality improvement suggestions) are reinforced with tangible incentives in addition to more traditional forms of appreciation. Jerry Riordan, vice president of quality, says, "We try to give them a quick response from the decision makers, as well as quick implementation for accepted ideas. Their incentive is the pleasure of getting changes made." The company is implementing a continuous improvement process that stresses response to ideas within ten days, as well as more formal recognition and reward procedures.

> **"Those who give and get praise at work have increased productivity."**
>
> —Findings from The Gallup Organization

B ob Vassallo, manager of employee relations at the Thomas J. Lipton Company, maker of food products in Englewood Cliffs, NJ, reports having an Open Vending Machine Day in which employees are allowed free access to plant cafeteria vending machines for reaching certain manufacturing goals, such as productivity, quality, and safety.

N oncommission employees who have achieved peak performance at the *Portland Business Journal* in Portland, OR, are recognized monthly. Special voice-mail messages on the main switchboard announce their names, the high sales results, and the gains in circulation, and cash bonuses are distributed.

A t 3M in St. Paul, managers give the "Golden Step Award," inspired by the Greek god Hermes's winged slipper, to those who make a new line of business profitable, initiate a new product or service, or create a new market niche. These tacky, plastic, gold-colored shoes are highly valued by employees.

_____

NCO Financial Systems in Horsham, PA, started a bonus system for data-entry clerks, encouraging them to work as a team to eliminate backlogs in paperwork. Each clerk receives a point for each day without backlog, and monthly prizes (up to $250 in value) are awarded based on the number of accumulated points. Those who don't win top prizes are also entered in a random drawing for $100. Productivity has increased 25 percent with this system, with no drop in quality.

_____

Motorola in Schaumburg, IL, has awards breakfasts at which factory workers who have met certain quality goals are recognized by senior managers.

_____

The Outstanding Teller Service Award at the First-Knox National Bank in Mt. Vernon, OH, tries to tie productivity and customer service awards to measurable goals. The program selects one outstanding teller from each branch using a system based 33 percent on tellers' choice, 34 percent on customer satisfaction (selection cards are included in customers' bank statements), 11 percent on balancing record, 11 percent on number of transactions, and 11 percent on supervisory rating.

_____

> **❝**I thought, my God, if I can get people pumped up, wanting to come to work, what an edge that is! That's the whole secret to increasing productivity. I saw them push and accomplish things they never thought were possible. I saw satisfaction on a daily basis.**❞**
>
> —JACK STACK,
> CEO,
> SRC Corp.

A CASE STUDY IN QUALITY IMPROVEMENT

The Tennant Company, a provider of nonresidential floor maintenance equipment, floor coatings, and related products based in Minneapolis, began its quality improvement push by defining an objective "to recognize superior quality performers in their organization." Because different people respond to different kinds of rewards and recognition, they developed a three-dimensional program.

First is the formal awards program, in which honored employees (up to 2 percent of the workforce each year) receive a 10-karat gold and diamond ring, and a plaque at an annual banquet. The peer-driven program has three rules governing the selection of award recipients:

1. The company's established criteria for selecting recognition recipients are printed on the nomination forms.

2. An employee can nominate anyone, with the exception of people he or she reports to directly.

3. Recognition recipients are selected by a committee of employees of different rank and from different departments of the company.

Second, an additional "formal" award grew out of employee feedback for more frequent recognition. Winners of the Koala T. Bear (a play on the word *quality*) are visited by a costumed bear and recognition committee. Each

> **❝**I don't think it's possible to make a great quality product without having a great quality work environment. So it's linked—quality product, quality customer service, quality workplace, and quality of life for your employees.**❞**
>
> —YVON CHOUINARD,
> CEO,
> Patagonia

recipient receives a stuffed Koala T. Bear and a certificate of his or her achievements. There's a less stringent nomination process, and the awards are presented monthly.

Third is the informal rewards program, designed to recognize people who meet specific goals. It is flexible and can be tailored to meet the needs and preferences of individuals and groups. Informal recognition is immediate recognition given by manager and supervisors to those employees doing something right.

While any one of these dimensions might be considered a complete program in many organizations, Tennant firmly believes that all three have to be present to maximize employee motivation and performance. According to former human resources manager Rita Maehling, "Like a three-legged stool, each dimension plays a critical role. Take away one leg of the stool and it falls."

A CASE STUDY IN IMPROVED PERFORMANCE

When Lou Gerstner became president of Travel Related Services (TRS) at New York–based American Express, the unit was facing one of its biggest challenges in AMEX's 130-year history. Hundreds of banks were offering or planning to introduce credit cards through Visa and MasterCard that would compete with the American Express card. And more than two dozen financial service firms were getting into the traveler's check business.

Within a week of his appointment, Gerstner brought together the people running the card organization and questioned all the principles by which they conducted their business. In particular, he challenged two widely shared beliefs— that the division should have only one product, the green card, and that this product was limited in potential for growth and innovation.

Gerstner also moved quickly to develop a more entrepreneurial culture, to hire and train people who would thrive in it, and to communicate clearly to them the organization's overall direction. He and other top managers rewarded intelligent risk-taking. To make entrepreneurship easier, they discouraged unnecessary bureaucracy. They also upgraded hiring standards and created the TRS Graduate Management program, which offered high-potential young people special training, an enriched set of experiences, and an unusual degree of exposure to people in top management. To encourage risk-taking among all TRS employees, Gerstner established a Great Performers program (similar to the program at Honeywell described earlier) to recognize and reward truly exceptional customer service, a central tenet of the organization's philosophy.

In the Great Performers program, life-sized posters showing famous people with their greatest achievements were displayed throughout the facilities for many weeks. Then the company began to picture American Express employees on posters, with a statement of a major accomplishment by each employee. Afterward the employee could take the poster home.

> **❝**The way managers treat their subordinates is subtly influenced by what they expect of them. If a manager's expectations are high, productivity is likely to be excellent. If his expectations are low, productivity is likely to be poor. It is as though there were a law that caused a subordinate's performance to rise or fall to meet his manager's expectations.**❞**
>
> —J. STERLING LIVINGSTON, *Harvard Business Review*

> 66There is no way a work force that is uninvolved and unrewarded will be quality-conscious, efficient, or innovative.99
>
> —AARON SUGARMAN,
> *Incentive*

Nominations were made by fellow employees, supervisors, and customers. Award winners were eligible to become Grand Award winners, named by the worldwide governing committee. There was no limit on how many people could win; in a recent year, thirty-eight employees garnered the award. Prizes for Grand Award winners included an all-expense-paid trip for two to New York, $4,000 in American Express traveler's checks, a platinum "GP" logo pin, and a framed certificate.

These initiatives quickly led to new markets, products, and services, and resulted in an increase in TRS's net income of 500 percent in eleven years, or about an 18 percent annual compounded rate. With a return on equity of 28 percent, the business outperformed many so-called high-tech, high-growth companies, as well as most low-growth but high-profit businesses.

Managers at Katzinger's Deli in Columbus, OH, made a deal with employees: if they reduced food costs, the company would split the savings with them. They ended up saving $30,000, and split $15,000 among themselves.

Attendance & Safety

In many ways, nothing is more important to a company than attendance and safety, especially in manufacturing firms. Offering effective attendance incentives to encourage employees to be prompt and not miss workdays, and effective safety incentives to ensure employee well-being and minimize accidents, is essential to the success of many companies.

A McDonald's in St. Louis gives first choice of work schedules to employees with the best attendance records. This promotes better attendance and—because many employees are students—gives people a chance to coordinate work and class schedules.

> 66It's no good saying you can't afford to look after your staff. You can't afford not to.99
>
> —JULIAN RICHER,
> Founder,
> Richer Sounds

———

Leone Ackerly, the owner of Mini Maid Service Company in Marietta, GA, gives employees an attendance bonus each pay period if they have come to work everyday on time and in uniform.

———

General Electric, headquartered in Fairfield, CT, offers a cash bonus for every six months of perfect attendance.

———

The Atlantic Envelope Company in Atlanta awards employees two hours' extra pay for every month of perfect attendance.

———

Rush-Copley Memorial Hospital in Aurora, IL, rewarded 128 employees with a buffet lunch, a certificate of achievement, and a ceramic coffee mug inscribed with "Perfect Attendance" and the year. A special gift certificate went to the employee with the longest perfect attendance.

———

Pella Corporation in Pella, IA, awards a $100 savings bond and arranges coffee time with top management for employees with one year of perfect attendance. The company, which mar-kets windows, even arranged a reception with the governor of Iowa for seven employees with twenty-five years' perfect attendance.

———

In the Instant Win Giveaway program at Todays Staffing, based in Dallas, temporary employees who have worked during the previ-ous six months are given a card with a scratch-off panel concealing the name of a prize. Prizes include a diamond watch, $100 or $50 cash, cal-culators, and six months of free long-distance telephone calls.

———

To recognize those with perfect attendance, Merle Norman Cosmetics, based in Los Angeles, offers the following gifts:

One year: a gold engraved watch

Two years: a video game, cookware set, or stainless flatware

Three years: a stereo or portable TV

Four years: a food processor

Five years: a camera

Six years: personal electronics

Seven years: a TV

Eight years: a microwave oven

Nine years: a specially designed ring

Ten years: a two-week, all-expense-paid trip to Hawaii for two

Fifteen years: a two-week, all-expense-paid trip to anywhere in the world for the employee and his or her spouse, relative, or friend

How well do these incentives work? In a given year, more than one-tenth of all hourly employees did not have a minute of absenteeism or tardiness, and eight employees had gone ten years without missing any time from work.

———

A large manufacturing firm with 7,500 hourly employees increased attendance by offering nonmonetary privileges, combined with progressive discipline for excessive absences.

———

> 66Positive reinforcement not only improves performance; it also is necessary to maintain good performance.99
>
> —R.W. REBER and G. VAN GELDER, Coauthors, *Behavioral Insights for Supervision*

In an effort to decrease absenteeism, New York Life Insurance Company holds a lottery for employees who have been at work every day each quarter. The first ten employees to have their names drawn earn a $200 bond; the next twenty earn a $100 bond; and seventy more receive a paid day off. A special lottery is held for employees with perfect attendance records for the entire year. Prizes are two $1,000 bonds and ten more paid days off. The company estimates that absenteeism is 21 percent lower than during the same period the previous year.

———

At Toyota Motor Company of America, every employee who has perfect attendance for the year gets a coupon to enter into a drawing for a free car. If an employee has two years of perfect attendance, he or she gets two tickets, for three years, three tickets, and so on. Six cars are awarded annually.

———

JP Morgan Chase & Company reported saving $820,000 in reduced absenteeism in one year alone by offering New York City employees backup child care. Employees are offered twenty free days of child care a year.

———

When Vic Anapolle was operations manager for a chemical specialties group at W. R. Grace in Atlanta (now Grace, headquartered in Columbia, MD), he implemented a new system for employee motivation. Starting with a nominal budget of $100 per person per year and using "Starperks" scratch-off coupons to reward safety practices, he set a safety goal of one million man hours without any injuries. Not only did he surpass the goal, motivating his group to exceed one and a half million man hours without any injuries, but his group was able to pass a surprise OSHA hazardous chemical inspection with flying colors.

> **❝Those who give and get praise at work have better safety records and fewer accidents on the job.❞**
> —Findings from The Gallup Organization

———

According to Dick Radell, vice president of human resources of The Marcus Corporation in Milwaukee, all the employees who work at a specific restaurant for one month without an accident are awarded a "megabuck" from the state lottery, in a program that is quite popular with employees.

———

At FedEx Freight West in San Jose, CA, safe workers and drivers receive a recognition gift (pins, watches, and rings, with diamonds added for continuous safety streaks) for safety milestones every five years. In addition, quarterly and annual President's Safety Awards in the form of cash and clothing, as well as a trip in the case of the annual winners, are given to four employees (one in each of four work groups) to recognize outstanding safety achievement. Contests are held for different locations, and winning work groups are recognized with barbecues or clothing.

———

> **"**The recognition program, along with good training and supervision, helps keep safety on the minds of all our workers—including management and supervisors. It helps keep us focused as a team.**"**
>
> —JIM RAINSBERGER,
> Superintendent,
> Pipeline Division Terminal,
> Quaker State

Southern New England Telephone, based in New Haven, CT, rewards employees who have driven one calendar year without a preventable accident. To be eligible, an employee must drive at least 12,000 miles annually or spend 25 percent or more of his or her work time operating or working out of a company vehicle. Employees amass certificates that are redeemed for products from one supplier.

———

At Furst-McNess Company in Freeport, IL, which manufactures premixed animal foods, Mark S. Fryer, director of human resources, says the company gives $25 to all personnel who are assigned a company vehicle and receive no moving violations for a calendar year. If an employee goes three years without any violations, he or she gets an additional $100 award. Accidents with company cars have been greatly reduced.

———

As an incentive for safe behavior, APG Electric in Clearwater, FL, gave employees with good safety records a chance to win a prize from $6,500 worth of cash and gifts, as well as a shot at the grand prize—a $13,500 Chevrolet pickup truck.

———

Southern Wine & Spirits, a distributor of bottled waters, juices, and alcoholic beverages, has a recognition award that has helped reduce safety-related financial losses by 70 percent—from almost $1 million annually to only a few hundred thousand dollars per year. The award is a Super Bowl–style gold and diamond ring, presented to drivers who steer clear of safety-related problems for five years in a row. A 1-carat diamond is added to that ring for each year of continued safety. Driver Alex Barnes says proudly, "It's truly an honor to wear the ring."

PART VI

FORMAL ORGANIZATIONAL REWARD PROGRAMS

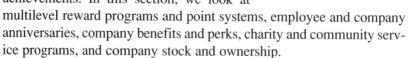

The formal rewards and recognition programs in this chapter are part of even more complex and structured systems than the ones for specific achievements. In this section, we look at multilevel reward programs and point systems, employee and company anniversaries, company benefits and perks, charity and community service programs, and company stock and ownership.

Tim Puffer, of Puffer & Associates marketing and public relations in St. Paul, describes eight general guidelines for conducting a successful rewards and recognition program: (1) define objectives; (2) lead by management example; (3) develop specific criteria; (4) use meaningful rewards; (5) involve employees; (6) keep communications clear; (7) reward teams; and (8) manage the long term.

Multilevel Reward Programs & Point Systems

Most companies have one or more formal reward programs for recognizing employee performance, often integrated to address the needs of different levels and types of employees. Although such programs typically recognize only a small number of people, the experience is significant and motivating, and the public example helps to shape the future aspirations of other employees.

Banister Shoe in White Plains, NY, uses a combination of programs to reward and recognize employees at all levels and for various achievements. Formal award programs include Manager of the Year; District Manager of the Year; the Leadership Achievement Award, also known as the "eagle ring," in which an employee first receives an onyx ring and then diamonds for it with each additional recognition event; the Achievement Award or "pyramid pen"; and membership in the President's Club for store managers.

More informal programs include "hero meetings," which are held once a month in the central office to announce achievements and

> ❝Employees will be more receptive to formal, organization-wide programs if they believe that the company really cares about them on a personal, day-to-day basis.❞
>
> —ROSALIND JEFFRIES, Rewards and Recognition Consultant

encourage employees to praise one another, and also include spontaneous standing ovations for various achievements by individuals.

———

Catherine Meek of Meek and Associates, a compensation consultant firm in Ojai, CA, mentions a hospital she worked with: "At any one time they had twelve to fifteen employee recognition programs going, each developed by employees. The janitors and housekeeping staff came up with the Golden Broom Award. They have these little cards made up with a golden broom on them, and if someone is seen picking up trash—other than a janitor—he or she gets this award. After someone receives ten cards, he or she gets something else—nothing really expensive or big, but it gets the message across.

"Another program," Meek says, "is called the Guaranteed Service Program. It refunds a patient's money for nonsurgical procedures if the patient is not totally satisfied with the services. This hospital has a fund for this, and every quarter of what isn't returned to patients is raffled off to employees. What that does is focus employees on providing the best possible patient care, because the better the care, the higher the fund and the more money in their pockets.

"Another program is called 'Caught in the Act of Caring.' Employees get little cards that say, 'I was caught in the act of caring.' After you get a certain number of these cards, you can trade them in for various merchandise, such as electronics equipment.

"None of this takes all that much time as long as you have employees involved in these various programs. The hospital doesn't really think of the time; it's just the way they do business."

Inspired by the slogan "At Ross, You're in the Company of Excellence," president Dick Gast decided that Ross Products, based in Columbus, OH, needed a recognition program to enhance its tradition of superior products and services.

Since much excellence is subjective, Gast decided to put it into more concrete terms by allowing employees to participate in defining and recognizing it. He specified that the program be open to all 4,100 employees, from line workers to executives, and that it be employee-driven. All company employees should be eligible to win and participate in selecting winners.

The program designates three levels of achievement with rising prestige and increasingly valuable awards. At each facility, it is administered according to the number of people and their particular preferences. Any full-time Ross employee may nominate another full-time employee, whether subordinate or supervisor, for an award. Employees may even nominate themselves.

All nominations are considered by a screening committee of twelve to twenty-five workers in each area. The committee considers all nominations and selects the most deserving people to be voted on by employees in their area. Although managers can serve on the selection

> **"Create a dynamic work environment by varying load, having a formal job rotation program so people don't become stale in their current positions, and by offering opportunities for personal and professional development."**
>
> —RON ROSENBERG,
> Founder,
> Drive-You-Nuts.com,
> the customer service
> how-to Web site

committee, they have no more clout than any other members in determining final selections. Service on the committee is voluntary and may not exceed two years.

The Award of Excellence program gives employees many chances for recognition. At the end of each quarter, the screening committee reviews all nominations submitted during that period. Nominees affirmed by the committee and verified by the personnel department as employees in good standing automatically become Level I winners. Their names are announced at a general meeting, during which they receive a two-ounce silver ingot engraved with the Ross Award of Excellence logo on the front and the original Ross milk truck logo on the back. The ingot is encased in a clear plastic base and can be used as a paperweight or desk ornament. The award costs approximately $50. The number of first-time winners varies depending on the number of area workers, although it is generally between ten and fifteen per quarter.

Each quarter, area employees select four Level II winners from among the Level I winners. Those four winners receive a five-ounce silver ingot with the same Level I imprints, but in the shape of an Olympic-style medal, complete with a ribbon. The award is encased in a black-velvet-covered box and costs approximately $100. Level II winners also receive a letter of congratulation from the division president. At the end of the year, a recognition dinner is held at each Ross location for all Level II winners.

At the end of the fourth quarter, an election is held to select Level III winners from among the Level II winners. Level III winners get together for a three-day trip to celebrate their achievements. Activities include a visit to the company's headquarters for a reception hosted by the president, a double-decker bus tour around the city and a free afternoon, followed by a president's celebration dinner. Each Level III winner is awarded a Waterford crystal decanter with six glasses, as well as a $250 gift certificate to be used toward his or her choice of merchandise from a catalog. The estimated cost of the Level III festivities is about $20,000.

"An excellent employee is someone other employees look forward to working with because that person is pleasant, easy to get along with, and does everything possible to make each working day a productive and pleasant experience for everyone," says Mike Strapp, director of marketing and financial services and Award of Excellence program chairman. "Fun is an important element in the definition of excellence.

"With any recognition program," says Strapp, "the goal is to encourage other employees to strive for the same kind of excellence as those who are recognized. Recognition from your peers is a great motivator."

"If you feel appreciated, you're going to go out of your way, too," says Maria Rossi, the company's receptionist, who became one of the company's first thirty-six Level III winners. "I have always appreciated my job, but this made me feel appreciated back."

> **❝A solid performance-improvement program pays for itself out of the profits it generates.❞**
> —The MBF Group, Inc.

Radisson Hotels & Resorts, based in Minnetonka, MN, have a program designed to increase employee retention and to improve service. The hotels award points for being on time, providing good service to guests, improving quality in hotel operations, reaching department profit and production goals, and referring new employees. The points are awarded by managers; customer service points are also tabulated from comment cards and quarterly evaluations by supervisors. Managers are rewarded for reducing turnover and costs, increasing the return rate on guest comment cards, and implementing suggestions.

The highlight of the program is its prize structure. "We're offering standard merchandise prizes like TVs, toasters, and golf clubs," says Sue Gordon, vice president of human resources. But workers can also choose more practical rewards, such as bus passes, free child care at local day-care centers, tuition reimbursement, and educational funds.

———

Newstrack Executive Information Service in Pitman, NJ, uses an Employee Recognition Coupon system that helps foster teamwork, better morale, and employees' appreciation of one another's contributions.

Each employee receives twenty coupons. When he or she sees a coworker doing something extraordinary, the employee fills out the coupon with some words of praise and gives it to the coworker. Employees save the coupons (a maximum of twenty per year) and redeem them for special awards:

1 coupon: certificate for free car wash

5 coupons: $25 gift certificate for dinner

10 coupons: $50 gift certificate for Macy's

15 coupons: one-night stay for two in Atlantic City

20 coupons: one-year membership to Four Seasons Health Spa

A CASE STUDY IN POINT SYSTEMS

A survey of employees at Cascades Diamond in Thorndike, MA, indicated that 79 percent thought they were not being rewarded for good work, 65 percent believed management did not treat them respectfully, and 56 percent approached their work with pessimism..

To change these perceptions, the company developed a program called "The 100 Club," which stresses attendance, punctuality, and safety among the rank and file. An employee earns 25 points for a year of perfect attendance, 20 points for going through a year without formal disciplinary action, and 15 points for working a year without losing time due to an injury. For each day or partial day of absence, the company deducts points. A worker also earns points for making a cost-cutting or safety suggestion to management as well as for community service,

> **"Well-constructed recognition settings provide the single most important opportunity to parade and reinforce the ... new behavior one hopes others will emulate."**
>
> —TOM PETERS,
> Author and
> Management Consultant

such as participation in a blood drive, the United Way, or Little League.

When an employee reaches 100 points, he or she gets a nylon jacket with the Diamond logo and the words "The 100 Club." A teller at a local bank described a woman who came into the bank and modeled her baby-blue 100 Club jacket for customers and employees. She said, "My employer gave me this for doing a good job. It's the first time in the eighteen years I've been there that they've recognized the things I do every day."

During those years she had earned $230,000 in wages, which had paid for cars, a home mortgage, food and other essentials, vacations, and college educations. In her mind, she had provided a service for her earnings. The money wasn't recognition for her work, but the 100 Club jacket was.

In the first year of the program, the division saved $5.2 million and increased productivity by 14.5 percent, and quality-related mistakes declined by 40 percent. In a new survey, 86 percent of employees reported that they thought the company and management considered them "important" or "very important"; 81 percent responded that they got "recognition by the company"; and 73 percent said the company showed "concern for them as people." On average, 79 percent said their own attitude toward work quality had improved.

A CASE STUDY IN MULTILEVEL RECOGNITION PROGRAMS

The MidMichigan Regional Medical Center in Midland has a number of formal recognition programs at the hospital and departmental levels.

At the corporate level, employees, volunteers, and physicians at the Medical Center can nominate another employee, volunteer, or physician for an Apple Award for anything they did that went beyond the normal scope of their jobs. These nominations go to a committee to ensure that they meet established criteria. When they are approved, the nominee receives a red apple lapel pin. After an employee receives five red apples, he or she gets a silver apple; and after five silver apples, a gold apple is awarded. At the silver and gold levels, there are formal presentations and gift certificates.

An employee is chosen each month as Most Valuable Person from nominations by other employees. At the end of the year, the staff is asked to vote for one of the twelve, who then becomes the Most Valuable Person of the Year. Each month, the MVPs' pictures are posted at the two main entrances to the Medical Center and write-ups appear in the Medical Center newsletter and the local newspaper.

At the departmental level, the Pharmacy Department has developed a "recognition sheet" that anyone can complete. It has space for an employee's name, the date, an explanation of the employee's activity or productivity, and the name of the person completing the sheet. The

> **"**It's not enough to tell people they should be happy to have a job here. At a time when people are asked to really stretch themselves with fewer resources, you want to reward them for that stretch.**"**
>
> —BRUCE DONATUTI, Director of Human Resource Policy, Citibank

completed sheet is routed to the manager of the department. The recognition sheets are used to select an internal Employee of the Month chosen for what he or she did, not by the number of recognition sheets that were completed. The Employee of the Month receives a $25 gift certificate. Recognition sheets are also typed up in a summary report that is distributed at the monthly staff meeting. At the end of the year, a contest is held for Employee of the Year. Each of the twelve recognized employees has his or her picture on the wall in the department, and everyone votes. The winner receives a gift.

The business office keeps a Praise and Recognition Board. Praise and Recognition forms are available throughout the department. Employees are encouraged to take a minute to recognize their coworkers, and the forms are posted on the board if the employee chooses. All forms go into a drawing each month; the prize is a gift certificate.

The Family Practice Center uses numerous recognition methods. Each staff meeting starts with thanks among coworkers. When a staff person is noticed doing something well or performing a special task, a Family Practice Center Flower is delivered to that person with a preprinted card from the department. Staff lunches are also provided at intervals.

The Medical Records Department has a "Good Deed Slip" that employees are encouraged to fill out. Half the slip goes to the employee, and half goes into the suggestion box. The employee with the most slips that month becomes Employee of the Month; there is also an Employee of the

Year. The department also hires new employees using an interview team. The manager and supervisors are on the team, and the remainder of the team is nominated and voted on by fellow employees. At the end of the interview process, the team is treated to lunch or dinner.

In the Information Resources Department, a Good News Reporter is assigned monthly. The reporter actively seeks out information about good performance by interviewing customers and peers. They have been very creative with their presentations: a professional singer was brought in to sing a rap song; children were videotaped announcing the good deeds of the month in a TV news format; a *National Enquirer* format was used to spread the news; and one session was modeled after the Emmys.

The Medical Center has many cross-functional and cross-departmental teams that are encouraged to celebrate their successes. Numerous departments and teams have lunches and pizza parties. After meeting for a year and a half, the Educator Resource Team had two major accomplishments. Its quarterly meeting became a surprise celebration at which each member received a mug that said he or she was a charter member of the team. Team members also received a letter signed by the president of the Medical Center, and the chairperson for the team congratulated them on their accomplishments and teamwork. The team leaders for the subgroups received gift certificates.

> **❝**Incentive awards are not compensation—they are recognition—a meaningful way to say thank you, while focusing attention on your company goals. They must carry a hassle-free guarantee of satisfaction.**❞**
>
> —The MBF Group, Inc.

FedEx has a host of awards for individual and team efforts:

✔ The Circle of Excellence Award, presented monthly to the best-performing Federal Express station, emphasizes teamwork.

✔ The Golden Falcon is awarded to employees who go above and beyond to serve their customers. Honorees receive a gold uniform pin, a congratulatory phone call from a senior executive, and ten shares of stock.

✔ The Bravo Zulu (Navy talk for "well done") Program allows managers to award a dinner, theater tickets, or cash to any employee who has done an outstanding job.

Phil Hughes, director of human resources for Acapulco Restaurants in Long Beach, CA, reports how hourly and salaried employees are rewarded:

✔ $100 for hourly new hire referrals after ninety days.

✔ $300 for management new hire referrals after ninety days.

✔ The Employee of the Month receives $50 cash, one day off, and a parking space by the front door for thirty days.

✔ The Bright Ideas Program rewards up to $1,000 for money-saving ideas.

✔ A President's Award plaque and a check for up to $2,500, signed and presented by the company president, for an act of outstanding service.

✔ Employees are treated to lunch by the department head for a job well done. Breakfast is prepared by the management staff for the line staff.

✔ Theme days throughout the year (Cinco de Mayo, Fourth of July, Halloween, Christmas) include various giveaways, trips, cash, and limo rides.

✔ Casual dress is allowed in the office every Friday and all week from Memorial Day to Labor Day.

✔ Monthly cash contests are held in the restaurants for the best server, bartender, busser, etc.

The company rewards its salaried employees as follows:

✔ QSC (Quality Service Control) Monthly Award for highest score ($1,000)

✔ QSC Award for 95 percent or better ($100 each month)

✔ Safety Lotto ($500 each month; restaurant must remain accident-free that month to be eligible)

✔ General manager referral ($1,000 per referral)

✔ General Manager of the Year ($5,500 trip and one week of vacation)

✔ President's Club (plaque and recognition in company publication)

✔ President's Honor Roll (plaque and recognition in company publication)

> **❝**The best programs get participants 'hunting when the ducks are flying.'**❞**
>
> —*Incentive*

Company Benefits & Perks

In deciding on jobs, a company's benefits, such as health care or child care, are often significant factors. On the job, however, such benefits do little to motivate employees to perform at higher levels over the long term. Company perks described in this chapter (as opposed to the personal perks in Part III) are offered to all employees and involve a financial cost to the organization. Following are a variety of unusual organizational benefits and perks being offered today, which, if tied to desired employee behaviors or performance, can become important motivators.

> **❝We used to call them 'fringe benefits,' but we quit using the term 'fringe' when we saw the magnitude of that figure.❞**
>
> —JAMES MORRIS, Director of Survey Research, U.S. Chamber of Commerce

Quill Corporation office supplies and equipment in Lincolnshire, IL, tries to lower health care costs by rewarding employees. The company forecasts its health care costs for six months and places the money in a pool. If funds remain in the pool at the end of the six months, they are divided equally among participating employees. Health care costs for the company have declined approximately 35 percent in each of the first two years of the program.

At Paychex, the wellness program, called "Well Power," is a long-running effort that publishes a quarterly newsletter, *Personal Best,* which has tips on health awareness, tests, exercise, nutrition, and obtaining good health care. More importantly, the company pays for a Health Risk Assessment performed by a mobile testing unit that visits each branch. Employees can call the Personal Wellness Coordinator for help in understanding the tests and their implications, researching related health issues, and building a health improvement plan. Almost half of Paychex's employees participate.

> **"The way positive reinforcement is carried out is more important than the amount."**
> —B. F. SKINNER, Psychologist

George MacLeod, a restaurant owner in Bucksport, ME, allows his employees to run the restaurant by themselves one Sunday every month, and split the profits among themselves to help pay for their health insurance. Participating employees have made enough money to cover the entire cost of their insurance premiums. IKEA distributes all profits from the day's sales as a bonus to employees, one day a year.

Hi-Tech Hose, makers of flexible hoses and ducting products in Georgetown, MA, lumps all vacation time, holidays, and sick days into a single account. Employees can take time off whenever they need it.

IBM provides health classes and physical examinations. Employees at Johnson & Johnson have access to a large fitness center with an option to enroll in a comprehensive program that includes a physical examination and professionals that guide enrollees in a physical fitness regimen. As an incentive for staying healthy, Johnson Wax deposits $300 in every employee's flexible health plan at the beginning of each year to be used to pay for health care charges not covered by the company's health plan. Unused money in the account at the end of the year is paid to the employee in cash.

———

❝It is not the dollar cost of the award, but sometimes the novelty of it," says Terry L. Curry, manager of human resources for Muscatine Power and Water in Muscatine, IA. Employees there take part in two rounds of "wellness" team events during the summer. First-round participants receive T-shirts. They receive shoelaces as well if they participate in both rounds. The company has also given away stadium cushions for participation in late summer or early fall wellness events.

———

Gail Sneed, resource coordinator for the City of Dallas, suggests offering a Free Month of Wellness for employees who must otherwise pay to use fitness equipment and take classes.

———

Pioneer Natural Resources Company, an Irving, TX, oil and gas company, gives workers up to $700 a year in bonuses if they exercise three times a week, don't smoke, don't take sick days, and don't submit major medical claims. Since the program started, the company has cut health care costs to 25 percent below the industry average.

———

Westinghouse in Monroeville, PA, gives $200 annual bonuses to workers who do ten minutes of aerobic exercise three times a week for at least nine months a year. The company estimates that it saves $1,715 annually on every fit employee.

———

Reader's Digest reimburses up to 50 percent (up to $250 per year) of the cost of health club memberships for its employees. Employees who choose to take sports instruction or participate in a sport can also be reimbursed for part of these fees. Time Inc. does the same if the club has a cardiovascular fitness program.

———

Steelcase, Inc., based in Grand Rapids, MI, has a minihospital staffed by nineteen nurses and two physicians. The company also employs a psychologist and two social workers to counsel people on their personal problems, at no cost, on company time or after hours.

———

PricewaterhouseCoopers provides a resource and referral program for employees who need child care information. One senior consultant used the service to find suitable care when her nanny quit just as she was closing a half-million-

dollar deal. She was able to interview candidates immediately and not miss a day of work. The cost: $150. Nearly thirty PricewaterhouseCoopers offices provide subsidized weekend child care during the busy tax season.

———

Southern California Edison has twelve staff physicians and part-time specialists to take care of its employees. The company also gives employees 25 percent off their electric bills.

———

Ryder System runs a subsidized day care center across the street from its Miami headquarters to attract and retain talented employees who might have small children. Now the company is constructing a $5 million public charter elementary school next door. "We want to be the employer of choice in South Florida," says Anthony Burns, chief executive of the truck leasing and logistics firm. The proximity of the school will mean productivity gains for Ryder, since teacher conferences and soccer games will be right across the street. Ryder employees' children will have first claim to the school's 300 seats. As of 2005, Florida is the only state that allows schools to give preference to a company's employees' children.

———

Motorola is constructing an on-site day-care center near its facility in Boynton Beach, FL, to help workers with young families.

———

In Houston, the Medical Center Charter School is adjacent to the hospital, clinics, and medical schools. Children of the medical center's employees account for nearly the entire enrollment, although it is open to the public.

———

NationsBank, headquartered in Charlotte, NC, provides five different on-site or nearby child-care centers for its 100,000 employees. They also have a chartered public school for 150 students from kindergarten to third grade in Jacksonville, FL. Finally, new parents can work part-time for up to six months after maternity leave is over.

———

First International Bank & Trust in Watford City, ND, opens its conference room to employees' school-age children every afternoon. They are free to turn on the big-screen TV, have snacks, and start on their homework while their parents finish up the workday. Dennis Walsh, the bank president, reports that it's been at least four or five years since anyone has left the company.

———

Baxter International Inc., which sells health-care products, systems, and services, provides priority access for its employees at over 150 day-care centers around the country at a reduced rate. The company pays for up to a year's worth of counseling for employees.

———

> ❝Many employers of all sizes are exploring the next generation of full-blown flexible benefit plans, which I call life-cycle programs. These plans start with the premise that employees are best suited to tailor a benefit program to their own needs and at the same time work within employer-established parameters. The outcome can be a win-win, with employees utilizing a varying set of benefits throughout their worklife.❞
>
> —GARY KUSHNER, President, Kushner and Co.

> **❝By providing part-timers with insurance, we've helped bring turnover to below 50% in an industry where it typically runs more than 100% annually. Thanks to lower turnover, we've saved more in training costs than we've spent on insurance.❞**
>
> —HOWARD SCHULTZ,
> CEO,
> Starbucks Coffee Co.

Marriott International, based in Bethesda, MD, helps employees balance career and personal life through its Work-Life Program, which has established a child-development center; child-care discounts; family-care spending accounts; referral services for child, elderly, and family-care issues; and many other innovative programs.

JP Morgan Chase & Co., recently opened a lactation room for nursing mothers on its Wall Street trading floor so they would be able to return to work sooner after maternity leave.

Leo Burnett Worldwide, Inc. provides up to $3,000 in adoption assistance; H.B. Fuller, Herman Miller, and Medtronic Physio-Control provide $1,500; IBM and Procter & Gamble provide $1,000.

One night a year, Sears employees brought in immediate family members for a shopping spree using the employee discount.

Fel-Pro Inc., in Southfield, MI, provides an interest-free cash advance of up to $2,250 for full-time employees to buy computers, which they can repay within two years through payroll deductions. To date, Fel-Pro has financed computers for 367 employees.

Under Timberland's adoption assistance program, full- and part-time employees receive up to $10,000 ($12,000 for a special needs child) to help defray the costs of adoption. They also receive two weeks paid adoption leave and may take additional paid time off from their "Lifestyle Leave" account.

———

At Apple Computer, based in Cupertino, CA, all employees—from assembly-line workers to vice presidents—are loaned a computer just two months after joining the company in a program called "Loan to Own." Ten months later, the computer is theirs, no strings attached. One Christmas, all employees received a solar-powered calculator; the next year, they received personal electronics.

———

Eli Lilly & Company, headquartered in Indianapolis, pays 100 percent of employees' prescriptions for any Eli Lilly drugs.

———

Benjamin Moore & Company, based in Montvale, NJ, lets employees buy paint at wholesale prices. The company also sends crews to two employees' homes each year to paint them for free.

———

At Nissan's Smyrna, TN, plant, any employee with twelve months of service qualifies to

> **"Our early emphasis on human relations was not motivated by altruism, but by the simple belief that if we respected our people and helped them respect themselves, the company would make the most profit."**
>
> —THOMAS J. WATSON, JR., Former CEO, IBM

lease a Nissan car for $160 a month, which includes maintenance, tax, license, and insurance.

———

Robert Mondavi Winery in Napa, CA, gives every employee a case of wine at the end of each quarter. Anyone who works for Anheuser-Busch Companies, based in St. Louis, is entitled to two free cases of beer a month.

———

SeaWorld San Diego employees are given four free passes to the park per year, and are invited to bring friends and relatives to see the shows free once a year, during "Employee Night."

———

Other companies that reward employees with their own products include:
- ✔ General Cinema (now owned by AMC Entertainment): $1 movie passes for employees and their guests
- ✔ Mirage Resort: free tickets to Las Vegas shows; free lunch at the hotel's dining room once a month
- ✔ Southwest Airlines: free standby air travel for employees and their families
- ✔ Ben & Jerry's: three pints of ice cream for every worker

———

At the Exxon Mobil Corporation, employees get a 10 percent reduction in the price of Exxon gas and 15 percent off the price of TBA (tires, batteries, and accessories) from Exxon service stations. Gas is also sold at cost at FedEx, Liebert Corporation, Linnton Plywood, and Merle Norman Cosmetics, which sells its cosmetics at cost as well.

———

At Delta Airlines, employees and their spouses receive annual passes for unlimited travel anywhere on the Delta system, and reduced rates on other airlines after ten years of service. Employees at FedEx can fly free on the company's planes and at reduced rates on other airlines.

———

Random House offers all employees ten free books a year and a 50 percent discount on all Random House books.

———

REI (Recreational Equipment, Inc.), based in Kent, WA, allows employees to use rental equipment at no cost. It also gives first-edition, not yet released, pieces of REI gear or apparel as holiday gifts to each employee. They are personally delivered by a member of the senior team to each store and department. The stores take this time to hold staff meetings, pancake breakfasts, and pizza dinners. They also set up "Let's Talk" sessions between store leaders and the senior staff member, and between the staff member and front-line employees.

———

> **"**How companies treat employees says worlds about the quality of their management. And quality management usually translates into companies with a long and successful financial story. Whether it is demonstrated through superior benefits, family-friendly policies, safety records, or union relations, a strong record on employee relations is generally an indication of forward-thinking executives thinking creatively about running a business.**"**
>
> —STEVEN LYDENBERY,
> Research Director,
> Kinder,
> Lydenberg, Domini & Co.

Most employees of Westin Hotels receive free meals at work. Free rooms are also available to employees after one year's service. A ten-year employee and his immediate family can stay for fifteen nights at a Westin Hotel, with 20 percent off the cost of meals. Other employees get 50 percent off any hotel room rate.

———

At the end of each year, employees at Valassis receive holiday baskets. Recently, the gift had a back-in-time theme: it was a Radio Flyer red wagon filled with old-fashioned candy and toys. Other holiday "baskets" included coolers on wheels filled with barbecue tools, cookbooks, sauces, and foodstuffs; two-piece luggage sets; insulated bags filled with sports equipment; and large, decorative tin tubs filled with edibles.

———

Close to a thousand firms in the New York metropolitan area pass out TransitCheks to their employees for buses, subways, ferries, and commuter railroads. Champion International Corporation in Stamford, CT, offers $15 a month to van-poolers and also buys TransitCheks. About 20 percent of employees who drove to work now use car pools, van pools, or mass transit.

———

Interstate Electronics in Anaheim, CA, gives $20 a month to each person in a car pool and the same amount to employees who take the train from San Diego. Xerox Corporation in Stamford, CT, also gives workers discounts off monthly bus or train passes, subsidizes van pools, and provides preferential parking for car and van pools.

———

At *Reader's Digest,* employees can identify potential car or van pools in their areas through a computer access program that matches employees' transportation needs.

———

Medtronic Physio-Control Corporation subsidizes a bus service during off-hours on Fridays and weekends for employees who are working odd shifts.

———

At Nissan, office and factory employees are each provided with three work outfits at no expense. Wearing the work clothes is voluntary.

———

In its Dallas plant, Mary Kay, Inc., provides each production-line worker with three sets of work clothes a year. Women get a bright red jumpsuit as well as reddish outfits with printed blouses and slacks. Men get blue trousers and shirts and matching baseball caps.

———

Employees of the Los Angeles Dodgers receive the same gifts and promotional items—Dodger caps, jackets, bats—that are given to fans during the baseball season.

———

A SAMPLING OF PERKS OFFERED BY TIME WARNER

■ *If employees work past 8 P.M. in New York, they get $10 toward dinner, and a free cab ride home—even to New Jersey.*

■ *Employees get free copies of all Time Inc. magazines.*

■ *Fathers and mothers get parental leave up to one year.*

■ *Employees get free admission to the major museums in New York City.*

■ *After five years of service, employees get free physical exams.*

Flight attendants choose from a variety of uniform styles at Delta Airlines.

The City of Decatur gave each employee a "company jacket" with the city's logo on the front.

Shirley Kauppi, owner and manager of the King Copper Motel in Copper Harbor, MI, provides juice and pop, and fruit and snacks to the cleaning staff. Kauppi also allows spouses and children to use a designated motel room to watch TV or read until employees finish working.

Larry Hilcher of Larry Hilcher Ford in Arlington, TX, provides a catered lunch for employees at both Thanksgiving and Christmas and gives each person a box of steaks and a turkey.

Instill Corporation, a Redwood City, CA, Internet commerce firm, has an open account for employees at a local Peet's. They can walk to the local coffeehouse on their break to buy a cup of quality "Joe."

Liebert Corporation in Columbus, OH, which manufactures air-conditioning and power-supply systems for computer rooms, offers free popcorn to employees all day long.

Leo Burnett Worldwide, Inc., the largest ad agency in Chicago, keeps a bowl of red apples in the reception rooms on every one of its eleven floors. Burnett gives away 1,000 apples daily.

———

All 6,000 employees at the main branch of JP Morgan Chase in New York get a free lunch everyday. The perk costs the company $8 million a year. Employees of Northwestern Mutual, based in Milwaukee, also get lunch, which costs about $3 million a year.

———

A chef prepares a seven-course lunch daily for employees of Merle Norman Cosmetics, based in Los Angeles, at a minimal cost to the employee. There is no charge for snacks and beverages, which are spread out in the company dining room during morning and afternoon breaks. In the morning, employees can choose among muffins, pastries, and croissants, and in the afternoon they can pick from an assortment of pies or cakes, doughnuts, cookies, and ice cream.

———

Lunches are subsidized at Mary Kay, Inc., where a hot meal costs less than $3. Each table also has a white cloth and a vase of flowers. At *Reader's Digest,* employees may choose from a variety of cold and hot lunches, including a complete "Lite Line" selection menu, for as little as $2.20. The company also offers the convenience of a daily "take-out" dinner.

———

Every day at exactly 3:30 P.M., the Fox Chase Cancer Center in Philadelphia hosts high tea with cookies for all employees, patients, vendors, and guests who happen to be in the building. About 200 people a day enjoy this perk. Employee feedback on the daily tradition has been extremely positive. "It gives us the opportunity to get away from the routine, step outside, get fresh air, and recharge our batteries," says staff scientist Kathy Alpaugh. "It also gives you the chance to interact with your colleagues and try out your jokes," adds technical specialist Jack Zilfou. This tradition has endured through dramatic changes and challenges, and makes it a little easier for everyone to get through their day.

———

The International Mission Board, SBC, in Richmond, VA, gives all employees a card with candy at Thanksgiving. The gifts are delivered by managers carrying baskets. "People get so much at Christmastime," says Charlene Eshleman, staff development manager, "that this gift is more special."

———

Each Christmas, Remington Products gives out a turkey to each employee, and each year another item is added—cranberry sauce, stuffing mix, a coupon for a bottle of wine—all bagged by Remington executives.

———

Linda Fuller, supervisor of business development at Jevic in Delanco, NJ, reports: "Last year at Eastertime, I purchased plastic eggs and filled them with candy, a bit of pocket change (mostly pennies), and coupons to take off an hour early, come in an hour late, or have lunch with me (my treat). To be able to participate, my folks had to meet their weekly quota and then pick an egg out of a beautifully decorated basket. It made that Monday morning a little more exciting and set the tone for the whole week!"

> **"**What's more important than a company perk is having the employee value that perk.**"**
>
> —BOB NELSON

A CASE STUDY IN EMPLOYEE BENEFITS & PERKS

When Valassis, a marketing company headquartered in Livonia, MI, acquired NCH Marketing Services, headquartered in Lincolnshire, IL, with offices in the United Kingdom, Italy, Spain, Germany, France, and Mexico, the company's employee base went from about 1,600 to nearly 4,000 employees— and its profile expanded from a U.S.-based company to one with a global presence. On the first anniversary of the successful acquisition, the Valassis CEO sent flowers to all of the NCH locations, thanking them for a great year and looking forward to the future. Thank-you cards were also created by in-house graphic designers, translated into five languages, signed by Valassis and NCH CEOs, and sent to all NCH employees in the United States and abroad.

During work hours, employees at Valassis are invited to sell handmade crafts and wares to other employees during their free time, at an event called Art Mart, held in November. It has

> **"**Here is a simple but powerful rule ... always give people more than they expect to get.**"**
>
> —Nelson Boswell

been a well-received and highly anticipated annual event.

Employees are also encouraged to have their families join them for lunch, where the cafeterias are equipped with booster and high chairs. Valassis has a family room that provides privacy for nursing mothers and is equipped with a breast pump, refrigerator, TV/VCR/DVD, toys, bean bags, and other kid-friendly items for parents who may need to bring children to work on snow days and during day-care emergencies. Upon the birth or adoption of a child, Valassis offers parents-to-be free car seats.

Additionally, Valassis provides graduation gifts to employees' children when they graduate from high school. The gift includes an all-purpose carry-on bag filled with an atlas, snacks, and other goodies for the "places they will go." Then, when they head off to college, care packages are sent to their dorm rooms or apartments filled with necessities: detergent, a laundry bag, snacks, and phone cards so they can call home.

At their headquarters in Livonia, Valassis has an on-site hair and nail salon for employees. It also has an on-site doctor for office visits, who answers employee questions online. All employees get annual on-site, discounted flu shots.

Northwestern Mutual in Milwaukee has dozens of clubs, ranging from fishing and running groups to a company chorus. Retirees who continue to participate do not have to pay dues.

Hewlett-Packard employees anywhere in the world may make reservations to stay, at a modest cost for a limited number of days, at any of the company's recreation areas, which include Little Basin Park in the Santa Cruz Mountains, three facilities in Colorado, one resort in the Pocono Mountains of Pennsylvania, a beach villa in Malaysia, a lake resort in Scotland, and a ski-chalet complex in the German Alps.

Johnson Wax has nine resort facilities in different parts of the country for vacationing employees and their families, including the Lighthouse Resort in northern Wisconsin and resorts at Cape Cod and Lake Tahoe. Other companies that offer vacation spots include Springs Mill, a textile manufacturer in Fort Mill, SC, and Steelcase, the office furniture maker in Grand Rapids.

IBM offers highly discounted memberships to recreational facilities, including country clubs at Poughkeepsie, Sands Point, and Endicott, NY.

At 3M, the Tartan Park Clubhouse—a country club in Lake Elmo, MN—is for the exclusive use of 3M-ers for a nominal membership cost.

Nearly 10,000 Wilmington-area employees of E. I. du Pont de Nemours belong to the company's country clubs, which consist of four eighteen-hole golf courses, three in Wilmington and one in nearby Newark, DE, as well as tennis courts and facilities for dining and social gatherings.

———

Employee & Company Anniversaries

Celebrating anniversaries is an important way to acknowledge a long relationship between a company and its employees. Ninety-two percent of organizations have some type of reward for years of service, and about 50 percent of employees view such programs as very or extremely important to them. Although they recognize employee tenure rather than performance, employee longevity is itself crucial to the success and stability of most organizations.

Celebrating birthdays is another important, and more personal, way for companies to honor their employees, and a few examples are included here.

At Country Kitchen International, headquartered in Madison, WI, restaurant employees are given an embroidered gold star to wear on their uniform after three months of employment, and other stars at six and nine months, respectively.

At Minnesota-based Wilson Learning Corporation, each employee is given a Mickey Mouse watch after three months of

employment as a reminder to always have fun while working for the company. On the tenth anniversary, the employee is given a second Mickey Mouse watch—this time in gold.

———

Every Westin Hotel holds an annual banquet honoring employees with more than five years' service.

———

On their fifth anniversary with Mary Kay, Inc., employees receive 20 shares of stock; on their tenth, 80 shares; on their fifteenth, 120 shares.

———

The H.B. Fuller Company, a St. Paul maker of glues, adhesives, and sealants, extends a special bonus vacation every five years, starting on an employee's tenth anniversary. That is, at the tenth, fifteenth, and twentieth year, and every fifth year thereafter, a person gets an extra two weeks off with pay as well as an $800 bonus.

———

Griffin Hospital, in Derby, CT, wanted to do something special for employees who had worked there five years or more, resulting in its own version of *American Idol*—"Griffin Idol Fun Night." Eleven employees volunteered to be contestants, and their performances were taped at a local news studio.

———

Lands' End recognizes employees who have ten, twenty, and twenty-five-year anniversaries with the company. On the date of their anniversary, they receive their choice of merchandise and a framed and signed catalog cover from the year they began at Lands' End. In a recent year, all eligible candidates were asked how they wanted to celebrate their anniversary, with a choice among (1) a game show, (2) a Packer Party, and (3) a rock and roll celebration. The winning choice was the rock and roll celebration, so the company hired a band, served burgers and fries in a basket, decorated everything in pink and black, and covered it all with 1950s icons. The party included icebreakers, trivia, and all kinds of 1950s prizes and giveaways. To end the celebration, all honorees were sent off with old-fashioned root beer floats.

> ❝Brains, like hearts, go where they are appreciated.❞
>
> —ROBERT MCNAMARA, Former U.S. Secretary of Defense

❝One thing we do that is an especially big hit with the employees' families is sending flowers or cookie-grams to the place of business or to the home of all spouses on their birthdays and anniversaries," says Michael L. Finn, chairman and CRO (chief remover of obstacles) at Fortress Safe & Lock in Cincinnati. Every child (up to age sixteen) is also sent a birthday card with $20 in movie tickets. "Including the families has meant a lot to everyone," Finn concludes.

For its employment anniversary program, Arbitron went beyond the usual watches, pens, and pearls. They offered employees the chance to shop online for a wide range of products and services—from furniture to food to travel. One employee remarked that after twenty years of standing on her feet in the mail room, the company owed her a foot massager— and she got one!

Robert W. Baird's Quarter Century Club recognizes those who have been with the company for twenty-five years or more. There are now over 74 associates in the club, which is about 20 percent of all associates. When Baird conducted an associate opinion survey that asked: "If you have your way, how likely are you to be working at Baird five years from now?" 82 percent responded that they were very likely or somewhat likely to be with Baird.

When an employee reached her twenty-fifth anniversary with the Office of Personnel Management in Washington, D.C., she was asked what she would like to do to celebrate. She said she had always wanted to ride an elephant, so they asked the local zoo if it would be possible to arrange a ride. It was, and they did, taking pictures of the event and creating a day to remember for this loyal long-term employee.

Mel Powell, manager of the training department for the Kellogg Company in Battle Creek, MI, converted a conference room into an office for one of his senior trainers to recognize the trainer's twenty-fifth anniversary with the company.

———

At Hallmark Cards in Kansas City, MO, employees can invite coworkers to share their twenty-fifth anniversary cake. Two hundred to 1,000 people show up for each celebration.

———

Pitney Bowes, headquartered in Stamford, CT, gives employees with twenty-five years of service an extra month's vacation. The same benefit is then offered every fifth year.

———

The Employee Recognition Committee of the library at Wake Forest University needed to recognize each employee, but to do so in a cost-effective manner. Mary Lib Slate, government documents librarian, reports: "In our building, no food or drink is allowed, only water in a closed container. So we bought bottled water, and designed tags to tie around the necks with pretty ribbons. The tags had a picture of the building and said "Drink to Your Good Health," and could serve as bookmarks. The director or associate director presented the water to each employee on his or her birthday, which not only recognized their special days, but also gave them the opportunity to say a personal word to each employee. Total cost for 50-plus people was under $14."

———

West Texas Utilities in Abilene, TX, allows employees to celebrate their birthdays or special occasions by bringing in cakes or doughnuts to share with others during breaks. This gives them control over whether or not to celebrate, and costs the company nothing. Most employees participate.

———

Manny Fernandez, CEO of Gartner, Inc., a Stamford, CT, technology consulting and research firm, calls every employee on his or her birthday. Says Fernandez says, "It used to be a lot easier when we were small. Now I sometimes make twelve calls a day, but it's a great way to keep in touch with what's going on in the company and employees seem to enjoy it."

———

Martin Edelston, chairman and CEO of Boardroom Inc. in Greenwich, CT, personally signs a "Happy Birthday" card to each of his eighty-five employees and drops by to sing to them on their special day.

———

At the Veterans Administration Philadelphia Regional Office and Insurance Center, each employee has the privilege, during the month of his or her birthday, of giving a coworker the office's Extra Step Award, a $30 cash prize for employees who go out of their way to satisfy their coworkers.

———

The president of Merle Norman Cosmetics keeps track of everyone's birthday and makes a point of seeking out people to wish them well on that day. The company chef also bakes a birthday cake for the employee.

———

When four employees had birthdays on the same day at Porterville Developmental Center in Porterville, CA, coworkers blindfolded them and drove them to a restaurant, putting signs on their backs that read, "It's my party," and everyone in the restaurant stood up and sang "Happy Birthday."

———

Personal letters and cards are sent from headquarters in Laval, Quebec, to the stores of Dairy Mart, on people's birthdays and wedding anniversaries.

———

At the space-borne plant of Iteris, Inc., everybody's picture appears on a huge hanging calendar on his or her birthdate.

———

A Capital One Services office in Tampa, FL, recognizes employees' birthdays and anniversaries by placing Styrofoam cakes on top of people's cubicles during the month of the celebration.

———

☑ *Give all employees one rose for each year of employment on the anniversary of their start date.*

☑ *Present awards at appreciation dinners.*

☑ *Ask employees how they'd like to be honored for a long-term service anniversary.*

☑ *Engrave on a plaque the names of the employees who have reached ten, fifteen, twenty, or more years of service. Acknowledge individual achievements during a company meeting each quarter.*

Compass Bancshares in Birmingham, AL, plans a lunch outing for each birthday person. He or she gets to select the restaurant, and the manager picks up the tab. All other staffers are invited to attend on a "Dutch treat" basis.

H.B. Fuller Company and Recreational Equipment, Inc., (REI) give employees the day off on their birthdays. Lowe's Companies, a lumber and hardware supply retailer headquartered in Mooresville, NC, offers them a free lunch. All Mary Kay, Inc. employees receive a birthday card and a voucher for lunch for two.

When associates at Robert W. Baird turn forty they receive "birthday rocks" to keep on their desks until the next person turns forty. The rock has been making its way around the firm from desk to desk for years. One Baird manager lets associates leave a couple of hours early as well. Finally, every January, Robert W. Baird formally says "thank you" to all associates for their contributions and commitment to the company. The day starts with pastries and coffee and socializing with senior management. Throughout the day, managers present associates with bonus checks, and the firm closes early.

Boardroom Inc., the publisher of several of the country's leading newsletters, recently celebrated a company milestone in style. Chairman and CEO Martin Edelston says, "To

make life more fun, we had a Dixieland marching band to celebrate the company's anniversary in a new space, a team member's coming back from maternity leave, and another coming back from a honeymoon."

S pouses of employees at a Black & Decker office in Anaheim, CA, get flowers on the employee's birthday to thank them for their support. Flowers also go to the spouses of employees who travel extensively.

A t Leo Burnett Worldwide, Inc., an advertising agency headquartered in Chicago, every employee receives a gift on Anniversary Day. Gifts have included jams and jellies, a model train, statues, and customized bottles of wine. In addition, every employee receives one dollar for every year of the agency's life.

W hen Baxter International, Inc., had its fiftieth birthday, they celebrated by hosting fifty rank-and-file employee ambassadors from fifty facilities in eighteen countries who traveled to the Deerfield, IL, headquarters to mark the occasion.

F or Ryder System's fiftieth-anniversary celebration, employees shared a cake that was shaped like a truck and covered with yellow icing.

To mark the seventieth anniversary of a British subsidiary, Johnson Wax closed its Racine, WI, plant for a week, chartered a Boeing 747 jet, and flew the entire British workforce—480 people—to the United States, where they were put up in hotels, toured the company's facilities, shopped, and enjoyed a banquet. One night, employees in Racine picked up the British guests and brought them to their homes for dinner. The visitors also spent two days sightseeing in New York.

———

Alaska Airline's seventieth anniversary celebration consisted of a host of events:

✔ Trivia Contest: Employees who correctly answered questions about Alaska's history were entered into a drawing for a prize.

✔ Anniversary Luncheon: The company invited 70 of their senior employees to a luncheon at the Canadian Museum of Flight in Langley, British Columbia, to talk about the "good old days." Guest speakers included former and current CEOs of Alaska Airlines.

✔ Poem and Song Contest: Employees were invited to create a song or poem best depicting the airline's history. The winner received a vacation package to Alaska.

———

When Beneficial Management Corporation of America, based in Peapack, NJ, celebrated its seventy-fifth anniversary, the company wanted to produce a sizable increase in sales. To gain an extra edge, management decided to stimulate three levels of employees—branch associates, branch managers, and district/regional supervisors—with a merchandise incentive. Employees who achieved their goals won their choice of top-end merchandise from an attractive catalog. The company also promised to enter all participants in a drawing for prizes. A full 98 percent of the target audience signed up for the "Celebration Continues" campaign, and the insurance company's sales jumped 31 percent over a twelve-month period.

Charity & Community Service

E mployees appreciate companies that value their efforts in supporting charities and community service programs. Such behavior
reflects positively both on the individual and on the organization.

> **A business that makes nothing but money is a poor kind of business.**
>
> —Henry Ford,
> Founder,
> Ford Motor Company

L yn Hilbert, vice president of human resources for BlueCross BlueShield of North Carolina, reports: "The staff here is heavily involved in many charitable activities and staff members donate their personal time tirelessly. Recently, to thank them, a manager ordered a number of Lance Armstrong 'Live Strong' bracelets. Each staff member received one along with a personal note thanking them for their strength and letting them know that they have inspired the manager many times over to live strong."

W hen a Paychex employee is struck by a personal tragedy (major illness, death of a spouse or child), fellow employees often take up a contribution, sometimes involving multiple Paychex locations. The company matches part or all of the employee contributions.

Jeff Sack, manager of the partnership support tech department at Eastern Connection, a package shipping company based in Woburn, MA, implemented a program to reward outstanding contributions by employees. Whenever an employee is recognized, either through customer letters or internally, the company purchases a book in his or her name and donates it to a local school or library.

———

Santa Clara, CA–based VeriFone, a credit card transaction systems manufacturer, has a great way to help employees through hard times. They have implemented the VeriGift program, through which employees can donate unneeded vacation time to a "vacation bank." The time is distributed to employees who are experiencing personal hardships and have exhausted their own leave.

———

At Duncan Aviation, employees can wear blue jeans on Fridays if they donate to charity.

———

Valassis began a pen pal program to foster relationships among employees in Europe, Canada, Mexico, and the United States— through their children. The children sign up for the program, kick off the company's annual celebration of Bring Your Kids to Work Day, and have the option of communicating via e-mail or postal services.

———

> **"**When company executives get involved in charity work, it sends the message that the leaders are invested in their community, that there's more to life than making a profit, and that they care about their employees having balanced lives.**"**
>
> —DR. ANN MCGEE-COOPER,
> Consultant

Robert W. Baird recently introduced a new program that allowed associates to take one paid day each year to perform volunteer service. In addition, many of their departments and branches organize food drives and holiday gift-giving events and support fund-raising walks for local charitable organizations.

Several associates who served in the Middle East in recent years regularly received cards and care packages from coworkers while they were deployed. There were also several electronic newsletter articles posted on the Baird intranet about the reservists.

———

At Decision Analyst in Arlington, TX, the 200 employees choose a family to adopt for Thanksgiving and bring food to be delivered on the Tuesday preceding the holiday. Tom Thumb, the convenience store chain, also encourages each store to select a local family in need of assistance. The company then matches whatever funds employees can raise to help that family.

———

At BAE Systems North America in Rancho Bernardo, CA, a tuxedo-clad leadership team served a chicken lunch to more than 1,000 employees the week of Thanksgiving, with all tips, which totaled close to $1,500, being used to kick off a fund-raising effort to buy bicycles for military children for the holidays. The previous year, BAE employees bought 508 bicycles for the same cause.

———

Texas Utilities Company encourages its 13,000 employees to participate in charitable activities and gives time off for employees to volunteer for charities of their choice.

At Pfeiffer & Company, formerly located in San Diego, employees formed a holiday singing chorale and visited a local children's hospital to perform, accompanied by a piano-playing manager. They were given half a day off for this and other charitable deeds during the season.

Ford Motor Company in Dearborn, MI, encourages employees to participate in various activities held locally during Breast Cancer Awareness Month and Race for the Cure runs or walks. Employees sign up their own sponsors, who write checks directly to the charities involved.

At Lee Jeans' Merriam, KS, location, employees of participating divisions can "buy" the right to wear jeans to work for $5. All proceeds go to the Komen Foundation.

Ilana Farwell, general manager of the Comfort Inn in Ithaca, NY, wanted to motivate staff to use a newly instituted recycling program to reduce the amount of trash the hotel generates. At first, everyone just saw the program as additional work, so managers took

them on a field trip to a local recycling facility, where they learned about the importance of recycling, as well as other ideas for reducing waste. As an added incentive, all money collected from the bottle and can redemption center is used to purchase bottled water and soda for the staff. The hotel has experienced great savings from the program in just over a year and employees have been enthusiastic about reducing waste, saving money, and helping the environment all at the same time.

T imberland prides itself on its Passive Service Sabbatical Program. This program, available to employees who have worked for the company for three years, allows them to work for six months as a volunteer with a nonprofit organization, while Timberland continues to pay their salaries. Some employees have gone overseas and one went to work in an orphanage in Peru.

A CASE STUDY IN CHARITABLE RECOGNITION PROGRAMS

M eridian Health, a leading hospital system in central New Jersey, has a program called WIN, for "When in Need," an emergency fund set up by employees to help coworkers during times of crisis, from fires to foreclosures.

The need is real and the stories are a little more personal when you know it's a fellow employee. When a Meridian Health employee lacked the money to bury a parent, she turned to the WIN fund and got help. When another employee suffered from a fire, she was given security money for a new apartment. Yet another employee who was going to have her gas turned off in the midst of a financial crisis, got money to keep it on.

Even before the WIN fund's creation, Meridian Health employees had raised money for crisis-stricken coworkers in an ad hoc manner. However, while workers often contributed generously to employees they knew, they donated less often to those they didn't know, such as nightshift workers. According to John Sindoni, senior vice president for human resources. "We realized we needed to do more to make sure the distribution of funds was equitable, and we needed oversight over distribution as well."

To solve the problem, Meridian Health, a group of nonprofit health care organizations in central New Jersey, created the WIN fund in 2001. The program allows the 7,500 employees to contribute to a common fund through the Meridian Affiliated Foundations. Once a year, through a onetime contribution or a payroll deduction, employees can donate to a variety of programs that support the medical center, such as the Patient Comfort Fund, which provides financial support for patients in need, or the WIN fund. An employee committee at each Meridian Health site decides how to disburse the WIN funds.

Lorraine McLaughlin, a human resources representative, says, "We hear from employees all the time about how they appreciate the little things we do for them—especially when they

☑ *Give a department a day off to work in a homeless shelter or to help clean up a local park.*

☑ *Give employees time off to give blood.*

☑ *Make a donation in the name of an employee to the charity of his or her choice.*

most need those things. The WIN fund is a good example of this, and having the program funded and managed by employees makes it even more meaningful to them."

To use the WIN fund, employees must be past their initial ninety-day probation and must face their crises "through no fault of their own," according to Sindoni. The WIN fund pays for daily necessities such as utilities, food, and clothes. Even employees who do not donate to the fund can qualify for up to $1,000 in aid. Since 2001, 537 employees have contributed a total of $108,267, and in 2004 alone, the fund disbursed some $20,000 to employees in need.

As part of Meridian Health's Total Rewards program, which encompasses pay, benefits, work environment, culture, learning, development, and work/life balance, the WIN fund has helped keep the organization's nursing vacancy rate between 3 and 4 percent—compared to 8.4 percent in New Jersey and 13 percent nationwide. It also fits well with the organization's "Five Pillars of Excellence"—People, Quality, Service, Growth, and Finance—which help to make Meridian a workplace of choice for employees, a hospital of choice for patients, and an institution of choice for the community.

"Employees see us not only an employer, but like a family," Sindoni says. "We like to take care of our own and provide a supportive working environment for our staff." Doing so helps make this community of caregivers a little more caring.

The Levi Strauss Foundation makes a donation of $500 to community organizations in which an employee actively participates for a year. If an employee serves on the board of a nonprofit organization, the company will give that organization a grant of $500 if the organization has a budget of up to $100,000, $1,000 for a budget between $100,000 and $1 million, and $1,500 for budgets of more than $1 million.

> **"By matching an employee's donation to a charity of his or her choice, it shows the company values what the employee values."**
>
> —BOB NELSON

At Atlantic Richfield Company (ARCO), headquartered in Los Angeles, annual community service awards go to employees who have made outstanding contributions in the community, and the company matches two for one any employee's or retiree's donation to a social service organization or college.

At DDB Worldwide Communications Group, Inc., a New York–based advertising agency, employees are given time off to work in community service or on political campaigns.

At McCormick & Company, Inc., a manufacturer of seasonings, spices, and frozen foods based in Sparks, MD, employees are encouraged to work one Saturday each year, designated as Charity Day. They donate their pay—at time and a half—to a charity, and the company matches their earnings dollar for dollar. More than 90 percent of employees participate.

The Thurston-Dupar Inspirational Award is given by each Westin Hotel to employees who have not only excelled in their jobs but also made important contributions in community service. A company-wide winner is then selected to receive a two-week, all-expense-paid vacation for two at a Westin Hotel, $1,000 cash, and airfare and expenses to attend the announcement ceremonies at the annual management conference.

———

State Farm Insurance Company donated money to the Special Olympics and to the restoration of the Statue of Liberty, based on agents' sales levels in incentive programs.

———

Reader's Digest offers a community garden for employees to grow vegetables, and plows and fertilizes the land for a nominal cost. Syntegra in Arden Hills, MN, also has plots where employees can grow their own vegetables.

———

Cato Johnson, a promotion agency in Lombard, IL (now Wunderman, based in New York), offered an Adopt-A-Tree America kit with everything needed to plant a tree in one's backyard: a fertilizing peat pellet, a packet of seeds, gravel, and instructions. The tree species were selected according to geographic region.

———

Xerox has a sabbatical program that allows several employees each year to take paid leaves of absences and work for charitable organizations. Customer service engineer William Lankford worked for ten months building homes with Habitat for Humanity in the woods of southern Maryland. "People often come back with skills they didn't even know they had," says Joseph M. Cahalan, head of the Stamford, CT–based Xerox Foundation, which runs the program. American Express and Wells Fargo have similar programs.

———

Saskatchewan Telecommunications raffles off merchandise prizes to employees and places the proceeds in a "Help Our Own People Fund" for those who need special medical attention. So far, ten employees have used the fund, which raised as much as $23,000 in its first year.

———

> **"If you haven't got any charity in your heart, you have the worst kind of heart trouble."**
>
> —BOB HOPE, American Comedian

Company Stock & Ownership

O ne of the most powerful forms of recognition is to make employees owners of the company. This represents a long-term commitment to the individual, typically reserved for a select few.
Employees who share a stake in an organization behave a lot differently
from employees who don't.

According to one survey of American workers, 85 percent
rank stock options as a positive incentive. On average, companies that have employee stock ownership plans and engage in partic-
ipative management programs grow three to four times faster than
those that do not. For example, after Avis became an employee-owned
company, its complaint rate dropped 35 percent and its stock value
rocketed 400 percent in two years.

If every employee can be made to feel that he is working for his or
her own company, pride, effort, and performance will improve. The following exchange between Carl Buchan, founder of Lowe's Companies,
and a store manager illustrates the importance of giving employees a
sense of ownership.

"What is that?" asked Buchan.

"It's damaged merchandise, sir."

"Look at it more closely and tell me what you see."

"Well, that's a damaged water pump, and a dented refrigerator, and
windows with broken glass," replied the manager.

"That's not what I see when I look over there. What I see is
money—my money—because I paid for it. And before the year is out,
we're going to have a plan whereby part of that will belong to you and
the other employees. Then when you look you'll see money, too, and

you'll take better care of your money than you're doing now, and consequently you'll take better care of my money."

THE TEN LARGEST ESOPS*

Company	Business	Employees
Public Super Markets	Supermarkets	60,000
HealthTrust	Hospital management	23,000
Avis	Rental cars	20,000
Science Applications	Research and development	11,000
EPIC Healthcare	Hospital management	10,000
Charter Medical	Hospital management	9,000
Parsons Corporation	Engineering	8,600
Weirton Steel	Steel manufacturing	8,200
Avondale Shipyards	Shipbuilding	7,500
Dan River	Textiles	7,000

* ESOP: Employee Stock Ownership Plans
(at least 20 percent majority-owned).

At Bovis Lend Lease's Atlanta office, interest on a stock fund set up for employees back in 1983 pays for various employee rewards. They can earn movie tickets, flowers, special classes such as skydiving or cooking, lawyer or accountant fees, a day off to help a charity of their choice, emergency elderly or child care, or permission to bring family members on business trips.

Approximately 9,500 American companies —about 10 percent of the workforce— have employee stock-ownership plans. Procter & Gamble, J. C. Penney, Lockheed Martin, Polaroid, and Time Warner all offer employee stock ownership plans. Employees also own a large piece of the company at Federal Express, Hallmark Cards, Linnton Plywood, Lowe's, and Quad/Graphics.

Starbucks offers all employees "bean stock" each year, equivalent to 14 percent of their salaries. They are allowed to hold the stock for a minimum of five years. They can then keep the difference between the original price and the current price of the stock.

At Apple Computer, based in Cupertino, CA, the assembly-line workers received stock options for 200 shares (50 a year for four years), and middle managers received options ranging from 5,000 to 20,000 shares.

At Citibank's Diners Club, outstanding customer service can earn an employee $400 worth of stock.

———

Companies that participate in the profit-sharing Scanlon Plan include Dana Corporation of Toledo, OH, which manufactures and distributes components for trucks and industrial vehicles; Magna Donnelly Mirrors North America in Troy, MI; and Herman Miller, furniture manufacturers in Zee-land, MI. The plan has four principles: (1) Identity—everyone in the company must understand the business, its goals, and the need for profitability; (2) Participation—everyone in the company must have the opportunity to influence decisions; (3) Competence—each person must continually improve his or her abilities; and (4) Equity—returns should be shared with employees, investors, and customers, each receiving a fair share.

———

At LifeUSA (now owned by AllianzLife Insurance Company), an insurance company located in Minneapolis, all employees are owners, receiving approximately 10 percent of their compensation in the form of stock options, and are more efficient and effective than employees of competing firms. According to founder Robert W. MacDonald, "We'll write more business than probably 98 percent of the companies out there. And we'll do it with fewer people. Because they're owners, they're involved, they run the company." Employees control options on

> **"Our philosophy is to share success with the people who make it happen. It makes everybody think like an owner, which helps them build long-term relationships with customers and influences them to do things in an efficient way."**
>
> —EMILY ERICSEN,
> Vice President of
> Human Resources,
> Starbucks Coffee Company

"Why do I work until two-thirty in the morning and then come back for a breakfast at eight o'clock almost every day? Because I own a piece of this. We've built this, and I feel a tremendous commitment to seeing it continue.**"**

—A partner at Goldman Sachs

more than 1.8 million shares of stock, or approximately 4,500 per employee. To help them learn how to improve the value of their stock, LifeUSA conducts quarterly financial briefings for employees called "Share the Wealth" meetings, and classes in topics such as marketing, customer service, and "Working the Business" are regularly taught by senior staff.

———

At Lowe's Companies, employees own 25 percent of the company. Each store elects a representative to an advisory committee and holds monthly meetings for employees to discuss changes to operating procedures and merchandising. As a result, productivity at Lowe's is 200 to 300 percent above industry average and employee theft is less than one-sixth of the average. When Carl Buchan, founder of Lowe's Companies, died, his will specified that employees, through a profit-sharing plan and trust, had the option of buying all his stock.

———

Southwest Airlines developed the first profit-sharing program in the airline industry. It involves employees in company ownership by requiring that they invest at least one-fourth of their profit-sharing funds in company stock. They are provided with regular financial and performance data (such as profit-and-loss statements, revenue passenger miles, and so forth) to monitor the effectiveness of the operation. As a result, Southwest has won the industry's "triple crown" (fewest lost bags, fewest complaints, best on-time performance) a record eight times. In fact, Southwest is the *only* airline to have won the triple crown.

———

At Missouri engine rebuilder Springfield ReManufacturing Corporation (SRC), employees own the company. One way that SRC involves them in decision making is through the use of what is known as the Great Game of Business—the company's form of open-book management. Introduced by CEO Jack Stack, the Great Game of Business trains all employees to understand everything about the company's financial data. They are then invited to play the game by monitoring weekly income statements and cash-flow reports, and to compare actual results against projected results. Then, on a quarterly basis, employees receive bonuses that are based on selected financial goals such as return on assets. According to Stack, "What they learn is how to make money, how to make a profit. The more people understand, the more they want to see the result."

———

Science Applications International Corporation (SAIC) in San Diego, was founded on the principle of employee ownership. J. Robert Beyster knew that to own even a small stake in a business that is growing exponentially can be the most powerful incentive. Beyster has gone further than most companies, however, in relinquishing 98 percent of the company to employees.

———

> **"**You get a sense that you own the business. What that means is that you're going to spend a lot less time worrying about whose toes you're going to tread on and much more time worrying about how you're going to move that business forward.**"**
>
> —JAMES A. MEEHAN,
> Manager,
> General Electric

Appendix I

Where to Get Specialty Reward Items

A.C. Oehmich Leather Company
3390 Lanam Rd., Bloomington, IN 47408, (800) 903-0763, www.acoehmichleather.com. Manufacturer of high-quality, value-priced business and personal use leather goods. Makes luggage, memo/note pads, business card cases, travel kits, etc.

Action Images
7101 N. Ridgeway, Lincolnwood, IL 60645, (847) 763-9700, www.actionimagesinc.com. Published a color poster depicting statistics and program-cover art from every Major League Baseball All-Star Game going back to the game's inception in 1933.

American Express
Corporate Sales, 4315 S. 2700 West, Rm. 3520, Salt Lake City, UT 84184, (800) 666-7317, www.10.americanexpress.com. The American Express Gift Cheque is an impressive award that offers the flexibility of cash.

American Tool Companies Inc.
John Robert or Deb Schwan, 108 S. Pear St., DeWitt, NE 68341, (402) 683-2315 or (800) 838-7845. Sells tools and tool sets that can be custom imprinted, including Vise-Grip locking hand tools.

Bang & Olufsen
Peter Bangs Vej 15, P.O. Box 40 , DK-7600 Struer, Denmark, (45) 96 84 11 22, www.bang-olufsen.com. Offers high-end, visually appealing audio/video, speakers, and telephones.

Bass Pro Shops/ Outdoor World Incentives
2500 E Kearney St., Springfield, MO 65898, (417) 873-5075, www.owincentives.com. Offers customizable gift cards for Bass Pro Shops and Outdoor World.

Bennett Brothers, Inc.
30 East Adams St., Chicago, IL 60603, (800) 621-2626 or (312) 263-4800, www.bennettbrothers.com. Offers an annual catalog, *Choose-Your-Gift and Prize Book* with

50+ gifts that can be customized in each of 13 price levels, from $16 to $1,000.

Bill Sims Company
P.O. Box 21008, Columbia, SC 29221, www.billsims.com. Offers tax-free scratch-off Star Bucks. Award your performers with Star Bucks that can be redeemed for thousands of gifts. Also offers custom support posters, newsletters, and promotional logoed gifts.

Blockbuster Incentives
1201 Elm St., Dallas, TX 75270, (214) 854-3609, www.bbincentives. com. Offers custom-produced gift certifi-cates, debit cards, general merchandise.

BMG Special Products
1540 Broadway, New York, NY 10036, (877) 264-7744, www.bmgsp.com. Recipients can select CDs and cassettes from over 900 titles by top-name artists.

Bulova Corporation
National Sales Manager, Special Markets Division, One Bulova Avenue, Woodside, NY 11377-7874, (718) 204-4600 or (800) 423-3553, www.bulova.com. Offers solid brass miniature replicas of world-famous clocks and customized watches that you can add diamonds to as an award—one diamond at a time—by sending it back to Bulova.

California Awards and Designs, Inc.
865 Viadela Paz, #201, Pacific Palisades, CA 90272, (310) 230-1295, FAX (310) 230-1179, www.cdala.com. Quality crystal awards: engraved, laminated, and cast plaques; trophies, medallions, and unique gifts. Manufactures an engraved business card paperweight.

Coleman Company
3600 North Hydraulic St., Wichita, KS 67219, (316) 219-7598, www.coleman.com.

Offers camping gear, gas grills, and backyard products.

Concord/Movado Group
650 From Rd., Paramus, NJ 07652, www.concord-watch. com. Makers of luxury watches.

Craftsman Tools
Sears Industrial Special Markets, 3333 Beverly Rd., D3-196A, Hoffman Estates, IL 60179, (847) 286-2495. Designs custom tool sets conveniently packaged in a sturdy, versatile Craftsman tool box.

Crate and Barrel Corporate Sales
1860 W. Jefferson Ave., Naperville, IL 60540, (800) 717-1112, www.crateandbarrel. com. Home cookware, decorations, gift certificates, home furnishings, housewares.

Creative Oakery
6467 E. Pacific Coast Highway, Long Beach, CA 90803, (800) 224-4261.

Customizes baked goods—Bundt cakes decorated with ribbons, bows, balloons, flowers. Ships nationwide.

Custom Factory, The
211 N. 5th St., Columbus, OH 43215, (800) 596-9352 or (614) 454-2115, www.costumefactory. com. Offers six-foot-tall inflatable costume characters for meetings, conventions, and trade shows.

Dartnell Corporation
4660 N. Ravenwood Ave., Chicago, IL 60640, (800) 621-5463, FAX (800) 327-8635, www.dartnellcorp.com. Sells the spiral-bound Dartnell Desk Planner which can be custom imprinted in 24-karat gold.

Eastman Kodak
343 State St., Rochester, NY 14650-0519, (585) 724-4000, FAX (585) 724-1089. Presents its newest Fun Saver disposable camera, the Telefoto 35, which has a

telephoto lens and high-speed film. Offers the basic Fun Saver 35, an upgraded version with flash, the water-resistant Fun Saver, and a panoramic model that produces wide-angle pictures.

Express Visa Service
2233 Wisconsin Ave., Ste. 215, Washington, DC 20007, (202) 337-2442, FAX (202) 337-3019, www.expressvisa.com. Visa and passport services; provides legalization services.

Fighter Pilots USA
Lee Abernethy, 505 N. Lakeshore Dr., Ste. 5602, Chicago, IL 60611, (800) 56-TOP-GUN, www.fighterpilotsusa. com, fpusa@ concentric.net. Customers actually fly fighter jets and engage in aerial combat maneuvers. Mission includes one hour of ground school, one hour of combat flying and a one-hour debriefing that includes photos and videos of the flight.

Fontazzi (subsidiary of Metrovox Snacks) 6116 Walker Ave., Maywood, CA 90270, (217) 235-1750. Will custom imprint gourmet popcorn tins and gift baskets.

Fortune Cookie Division
Wonton Food Inc., 220-222 Moore St., Brooklyn, NY 11206, (800) 776-8889, www.wontonfood.com. Offers fortune cookies with personalized messages in several flavors.

Franklin Electronic Publishers
1 Franklin Plaza, Burlington, NJ 08016, (800) 266-5626, www.franklin.com. New *Big League Baseball Electronic Encyclopedia* contains more than one million statistics on the sport. Also sells *Crosswords,* an electronic crossword-puzzle aid.

Gargoyles, Inc.
521 8th St. SW, Ste. D, Auburn, WA 98001, (800) 426-6396 or

(253) 561-0400, www.gargoylesinc.com. G-FORCE, GXP and Gargoyles eyewear and a full line of eyewear accessories and repair kits.

Gingiss Formalwear
2101 Executive Dr., Addison, IL 60101, (630) 620-9050, FAX (630) 620-8840, www.gingiss.com. Tuxedo and formal wear rental and service.

G. Neil Companies
720 International Parkway, P.O. Box 450939, Sunrise, FL 33345-0930, (954) 846-8899, www.gneil.com. Personalized certificates, plaques, frames, and presentation folders.

GreenWorld Project, The
P.O. Box 177, Cohasset, MN 55721, (800) 825-5122, www. greenworldproject.net. Provides environmentally conscious gifts with customizable messages such as live tree seedlings wrapped in clear tubes and seed kits.

Haas-Jordan Company
1447 Summit Street, P.O. Box 1596, Toledo, OH 43603, (800) 536-0283 or (419) 243-2189, www.haas-jordan.com. Sells a personal beach umbrella imprinted with your company logo.

Harry and David
2500 S. Pacific Hwy., Business Division, Medford, OR, 97501-2675, (800) 248-5567, www.harryanddavid. com. Offers rewards from fresh fruits and meats to savory seafood and gift baskets.

Hertz Corp.
225 Brae Blvd., Park Ridge, NJ 07656, (800) 654-3131, www.hertz.com. Offers Award Check Vouchers good for car rentals, starting at $25.

Hillerich & Bradsby Company
Premium and Incentive Dept., P.O. Box 35700, Louisville, KY 40232, (800) 282-2287, www.slugger.com. Offers sporting equipment that can

be custom printed with your company name, logo, individual's name or promotional message, including baseball bats, baseball gloves, and golf clubs.

Hinda Incentives
2440 West 34th St., Chicago, IL 60608, (773) 890-5900, FAX (773) 890-4606, www.hinda.com. A full-service incentive company with in-house program administrators, creative and marketing professionals, merchandise recommendation and sourcing.

Historic Newspaper Archives
Dept. P, 1582 Hart St., Rahway, NJ 07065, (800) 221-3221, www. historicnewspaper.com. Original U.S. newspapers dating back to 1800. Encased in personalized gold-embossed binder with certificate of authenticity.

Houghton Mifflin Company
222 Berkeley, Boston, MA 02116, (617) 351-5000, www.hmco.com.

Offers books that can be customized with a personal message, company logo, or custom title.

Irwin Productions
6340 Hinson St., Las Vegas, NV 89118, (702) 616-4770, www. irwinproductions.com. Offers an Escapade show of singers and dancers who interact with the audience. The theme can be tailored to any corporate event.

J. C. Penney
Incentive Sales, 9701 W. Higgins Rd., Ste. 400, Rosemont, IL 60018, (800) 832-4438, www.jcpenneyincentives. com. Gift certificates good at all retail stores and through all catalogs.

Jet Lag Watch Company
4 Allston St., West Newton, MA 02465, (617) 965-1231, www.jetlag.com. Offers a watch that lets the user adapt naturally to a new time zone by running more slowly or more quickly during a flight.

John's Inc.
800 W. Johns Rd., Apopka, FL 32703, (407) 886-8850. Growing gifts—live plants that can be customized with your name or company logo. Minimum order of 200 pieces.

Kmart Corporation
Gift Certificate Administration, 3100 W. Big Beaver Rd., Troy, MI 48084, (800) 345-2497. Personalized "Cash Cards" in any denomination between $5 and $250.

La Crosse Technology
1116 South Oak Street, La Crescent, MN 55947, www. lacrossetechnology.com. Offers a sunrise, sunset wireless weather control station. Displays a forecast for the next 12 to 15 hours.

Lalique Crystal
400 Veterans Blvd., Carlstadt, NJ 07072, (888) 488-2580, www.lalique.com. A collection of crystal vases, perfume bottles, objets d'art and bases for award presentations that can be customized.

Legal Sea Foods
One Seafood Way, Boston, MA, 02210, (800) EAT-FISH, www.legalseafoods.com. Offers lobsters, clams, steaks, other delicacies, and custom-imprinted lobster pots.

Louisville Golf
2500 Grassland Drive, Louisville, KY 40299, (800) 456-1631, www.louisvillegolf.com. Offers a wide range of premium wood golf equipment, replica clubs, and desk items. Each Louisville Golf wood mallet putter is handcrafted with over 100 hand operations and can be adorned with laser-etched logos and emblems.

McArthur Towels
700 Moore St., P.O. Box 448, Baraboo, WI 53913, (800) 356-9168 or (608) 356-8922, www.mcarthur-towels. com. Personalized towels and robes.

Marketing Innovators
9701 W. Higgins Rd., Rosemont, IL 60018, (800) 843-7373, www.marketinginnovators.com. Freedom to Choose retail gift certificates.

Media Systems, Inc.
727 Wainee St., Ste. 201, Lahaina, HI 96761, (800) 398-2271, www.mediasystemsmaui.com. Photography, video, and computer graphics.

MHP International
6430 N. Hamlin, Lincolnwood, IL. 60712, (847) 675-2770, www.mhpinternational.com. Offers massage tables and massage chairs.

Multi Image Productions
8849 Complex Dr., San Diego, CA 92123, (858) 560-8383, www.multiimage.com. Produces custom multimedia shows.

NordicTrack
1500 S. 1000 West, Logan, UT 84321, (435) 750-5000, FAX (435) 750-3917, www.nordictrack.com. Features the new Back & Stomach Machine— a seat that rotates to exercise back, abdominals, and obliques.

Olympus/Mar-San
6045 N. Keystone Ave, Chicago, IL 60646, (773) 583-5700, ext. 17, www.mar-san.com. Offers a wide range of technology products such as digital cameras, voice recorders, printers, etc.

Omaha Steaks
10909 John Galt Blvd., Omaha, NE 68103, (800) 228-9872, www.osincentives.com. Sample packages of steaks, all cuts.

Oneida Silversmiths
Oneida Planning Guide, Sharon Mercier, Oneida, NY 13421-2829, (315) 361-3143. A catalog of gifts from $50 to $100 that can be personalized.

Orrefors Kosta Boda
Special Markets Group, 140 Bradford Drive, West Bretlin, NJ 08091, (800) 433-4167, www.kostaboda.se. Hand-crafted crystal awards that can be personalized.

Panasonic
Premium Sales Division, 1 Panasonic Way, Secaucus, NJ 07094, (201) 392-6198, www.panasonic.com. More than 400 electronic products from digital cameras to DVD players, from massagers to HDTV.

Parker Pen U.S.A. Ltd.
Sanford Business to Business Division, 2200 Foster Ave., Janesville, WI 53545, (608) 755-7000, www.sanfordb2b.com. Gift guide of pens that can be personalized with your company's logo or individual's name.

PC Nametag
124 Horizon Dr., Verona, WI 53593, (877) 626-3824 or (608) 845-1870, www.pcnametag.com. Name tags.

Physicians Sales & Service
4345 Southpoint Blvd., Jacksonville, FL 32216, (904) 332-3000, FAX (904) 332-3213, www.pssd.com. Medical products distribution.

Polaroid Corporation
1265 Main St., W2-2, Waltham, MA 02451, (800) 662-8337, ext. V049, www.polaroid.com. Offers customizable instant cameras.

Privacash, Inc.
Toledo, OH, (419) 255-2322, www.privacash.com. Offers a MasterCard gift card that can be used by millions of merchants worldwide.

Promo Direct
2301 W. 205th St., Ste. 104, Torrance, CA 90501, (800) 748-6150, www.promodirect.com. Offers huge selection of customizable items such as awards, plaques, pens, watches, golf balls, and portfolios.

PSP Sports Marketing
Custom Publishing Services, 355 Lexington Ave., New York, NY 10017, (212) 697-1460, www.pspsports.com. Offers personalized desktop diary featuring profiles and color photos of America's Olympic heroes.

The Quill Company, Inc.
P.O. Box 6608, Providence, RI 02940-6608, www.quillpen.com. Offers quality writing pens that can be custom engraved.

REI (Recreational Equipment Inc.)
1700 45th St. E., Sumner, WA 98390, (800) 258-4567 or (253) 891-2523, FAX (206) 891-2523, www.rei.com. Outdoor gear and clothing products and gift certificates.

Santa's World
Kurt S. Adler Inc., 1107 Broadway, New York, NY 10010-2872, (800) 243-XMAS or (212) 924-0900, www.kurtadler.com. Features more than 20,000 Christmas items including Disney and *Sesame Street* characters.

Seiko Corporation of America
The Premium Dept., 1111 MacArthur Blvd., Mahwah, NJ 07430, (800) 545-2783, www.seikousa.com. Offers watches for color imprinting and embossed customization.

Sentry
900 Linden Ave., Rochester, NY 14625, (800) 828-1438, www.sentrysafe. com. Customized fire-safe products for protecting valuables.

Sevylor U.S.A. Inc.
6651 E. 26th St., Los Angeles, CA 90040, (323) 727-6013, www.sevylor.com. Full line of inflatable sports products like air mattresses, canoes, boats, and snow products.

Sharper Image, The
650 Davis St., San Francisco, CA 94111, (800) 344-9919, www.sharperimage.com. Offers a wide range of

products such as air purifiers, foam neck pillows, travel products, etc.

Skip Barber Racing School
P.O. Box 1629, Lakeville, CT 06039, (800) 221-1131, www.skipbarber.com. Offers classes in formula race-car driving at more than 20 different racetracks. They will arrange lodging, catering, and professional photography.

Smith & Hawken
4 Hamilton Landing, Novato, CA, 94949, (800) 423-0117, www.smithandhawken. com. Garden catalog.

Sony Corporation
Park Ridge, NJ, (201) 930-1000, www. motivation.sony.com. Offers electronic equipment that can be used for incentives.

SportSource, Inc.
375 Commerce Dr., Fort Washington, PA 19034, (215) 283-9549, www.sport-source.com.

Offers customizable items such as basketballs, volleyballs, croquet sets, air hockey tables, tents.

Starbucks Coffee Co.
2401 Utah Ave. S., S-NV1, Seattle, WA 98134, (800) 611-1669, www.starbucks.com. Coffee and related items.

Starlite Originals
11908 Ventura Blvd., Studio City, CA 91604, (818) 761-7779, www.sollc.com. Supplies fine art sculptures in bronze, pewter, brass vermeil, and 24-karat gold vermeil.

Stock Yards Packing Co.
Dan Rost, 340 N. Oakley Blvd., Chicago, IL 60612, (800) 621-3687, FAX (312) 733-0738, www.stockyards. com. Catalog of gifts, such as steaks, seafood, and gourmet treats.

Subtle Media, Inc.
P.O. Box 6130, San Antonio, TX 78209, (800) 635-7261, FAX (210) 822-5959,

www.constantexposure. com. Customizes a wide range of merchandise and office supplies.

Sugardale's
Special Markets Division, 1888 Southway St. S.E., Massillon, OH 44646, (800) 860-5444, www.sugardale.com. Offers 130 gourmet food items, such as their signature "beauty ham." They will include a personalized gift card.

Swiss Army Brands, Inc.
1 Research Drive, P.O. Box 874, Shelton, CT 06484-0874, (800) 243-4066, FAX (800) 243-4025, www.swissarmypromo products.com. Can custom-imprint the Swiss Army Brand Watch and Swiss Army Knife.

Telescope Casual Furniture, Inc.
85 Church Street, Granville, NY 12832, (518) 642-1100, ext. 272, www. telescopecasual.com. Offers umbrellas, beach chairs, and a full line of director's chairs that

can be customized with your company name and logo.

Tiffany & Co.
727 Fifth Ave.,
New York, NY 10022,
(212) 755-8000,
www.tiffany.com. Will
custom-engrave a ster-
ling silver yo-yo, Swiss
Army Knife, key chain,
or other specialty item.

**Torrington Christie
Photography**
210 Post St., Ste. 901,
San Francisco, CA
94108, (415) 921-6333,
FAX (415) 986-3886,
www.sfphotopro.com.
Professional photo-
graphers.

**Travel Graphics
International**
1118 S. Cedar Lake Rd.,
Minneapolis, MN 55405,
(612) 377-1080, ext. 15,
FAX (612) 377-1420,
www.tgimaps.com.
Graphics of
promotional material
for destination, pocket
maps, posters.

Tucker-Jones House
P.O. Box 231, East
Setauket, NY 11733,
(800) 992-9883,

www.tavernpuzzle.com.
Metal puzzles offered.
Packaging for puzzles can
be personalized with
company names and
logos.

**Waterford
Wedgwood USA**
Incentive Division,
P.O. Box 1454, Wall, NJ
07719, (800) 933-3370,
www.waterford.com.
Features crystal and
china at all price levels.

Wells Lamont
6640 West Touhy Ave.,
Niles, IL 60714,
(800) 323-2830,
www.wellslamont.com.
Sells gloves that can be
customized with your
logo.

**Wilson Sporting
Goods Co.**
8700 W. Bryn Mawr
Ave., Chicago, IL
60631, (800) 432-0321,
www.wilsonsport.com.
Will imprint a golf ball
with your four-color
logo or name. Also
offers laser-engraved
putters and golf balls.

**Wittnauer
International**
Andrew Finn, Director

of Sales, Special Markets,
145 Huguenot Street,
New Rochelle,
NY 10801,
(800) 451-2242,
www.wittnauer.com.
Carries the Wittnauer
watch line and Zodiac
watch line. Will
customize products.

**Workman
Publishing Co.**
Special Markets
Department,
708 Broadway,
New York, NY 10003-
9555, (212) 614-7509,
www.workman.com,
jenny@workman.com.
Offers a full line of
gift books, cookbooks,
kids' books, and
calendars. Will create
customized books and
calendars (Page-A-Day
too) for corporate
promotions and
incentive programs.

**World Heritage
Incentives**
World Heritage
Travel Group, Inc.,
1211 Main St., Angels
Camp, CA 95222,
(209) 736-0933,
FAX (209) 736-0333.
Travel and video
production.

Appendix II

Companies That Arrange Unusual Reward Activities

Adam Productions
1520 Daytonia Rd.,
Miami Beach, FL 33141,
(305) 865-0363,
www.adamprod.com.
Offers themed events
such as Renaissance,
Pirate, or Patriotic
dinners complete with
amazing decorations
and staff dressed to
the theme.

Adventure Connection
P.O. Box 475, Coloma,
CA 95613,
(800) 556-6060
or (530) 626-7385,
www.raftcalifornia.com.
River trips, whitewater
rafting.

**Atlantis Submarines
International, Inc.**
210 West 6th Ave., Ste.
200, Vancouver, BC V5Y
1K8, Canada,
(604) 875-1367,

www.atlantisadventures.
com. Offers submarine
tour of the waters off
the Caribbean's only
desert island, Aruba.

**Balloon Aviation
of Napa Valley**
6525 Washington St.,
Ste. 7, Yountville,
CA 94599-1300,
(707) 944-4400.
Hot-air balloon tours.

**Balloons Above
the Valley**
5091 Solano Ave.,
Napa, CA 94558,
(800) 464-6824 or
(707) 253-2222, www.
balloonrides.com. Hot-
air balloon excursions.

**Black Canyon River
Adventures**
P.O. Box 60130,
Boulder City, NV,
89006, (800) 455-3490,

www.blackcanyon
adventures.com. Group
raft trips down the
Colorado River.

**Boundary Country
Trekking**
173 Little Ollie Rd.,
Grand Marais, MN
55604, (800) 322-8327,
www.boundarycountry.
com. Offers cross-
country ski trips in
winter, guided canoe
trips in summer, along
with dog-sled trips.

Brier & Dunn
2962 Fillmore St., San
Francisco, CA 94123,
(415) 346-7801,
www.brier-dunn.com.
Stages jungle theme
dinners at the San
Francisco Zoo.

Burnside Marina
680 W. Lakeshore Dr.,

Burnside, KY 42519, (606) 561-4223, www.burnsidemarina.com. Houseboat excursions.

California Leisure Consultants
77-530 Enfield Lane, Ste. C-1, Palm Desert, CA 92211, (760) 200-0112, www.accessdmc.com. Offers unique theme events including Indian-Western barbecues with stuntmen who stage a gunfight, or baseball games with players wearing vintage uniforms.

Canadian Pacific Hotels and Resorts
Fairmont Hotels & Resorts, 100 Wellington St. W., Ste.1600, Toronto, ON M5K 1B7 Canada, (866) 627-0642 or (416) 874-2600, www.cphotels.ca. A legendary 850-room castle in Banff Springs in the Canadian Rockies.

Carlson Marketing Group
P.O. Box 59159, Carlson Parkway, Minneapolis, MN 55459, (763) 212-4520, www.carlsonmarketing.com. Houseboating and other excursions.

Echo Bay Resort
North Shore Rd., Overton, NV 89040, (702) 394-4000. Houseboating excursions.

EGR International
30 Broad St., New York, NY 10004, (800) 221-1072, www.egrinternational.com. Houseboating excursions.

Feather River Rail Society
P.O. Box 608, Portola, CA 96122, (530) 832-4131, www.wplives.org/. Train fans and would-be engineers can go to the Portola Railroad Museum, the only place in the world where you can rent and drive a real locomotive. The museum also offers rides on cabooses and flatcars.

Incentives to Intrigue
652 Waller St., San Francisco, CA 94117, (415) 626-2950, FAX (415) 626-1445, www.incentivestointrigue.com. Organizes teams on a treasure hunt through San Francisco via streetcars.

Incredible Adventures
6604 Midnight Pass Rd., Sarasota, FL 34242, (941) 346-2603, www.incredible-adventures.com. Compete against friends or foes in a full-day aerial combat competition, Fighter Combat. The hangar facility at Fighter Combat International is tailor-made to provide group comfort.

Jamestown Resort and Marina
3677 S. Hwy 92, Jamestown, KY 42629, (270) 343-5253, www.flagshipmarinas.com. Houseboating excursions.

La Costa Resort and Spa
Costa del Mar Rd., Carlsbad, CA 92009, (800) 544-7483, www.lacosta.com. Offers a world-famous

spa, golf courses, tennis courts, and 300-seat nightclub.

Mana, Allison & Associates
1388 Sutter St., #525, San Francisco, CA 94109, (415) 474-2266, www.mana-allison.com. Offers an array of leisure activities for conferences and conventions coming to San Francisco, including Renaissance fairs.

Maritz Travel Company
1400 S. Highway Dr., Fenton, MO 63099, (636) 827-1519, www.maritztravel.com. Exclusively Yours Cheques, in denominations of $10 and $50 and redeemed for unique travel experiences including safaris, flying lessons, golf clinics, and baseball camps.

Marketing Innovators
9701 W. Higgins Rd., Ste. 400, Rosemont, IL 60018, (800) 543-7373, www.marketing innovators.com. Freedom to Choose retail gift certificates.

Marriott Hotels & Resorts
10400 Fernwood Rd., Bethesda, MD 20817, (301) 380-3000, www.marriott.com. Marriott Surfers Paradise Resort on Australia's Gold Coast features aquatic playground with beaches, lagoon, simulated coral reef, and water sports.

Micato Safaris
15 W. 26th St., New York, NY 10010, (800) 642-2861, www.africansafari.org. Offers tented safari camps in Kenya and Tanzania.

The Moorings
19345 U.S. Hwy. 19 N., Clearwater, FL 34624, (888) 952-8420 or (727) 535-1446, FAX (813) 530-9747, www.moorings.com. Yacht-chartering company.

Mountain Winery
14831 Pierce Rd., Saratoga, CA 95070, (408) 913-7122, www.mountainwinery. com/corporate.html.

Offers group events at this winery such as bridge building and casino parties.

Museum of Science and Industry
57th St. & Lake Shore Dr., Chicago, IL 60637, (800) 468-6674 or (773) 684-1414, www.msichicago.org. Meeting facility.

Mushing Magazine
Stellar Communications, Inc., P.O. Box 149, Ester, AK 99725, (907) 479-0454, www.mushing.com. Lists a number of companies offering dog-sledding trips.

Napa Chamber of Commerce
1556 First St., Napa, CA 94559-0636, (707) 226-7455, www.napachamber.org. Complete list of companies that provide hot-air balloon excursions in the Napa Valley.

Napa Valley Wine Train
1275 McKinstry St., Napa, CA 94559, (800) 427-2124 or (707) 253-2111,

FAX (707) 253-9264, www.winetrain.com. Scenic ride on 1915 Pullman train.

Pacific Whale Foundation
300 Maalaea Rd., Ste. 211, Wailuku, HI 96793, (808) 249-8811, www.pacificwhale.org. Offers whale and dolphin watching in Hawaii.

Paragon Guides
P.O. Box 130, Vail, CO 81658, (970) 926-5299, www.paragonguides. com. Weekend or six-day backcountry hiking trips.

PLAYTIME Inc.
P.O. Box 25022, Seattle, WA 98165, (877) 652-0875, www.playtimeinc.com. Participants skillfully combine the use of GPS and cutting-edge office technologies— PDAs, cell phones, laptops and digital cameras—to find a hidden cache of goods. Success will require both competition and collaboration. Teams must design a plan,

execute it, and reach the final goal, all without a predesignated leader.

QuizMaster Productions
9845 Bankside Dr., Ste. 1100, Roswell, GA, 30076, (770) 664-0648, www.quizmaster.com. Offers customized corporate contests.

Regent Sydney
Regent International Hotel, 199 George St., Sydney NSW 1220 AU, Australia, (800) 545-4000. Offers a camel safari and other exotic adventure packages.

Safaris, Inc.
PGI Destination Management Business & Events Communications, 44 Canal Center Plaza, Alexandria, VA 22314, (703) 528-8484, www.pgi.com. Re-creates the golden age of Hollywood for theme parties, including a theater marquee with your company name.

Sheraton Hotels & Resorts
1111 Westchester Ave., White Plains, NY 10604, (914) 640-8100, www.sheraton.com. Includes the Sheraton Parco de Medici, the first golf resort in Italy.

Soaring Adventures of America, Inc.
P.O. Box 541, Wilton, CT 06897, (800) 762-7464, www.800soaring.com. Sailplane and glider rides.

Space Camp
U.S. Space & Rocket Center, One Tranquility Base, Huntsville, AL 35805, (256) 837-3400, www.spacecamp.com. Experience astronaut training camp.

Star Clippers
4101 Salzedo, Coral Gables, FL 33146, (800) 442-0551 or (305) 442-0550, www.starclippers.com. Groups sail on the world's only modern-day clipper ship.

Sunrise Balloons
P.O. Box 891360,

Temecula, CA 92589, (800) 548-9912, www.sunriseballoons.com. Scenic balloon and helicopter tours and charters.

Team Building USA
229 Patricia Lane, Highland Village, TX 75077, (866) 351-8326, www.teambuildingusa.com. Offers fun events such as canoeing and wilderness adventures, scavenger hunts, and murder mystery games.

10th Mountain Trail Association
1280 Ute Ave., Aspen, CO 81611, (970) 925-5775, www.huts.org. Backcountry hiking trips.

Unix Group, Inc.
170 Cambridge St., Burlington, MA 01803, (800) 633-5200 or (617) 229-2755, FAX (617) 229-8886,

www.utix.com. Golf and ski tickets.

Vancouver Aquarium
P.O. Box 3232 Vancouver, B.C., Canada V6B 3X8, (604) 659-3474, www.vanaqua.org. Arranges activities such as breakfast with beluga whales, cocktails with killer whales, and dinner among octopuses, sea otters, and other aquatic creatures for groups of up to 1,000.

Venture-Up Mountain Expeditions
2415 E. Indian School Rd., Phoenix, AZ 85016, (602) 955-9100, www.ventureup.com. A corporate training and wilderness adventure company offers team-building courses.

Waterfall Resort
Mike Dooley,

Reservations, P.O. Box 6440 Ketchikan, AK 99901, (800) 544-5125, www.waterfallresort.com. Resort in Ketchikan, Alaska, offers mountain wildlife and salmon fishing. Also offers national wildlife trips and fly-fishing adventures.

Windridge Yacht Charters
2950 N.E. 32nd Ave., Fort Lauderdale, FL 33308, (954) 525-7724, www.windridgeyachts.com. Luxurious and elegant charter for corporate events or parties; 5-star-hotel dining quality.

World Yacht
Pier 81, W. 41st St. & Hudson River, New York, NY 10036, (212) 630-8100, FAX (212) 630-8899, www.worldyacht.com. Yacht charters.

Appendix III

Incentive Travel Coordinators

Activities, Inc.
53 Pennington-
Hopewell Rd.,
Pennington, NJ 08534,
(609) 466-4100 or
(609) 455-5414.

**ADI Meetings &
Incentives, Inc.**
1223 E. Broadway Rd.,
Ste. 100, Tempe, AZ
85282, (480) 350-9090,
www.adimi.com.

Ambassadors
1071 Camelback St.,
Newport Beach,
CA, 92660,
www.ambassadors.com.

**Atlantis
Submarines
International, Inc.**
210 West 6th Ave., Ste,
200, Vancouver,
BC V5Y 1K8, Canada,
(604) 875-1367,
www.atlantis
adventures.com.

ATS Pacific
P.O. Box A2494, Sydney
South, NSW 2000,
Australia,
(612) 9268 2111,
www.atspacific.com.

Bateaux Parisiens
Sodexho Loisirs, Port
De la Bourdonais,
75007 Paris, France,
(314) 411-3344,
FAX (314) 566-0788,
www.bateauxparisiens.
com/english/main.htm.

Bell Tours, Inc.
12894 16th Ave., White
Rock, BC V4A 1N7,
Canada, (604) 536-8488,
FAX (604) 538-6646,
www.belltours.com.

**Canadian
Pacific Hotels
and Resorts**
Fairmont Hotels
& Resorts,
100 Wellington St. W,

Ste. 1600, Toronto,
ON M5K 1B7, Canada,
(866) 627-0642 or
(416) 874-2600,
www.cphotels.ca.

**Carlson Marketing
Group**
P.O. Box 59159,
Carlson Parkway,
Minneapolis, MN 55459,
(763) 212-4520, www.
carlsonmarketing.com.

Cruzan Yacht
3375 Pan American
Dr., Coconut Grove,
FL 33133,
(800) 628-0785,
www.cruzan.com.

**Classic Cruise &
Travel Co.**
19720 Ventura Blvd.,
Ste. A, Woodland Hills,
CA 91364,
(800) 688-8500 or
(818) 346-8747,
www.classic-cruise.com.

Convention Consultants
117 W. Perry St.,
Savannah, GA 31401,
(912) 233-4088,
www.savtours.com.

Cornerstone
86 Pleasant St.,
Marlboro, MA 01752,
(800) 825-5494 or
(508) 460-1900,
FAX (508) 460-9996.

Creative Group Travel
621 N. Lyndale Dr.,
Appleton, WI 54914-
3022, (920) 739-8550,
FAX (920) 739-8817.

Creative Travel Planners, Inc.
5855 Topanga Canyon
Blvd., Ste. 220,
Woodland Hills,
CA 91367,
(800) 255-3070 or
(818) 704-7033,
FAX (818) 347-4113.

Curacao Chamber of Commerce and Industry
Kaya Junior Salas #1,
P.O. Box 10, Willemstad,
Curacao, N.A. 611451,
(599) 461-1451,
FAX (599) 461-5652,
www.curacao-
chamber.an.

Destination Sherbrooke
2964 King St. W.,
Sherbrooke, Quebec
J1L 1Y7, Canada,
(819) 821-1919,
www.sdes.ca/tourism.

Diethelm Travel
Diethelm & Co., Ltd.,
Kian Gwan Bldg. 11,
140-1 Wireless Rd.,
Bangkok, Thailand
10330, (662) 255-9150,
FAX (622) 254-9018,
www.diethelm-travel.
com.

Diners Fugazy Travel
105 W. Adams St.,
Chicago, IL 60603,
(312) 263-4212.

Dittman Incentive Marketing Corp.
108 Church St.,
New Brunswick,
NJ 08901,
(732) 745-0600.

EGR International Meetings & Incentives
30 Broad St., 14th Fl.,
New York, NY 10004,
(212) 949-7330.

Empire Force Events
71 W. 23rd St., Ste.
1610, New York,
NY 10010-4102,

(212) 924-0320, FAX
(212) 675-9106,
www.empireforce.com.

Four Seasons Hotel Sydney
199 George St., Sydney,
NSW 2000, Australia,
61 (2) 9238-0000,
FAX 61 (2) 9251-2851,
www.fourseasons.com.

Frazier & Hoyt Incentives
1505 Barrington St.,
Ste. 107, Halifax,
NS B3J 3K5, Canada,
(902) 421-1113.

Greater Lansing Convention & Visitors Bureau
1223 Turner St., Lansing,
MI 48906-5066,
(800) 648-6630,
www.lansing.org.

Helen Moskovitz Group
95 White Bridge Rd.,
Ste. 500, Nashville, TN
37205, (615) 352-6900,
www.nashdmc.com/
index2.html.

H.M.I. Holiday Models, Inc.
5830 W. Flamingo Road,
Suite 229, Las Vegas,
NV, 89103-2310, www.
holidaymodels.com.

Holt Paris Welcome Service
12 Rue du Helder, 75009 Paris, France, (452) 308-14, FAX (474) 919-89, www.holtfrance.com.

HotelLocators.com
919 Garnet Ave., Ste. 216, San Diego, CA 92109, (800) 576-0003 or (858) 581-1315, www.hotellocators.com.

Hotels of Switzerland
104 S. Michigan Ave., Ste. 802, Chicago, IL 60603, (773) 782-1912, FAX (773) 262-9323, www.swissplan.com.

Incentive Holland Group
Dukatenburg 86A, 3437 AE, Nieuwegein, Netherlands, www.incentive.nl.

Incentive Solutions
2136 Westlake N., Ste. 1, Seattle, WA 98109, (206) 283-7176, FAX (206) 283-5508.

Incentive Travelers Cheque International
505 N. Lakeshore Dr., Ste. 6601, Chicago, IL 60611, (877) 267-9139, www.jfainc.com.

INCOMA/Incentive Congress & Marketing Service
Nieder-Roeder-Weg12, Heusenstamm, Germany DW-6056, (061) 046-5024, FAX (061) 046-7774, www.incoma.de.

Intermedia Convention & Event Management
P.O. Box 1280, MILTON QLD 4064, Australia, +61 (0)7 3858 5400, FAX +61 (0)7 3858 5510, www.ice.im.com.au.

International Travel Associates Group
4800 Westown Pkwy., Regency West 3, West Des Moines, IA 50266, (800) 257-1985 or (515) 224-3400, FAX (515) 224-3552, www.itagroup.com.

International Travel Incentives, Inc.
1921 E. Carnegie Ave., Ste. 3H, Santa Ana, CA 92705, (949) 757-0490, FAX (949) 757-0926, www.intltravelincentives.com.

Jecking Tours & Travel, Ltd.
304A 3/F Oriental Centre, 67 Chatham Road, Kowloon, Hong Kong SAR, (852) 739-1188, FAX (852) 721-2748.

JNR Inc.
2603 Main St., 2nd Fl., Irvine, CA 92614, (949) 476-2788.

The Journeymasters, Inc.
254 Jessex St., Salem, MA 01970, (800) 875-3422 or (978) 745-4500, FAX (978) 741-4816, www.journeymasters.com.

Kirby Tours
719 Griswold St., Ste. 100, Detroit, MI 48226, (313) 278-2000, www.kirbytours.com.

Krebs Convention Management Services
657 Carolina St., San Francisco, CA 94107, (415) 920-7000, FAX (415) 920-7001, www.krebs.lenos.com.

Kuoni Travel Ltd.
Neue Hard 7, CH-8010

Zurich, Switzerland, (0041) 1 277 44 44, FAX (0041) 1 271 52 82, www.kuoni.com.

Kushner & Associates
3444 Cloudcroft Drive, Malibu, CA 90265, www.kushnerdmc.com.

Landry & Kling Cruise Specialists
1390 S. Dixie Hwy., Ste. 1207, Coral Gables, FL 33146, (800) 448-9002 or (305) 661-1880, FAX (305) 661-0977, www.landrykling.com.

Leaders in Travel
200 Middleneck Rd., Great Neck, NY 11021-1103, (800) 327-5947 or (516) 829-0880, FAX (516) 829-0895, www. leadersintravel.com.

Longue Vue House & Gardens
7 Bamboo Rd., New Orleans, LA 70124, (504) 488-5488 FAX (504) 486-7015, www.longuevue.com.

Mandarin Oriental Hotel Group
345 California St., Ste. 1250, San Francisco, CA

94104, (415) 772 8800, FAX (415) 782 3778, www.mandarin-oriental.com.

Maritz McGettigan
100 Penn Square E., 11th Fl., Philadelphia, PA 19107, (215) 422-1000, (215) 422-1283.

Marriott Hotels & Resorts
10400 Fernwood Rd., Bethesda, MD 20817, (301) 380-3000, www.marriott.com.

Monark Turismo
Praca dom Jose Gaspar, 134, 11 andar, Sao Paulo, Brazil, (11) 3235-4322, (11) 3235-4332, www.monark.tur.br.

MotivAction
16355 36th Ave. N., Minneapolis, MN 55446, (800) 326-2226, www.motivaction.com.

Mount Snow Vermont Tours
New England Vacation Tours, P.O. Box 560, Rt. 100, West Dover, VT 05356-0560, (800) 742-7669 or (802) 464-2076, FAX (802) 464-2629.

Newtours & CMO
Via. A. Righi, 8-50019 Osmannoro, Sesto Fiorentino, Florence, Italy, (039) 55 33611, FAX (039) 55 3361250/350, www.newtours.it/nwt/enazie0d.htm.

Norwegian Cruise Line
7665 Corporate Center Dr., Miami, FL 33126, (305) 436-4000, FAX (305) 436-4111, www.ncl.com.

Olsen O'Leary Travel, Inc.
565 Epsilon Dr., Pittsburgh, PA 15238, (412) 963-7272, FAX (412) 963-9773.

Orange County Convention Center
9800 International Dr., Orlando, FL 32819, (800) 345-9845 or (407) 685-9800, FAX (407) 345-9876, www.orlando convention.com.

Paragon Guides
P.O. Box 130, Vail, CO 81658, (970) 926-5299, www.paragonguides. com.

PGI Events & Co.
504-68 Water St., 425
Carrall St., Ste. 400
Vancouver, BC V6B 1A4,
Canada, (604) 689-3348,
FAX (604) 689-5245.

**Remington Hotel
Corporation**
14185 Dallas Pkwy, Ste.
1150, Dallas, TX 75254,
(972) 980-2700, FAX
(972) 980-2705, www.
remingtonhotels.com.

**Resort at Port
Ludlow, The**
1 Heron Rd., WA
98365, (877) 805-0868
or (360) 437-7000,
FAX (360) 437-0310,
www.portludlow
resort.com.

Silkway Travel Ltd.
4012-4018 Cambie St.,
Vancouver, BC V5Z
2X8, Canada,
(604) 656-1000,
FAX (604) 879-8780,
www.silkway.com.

Sino-American Tours
37 Bowery,
New York, NY 10002,
(800) 628-1168 or
(212) 966-5866,
FAX (212) 925-6483,
sinortours@ix.
netcom.com.

Sita World Travel
16250 Ventura Blvd.,
Se. 300, Encino, CA
91436, (818) 990-9530
or (800) 421-5643,
www.sitatours.com.

**Sitework Associates,
Inc.**
P.O. Box 20068,
Sarasota, FL 34276,
(941) 927-5400,
sitework@worldnet.
att.net.

**Sheraton Hotels
& Resorts**
1111 Westchester Ave.,
White Plains, NY 10604,
(914) 640-8100,
www.sheraton.com.

**Smith Design
Associates**
205 Thomas St.,
Bloomfield, NJ 07003,
(973) 429-2177,
FAX (973) 429-7119,
www.smithdesign.com.

Space Camp
U.S. Space & Rocket
Center, One Tranquility
Base, Huntsville, AL
35805, (256) 837-3400,
www.spacecamp.com.

**Spectacular
Sport Specials**
5813 Citrus Blvd.,

New Orleans, LA
70123-5810,
(800) 451-5772
or (504) 734-7075,
www.spectacularsport.
com.

Star Clippers
4101 Salzedo, Coral
Gables, FL 33146,
(800) 442-0551
or (305) 442-0550,
www.starclippers.com.

**State of Tennessee
Department of
Tourist Development**
320 6th Ave., 5th Fl.,
Nashville, TN 37243,
(615) 741-2159,
www.state.tn.us/
tourdev/.

**Successful Incentive
Travel**
Allied World Travel,
899 Skokie Blvd.,
Northbrook, IL 60062,
(800) 323-8268,
(847) 272-4800.

**Sunbelt Motivation
& Travel, Inc.**
5215 N. O'Connor
Blvd., Ste. 950, Irving,
TX 75039,
(214) 638-2400,
FAX (214) 630-6642,
www.sunbeltmotivation.
com.

Sunquest Incentive Travel
130 Merton St.,
Toronto, ON M4S 1A4,
Canada, (416) 485-1700,
FAX (416) 485-6506,
www.sunquest.ca.

10th Mountain Trail Association
1280 Ute Ave.,
Aspen, CO 81611,
(970) 925-5775,
www.huts.org.

Transeair Travel, Inc.
2813 McKinley Pl. NW,
Washington, DC
20015, (202) 362-6100,
FAX (202) 362-7411.

Travel and Transport, Inc.
2120 S. 72nd St.,
Omaha, NE
68124-6310,
(800) 228-2545
(402) 399-4500,
FAX (402) 398-9290,
www.tandt.com.

Travel New Orleans, Inc.
400 Poydras St., Ste.
1720, New Orleans, LA
70130, (800) 535-8747
or (504) 561-8747,
FAX (504) 565-3550,
www.travelneworleans.
com.

Travelmore/Carlson
212 W. Colfax Ave.,
South Bend, IN 46601,
(877) 543-5752,
www.travelmore.com.

USA Hosts
1055 E. Tropicana, Ste.
625, Las Vegas, NV
89119, (800) 634-6133
or (702) 798-0000,
FAX (702) 798-5396,
www.usahosts.com.

United Travel Group
International Tours,
African Tours, 1 Bala
Plaza, Ste. 414, Bala
Cynwyd, PA 19004,
(800) 223-6486 or
(610) 617-3300, FAX
(610) 617-3312,
www.unitedtour.com.

Vacation Connection
5535 Stearns, Long
Beach, CA 90815,
www.ta2000.com.

Vantage Adventures
1324 E. North St.,
Greenville, SC 29605,
(803) 233-7703, FAX
(803) 233-3864, www.
travelvantage.com.

Virginia Escape Ltd.
1215 McLaws Cir.,
Williamsburg, VA 23185,
(757) 229-1161,

FAX (757) 229-4207,
www.vaescape.com.

Vista Travel, Inc.
229 Binney St.,
Cambridge, MA 02142,
(617) 621-0110, FAX
(617) 621-0101.

Walther's Tours Pty. Ltd.
P.O. Box 3247,
Randburg, South Africa
2125, (271) 789-3623,
FAX (271) 789-5255,
www.walthers.co.za.

Waterfall Resort
Mike Dooley,
Reservations,
P.O. Box 6440,
Ketchikan, AK 99901,
(800) 544-5125,
www.waterfallresort.
com.

World Heritage Incentives
World Heritage
Travel Group, Inc.,
1211 Main St., Angels
Camp, CA 95222,
(209) 736-0933,
FAX (209) 736-0333.

Appendix IV

Motivational and Incentive Companies and Associations

Abercrombie & Kent
1520 Kensington Rd., Ste. 212, Oak Brook, IL 60523, (800) 323-7308, www.abercrombie kent.com. Offers luxury travel all over the world.

Adcentive Group, Inc.
4801 Viewridge Ave., San Diego, CA 92123, (858) 278-9200, FAX (858) 278-9079, www.adcentive.com. Unique employee recognition and motivational programs.

All Star Incentive Marketing
208 Charlton Rd., Sturbridge, MA 01566, (800) 526-8629, www.incentiveusa.com. Incentive marketing company.

American Rental Association
1900 19th St., Moline, IL 61265, (800) 334-2177 or (309) 764-2475, FAX (309) 764-1533, www.ararental.org. Trade association.

Association of Retail Marketing Services, Inc.
10 Dr. James Parker Blvd., Ste. 103, Red Bank, NJ 07701-1500, (732) 842-5070, FAX (732) 219-1938. Trade association.

BI Performance
7630 Bush Lake Rd., Edina, MN 55439, (952) 835-4800, www.biworldwide.com. Incentive consulting company.

Edward Enterprises, Inc.
641 Waiakamilo Rd., Honolulu, HI 96817, (808) 841-4231, FAX (808) 841-7707, www.ee3.com. Convention printing, newsletters, programs.

Excellence In Motivation, Inc.
Six North Main St., Ste. 370, Dayton, OH 45402, (937) 222-2900, www.eim-inc.com. Offers wide range of motivating incentives such as travel, debit cards, and merchandise.

Extraordinary Events
7447 Conroy Rd., Orlando, FL 32835, (407) 290-1509, FAX (407) 296-7742, www.extraordinary events.net.

The Golf Card
164 Inverness Dr. E.,
Englewood, C0 80155,
(800) 321-8269,
www.golfcard.com.
Golf discount card.

**Destination
Sherbrooke**
2964 King St. W.,
Sherbrooke,
QC JIL IY7, Canada,
(819) 821-1919,
www.sdes.ca/tourism.
Trade association.

Incentive Magazine
355 Park Ave. So.,
New York, NY 10010,
(646) 654-5447,
www.incentivemag.com.
Magazine.

**Intermedia
Convention & Event
Management**
11/97 Castlemaine St.,
P.O. Box 1280, Milton
QLD 4064, Australia,
+61 (0)7 3858 5400,
FAX +61 (0)7 3858
5510, www.
ice.im.com.au.
Conference organizers.

Kohala Coast Resort
H002 Box 5300,
Kohala, HI 96743-5000,
www.kkra.org. Resort
association.

**KVL Audio Visual
Services, Inc.**
466 Saw Mill River Rd.,
Ardsley, NY 10502,
(800) 862-3210,
FAX (914) 479-3395,
www.kvlav.com.
Event staging, video
production.

**Howard Lanin
Productions, Inc.**
59 E. 54th St.,
New York, NY 10022,
(212) 752-0960,
FAX (212) 752-7065.

**Mana, Allison &
Associates**
1388 Sutter St., #525,
San Francisco, CA
94109, (415) 474-2266,
FAX (415) 474-1989,
www.mana-allison.com.
Motivational consultants.

Marden-Kane Inc.
36 Maple Pl., Manhasset,
NY 11030-1962,
(516) 365-3999,
FAX (516) 365-5250,
www.mardenkane.com.
Promotional firm.

Maritz Inc.
1375 N. Hwy. Dr.,
Fenton, MO 63099,
(636) 827-1519,
www.maritz.com.
Motivational consulting.

Marketing Innovators
9701 W. Higgins Rd.,
Rosemont, IL 60018,
(800) 543-7373,
www.marketing
innovators.com.
Freedom to Choose
retail gift certificates.

Media Systems, Inc.
727 Wainee St.,
Ste. 201,
Lahaina, HI 96761,
(800) 398-2271 or
(808) 667-2271, www.
olahamoment.com.
Computer graphic
production.

**Mount Snow
Vermont Tours**
New England Vacation
Tours, P.O. Box 560,
Rt. 100, West Dover,
VT 05356-0560,
(800) 742-7669 or
(802) 464-2976,
FAX (802) 464-2629.
Independent meeting
planners.

**National 4-H
Center**
Natl. 4-H Council,
7100 Connecticut Ave.,
Chevy Chase,
MD 20815-4999,
(301) 961-2840,
FAX (301) 961-2894.
Trade association.

**Orange County
Convention Center**
9800 International Dr.,
Orlando, FL 32819,
(800) 345-9845 or
(407) 685-9800,
FAX (407) 345-9876,
www.orlando
convention.com.
Convention facility.

PGI Events
425 Carrall St., Ste.
400, Vancouver,
BC V6B 6E3 Canada,
(604) 689-3448,
FAX (604) 689-5245,
www.pgicanada.com.
Supplier of theme
decor, entertainment
and corporate events.

Playfair
2207 Oregon St.,
Berkeley, CA 94705,
(800) 750-5439 or
(510) 540-8768,
www.playfair.com.
Humor and
motivational
consultants.

Robbins Company, The
400 O'Neil Blvd.,
Attleboro, MA 02703,
(508) 222-2900, www.
therobbinsco.com.
Recognition and
reward programs.

**Sitework
Associates, Inc.**
P.O. Box 20068,
Sarasota, FL 34276,
(941) 927-5400.
Conference site
finding services.

**Society of
Incentive Travel**
401 North Michigan
Ave., Chicago, IL 60611,
(312) 321-5148,
FAX (312) 527-6783,
www.site-intl.org. Travel
incentive information,
promotional and
research society.

**Starr-Seigle
Communications**
1001 Bishop St.,
Pacific Tower, 19th Fl.,

Honolulu, HI 96813,
(808) 524-5080, FAX
(808) 523-7443,
www.starrseigle.com.
Advertising for group
conventions.

**The Sweepstakes
Center**
P.O. Box 16350,
Rochester, NY 14616,
(585) 256-0080,
www.thesweepstakes
center.com. Sweep-
stakes and contest
consulting and
administration.

USMotivation
7840 Roswell Rd.,
Bldg. 100, 3rd Fl.,
Atlanta, GA 30350,
(770) 290-4700,
ext. 4757,
www.usmotivation.com.
Full-service incentive
company.

Appendix V

Featured Companies

American Association for Retired People (AARP), *p. 20*
Washington, DC.
Retirement association

Abbott Laboratories, *p. 130*
Abbott Park, IL.
Pharmaceuticals

Acapulco Restaurants, *pp. 282–283*
Long Beach, CA.
Restaurant chain

Accenture, *pp. 70, 145*
Hamilton, Bermuda.
Management and technology consulting

Access Destination Services, *pp. 200–201*
Long Beach, CA.
Design management and event production

ACCO Brands, Inc., *p. 223*
Lincolnshire, IL.
Manufactures office products

Accudata, *pp. 120–121*
Ft. Myers, FL.
Mailing lists, data solutions

Action Management Associates, *p. 77*
Dallas, TX.
Training company

Advanced Micro Devices, *pp. 156, 194, 220*
Sunnyvale, CA.
Manufactures and markets complex monolithic circuits

Advanta Corporation, *pp. 79, 94, 139–140, 241–242*

Horsham, PA.
Financial services.

ADVO, Inc., *p. 147*
Windsor, CT.
Direct mail services

U.S. Air Force, *p. 99*
Arlington, VA.
Military

Akili Systems Group, *p. 48*
Dallas, TX.
Software and consulting company

Alaska Airlines, Inc., *pp. 105–106, 195, 312*
Seattle, WA.
Airline

Amazon.com, Inc., *p. 90*
Seattle, WA.
Online store

Armstrong International,
p. 91
Three Rivers, MI.
Manufactures air, water, energy and humidification systems

U.S. Army,
pp. 14–15
Ft. Lesley J. McNair, Washington, DC.
Military

Arthur Andersen,
p. 197
Chicago, IL.
Accounting firm

AT&T (American Telephone & Telegraph Company),
pp. 37, 79
Harrisburg, PA.
Communications

AT&T Universal Card Services,
p. 57
Sioux Falls, SD.
Credit card

Atlanta Business Chronicle,
p. 217
Atlanta, GA.
Regional business newspaper

Atlanta Consulting Group,
p. 8
Atlanta, GA.
Consulting services

Atlantic Envelope Company,
p. 264
Atlanta, GA.
Manufactures business and specialty envelopes

Atlantic Richfield Company (ARCO),
p. 321
Los Angeles, CA.
Oil and gas exploration and production.

Au Bon Pain,
p. 83
Boston, MA.
Retail bakery

Augusta Technical Institute,
p. 173
Augusta, GA.
Vocational technical school

Automatic Answer,
p. 213
San Juan Capistrano, CA.
Automated phone systems

Avis Rent A Car,
pp. 106, 325
Parsippany, NJ.
Rental cars

Avondale Shipyards,
p. 325
New Orleans, LA.
Ship building

BAE Systems,
p. 316
Hampshire, United Kingdom.
Defense contractor

Bagel Works,
p. 126
Keene, NH.
Bagel store

Baltimore Orioles,
p. 10
Baltimore, MD.
Professional baseball team

Banister Shoe,
pp. 271–272
White Plains, NY.
Retail shoe products

Bank of America Corporation,
pp. 29, 177
Charlotte, NC.
Financial services

Burger King,
pp. 83, 117
Miami, FL.
Fast food
restaurant chain

Busch Gardens-Tampa,
*pp. 22, 96, 118,
229–230*
Tampa, FL.
Entertainment

**Busch
Stadium,**
pp. 239–240
St. Louis, MO.
Sports stadium

**Business First of
Columbus,**
pp. 112, 163–164
Columbus, OH.
Regional business
newspaper

**Business First of
Louisville,**
p. 29
Louisville, KY.
Regional business
newspaper

**California
Public Employees'
Retirement System
(CalPERS),**
p. 19
Sacramento, CA.
Pension system

Cal Snap & Tab,
pp. 164–165
City of Industry, CA.
Produces business
forms

Canon USA,
pp. 128–129
Lake Success, NY.
Marketing and
distribution of
printers and
copiers

Capital One Services,
pp. 174, 309
McLean, VA.
Credit card services

**Carlson Marketing
Group,**
pp. 49, 133
Minneapolis, MN.
Trading stamp,
coupon redemption;
manufactures and
distributes telescopes
and binoculars

**Carmel Clay Public
Library,**
pp. 167–169
Carmel, IN.
Local public library

Career Track,
p. 66
Kansas City, MO.
Public seminar
company

**Cascades
Diamond, Inc.,**
pp. 277–278
Thorndike, MA.
Manufactures egg
cartons

**Cato Johnson
(Wunderman),**
p. 322
Lombard, IL.
Promotion agency

**CDA Management
Consulting,**
p. 73
Chagrin Falls, OH.
Management and
organizational
consulting

**CEDRA
Corporation,**
p. 105
Austin, TX.
Bioanalytical chemical
services

**Celestial
Seasonings, Inc.,**
p. 119
Boulder, CO.
Herbal tea
company

Cellular One,
pp. 240–241
Indianapolis, IN.
Cellular phone
service provider

Cobb Electric Membership Corporation,
p. 23
Marietta, GA.
Electric utility

Coca-Cola,
p. 179
Atlanta, GA.
Soft drink distributor

Colin Service Systems,
pp. 77, 79
White Plains, NY.
Janitorial services

Collins & Aikman Floorcoverings, Inc.,
pp. 41, 81
Dalton, GA.
Manufacturers of commercial floor coverings

Columbo (General Mills, Inc.),
p. 134
Minneapolis, MN.
Frozen yogurt company

Comfort Inn Ithaca,
pp. 317–318
Ithaca, NY.
Hotel

Compass Bancshares, Inc., *p. 310*
Birmingham, AL.
Financial services

The Container Store,
pp. 57, 61–63, 73
Copell, TX.
Storage and organizational solutions retail store

Continental Airlines,
pp. 238–239
Houston, TX.
Airline

Cooper Tire & Rubber Company,
p. 36
Findlay, OH.
Manufactures and distributes rubber products

Coronet/MTI Film and Video, *p. 218*
Deerfield, IL.
Production and distribution of educational films

Country Kitchen International,
p. 303
Madison, WI.
Restaurant chain

Crate & Barrel (Euromarket Designs, Inc.),
p. 66
Northbrook, IL.
Home décor retail store

Crillon Importers, Ltd.,
p. 46
Paramus, NJ.
Importers of Absolut vodka and other liquors

Cumberland Farms,
p. 83
Canton, MA.
Convenience stores

CUNA Mutual Group,
p. 107
Madison, WI.
Offers life insurance, investment advisory and information technology to credit unions

Cunningham Communications,
p. 76
Palo Alto, CA.
Public relations firm

Cuno, *p. 188–189*
Meriden, CT.
Manufactures water filtration and purification systems

Cyanamid Canada,
p. 252
Mississauga, Ontario, Canada.
Manufactures pharmaceuticals

Cygna Group, p. 66
Oakland, CA.
Engineering and
consulting

D'Agostino's,
pp. 94, 113, 126–127
Larchmont, NY.
Supermarket chain

**Daired's Salon and
Spa Pangéa,** p. 89
Arlington, TX.
Spa

**Dairy Mart
(Alimentation
Couche-Tard, Inc.),**
p. 309
Laval, Quebec, Canada.
Convenience stores

**Dallas Business
Journal,** p. 118
Dallas, TX.
Regional business
newspaper

Dallas, TX. p. 286
Local government

Dan River Company,
p. 325
Danville, VA.
Textile mill

Dana Corporation,
p. 327
Toledo, OH.
Manufactures and

distributes components
for truck and industrial
vehicles

**Dan Dipert
Tours & Travel,**
p. 69
Arlington, TX.
Travel agency

**Danis Environmental
Industries, Inc. (DEI),**
p. 51
Dayton, OH.
Designs water and
wastewater treatment
facilities

**DDB Worldwide
Communications
Group, Inc.**
pp. 136, 196, 321
New York, NY.
Advertising agency

Decatur, IL,
p. 296
Local government

**Decision Analyst,
Inc.,**
p. 316
Arlington, TX.
Market research and
consulting services

Deere & Company,
pp. 246–247
Moline, IL.
Farm equipment

Del Taco,
p. 230
Atlanta, GA.
Fast food chain

**Deland, Gibson
Insurance Associates,**
p. 72
Wellesley Hills, MA.
Insurance services

**Deloitte Touche
Tohmatsu,**
p. 71
New York, NY.
Accounting services

Delta Airlines,
pp. 158, 237, 293, 296
Atlanta, GA.
Airline

**U.S. Department
of Energy,**
p. 246
Washington, DC.
Government agency

Designer Checks,
p. 176
Colorado Springs, CO.
Manufactures designer
checks

**Developmental
Disabilities Resource
Center,**
p. 246
Lakewood, CO.
Disability services

**Dole Food
Company, Inc.,**
p. 179
Westlake Village, CA.
Produce producer

Domino's, Inc.,
p. 187
Ann Arbor, MI.
Fast food chain

**Dow Chemical
Company,**
p. 199
Midland, MI.
Chemical products,
plastic products,
consumer products

**Dr. Pepper/
Seven-Up, Inc.**
p. 206
Plano, TX.
Soft drink
manufacturer

**Duncan
Aviation,**
pp. 84, 90, 315
Lincoln, NE.
Services business
aircrafts

**Eastern
Connection,**
p. 315
Woburn, MA.
Parcel delivery
services in the
eastern U.S.

**Eastman Kodak
Company,**
pp. 52–53, 179, 246
Rochester, NY.
Photographic
products and
services, chemicals,
imaging, information
services

Eddie Bauer, Inc.,
p. 68
Redmond, WA.
Retail clothing stores

**E. I. du Pont de
Nemours and
Company,**
pp. 126, 302
Wilmington, DE.
Energy, consumer
products, insecticides,
firearms,
pharmaceuticals,
industrial chemicals,
medical products

**El Torito Restaurants
(Acapulco Acquisition
Group),**
pp. 108–109
Long Beach, CA.
Food service

**Electronic Data
Systems (EDS),**
p. 140
Plano, TX.
Computer outsourcing
services

ELetter,
p. 214
Portland, OR.
Direct mail marketing
services

**Eli Lilly &
Company,**
p. 291
Indianapolis, IN.
Pharmaceuticals

Elizabeth Arden, Inc.,
p. 228
Miami Lakes, FL.
Personal care products

**EMC Mortgage
Corporation,**
p. 19
Irving, TX.
Mortgage financial
services

**Emerald
Publications,**
p. 144
San Diego, CA.
Financial seminars
and direct mail
services.

**Emerson Process
Management Power &
Water Solutions, Inc.,**
pp. 104–105
Pittsburgh, PA.
Power generation and
water/wastewater
treatment services

Emporio Armani,
p. 48
Milan, Italy.
Retail clothing stores

Enterprise Rent-A-Car Company, *p. 47*
St. Louis, MO.
Rental cars

The Estée Lauder Companies, Inc.,
p. 12
New York, NY.
Personal care products

Exxon Mobil Corporation,
pp. 292–293
Irving, TX.
Petroleum products, exploration and refining, coal mining, chemical products

Famous-Barr (May Department Stores),
p. 10
St. Louis, MO.
Department stores

Fargo Electronics,
p. 30
Eden Prairie, MN.
Card identity systems

Farmers Insurance Group, *p. 71*
Los Angeles, CA.
Insurance Company

Federal Express,
pp. 37, 48, 54, 83, 92, 282, 293, 326
Memphis, TN.
Delivery services

FedEx Freight West, Inc.,
pp. 88, 100–101, 148, 185, 267
San Jose, CA.
Trucking company_ freight carrier

FedEx Kinko's, Inc.,
p. 245
Dallas, TX.
Printing services

Fel-Pro (Federal-Mogul),
pp. 252, 290
Southfield, MI.
Manufactures components for cars, trucks and construction vehicles

Firmani & Associates,
p. 193
Seattle, WA.
Public relations and marketing firm

First Capital Life,
p. 190
La Jolla, CA.
Life insurance company

FirstEnergy Corporation,
p. 23
Akron, OH.
Electric utility

First International Bank & Trust,
p. 289
Watford City, ND.
Financial services

First-Knox National Bank, *p. 258*
Mount Verson, OH.
Financial services

Five Star Speakers & Trainers, LLC,
p. 192
Overland Park, KS.
Training and seminar services

Florida Power and Light Company, *p. 32*
Juno Beach, FL.
Electric utility

FMC Lithium Division,
p. 238
Bessemer City, NC.
Industrial chemicals, machinery, precious metals, defense systems

Focus2, *p. 147*
Dallas, TX.
Brand development services

Ford Motor Company,
pp. 37, 80, 179, 317
Dearborn, MI.
Manufacture and sale
of cars, financial
services

Fordham University,
p. 186
Career Planning and
Placement Office,
New York, NY.
Educational services

**Fortress
Safe and Lock,**
p. 305
Cincinnati, OH.
Manufactures locks,
safes, and access
control systems

**Founders Title
Company,**
p. 205
Salt Lake City, UT.
Title company

**Four Pi Systems
(Hewlett-Packard),**
p. 256
San Diego, CA.
Developer of
manufacturing test
equipment

**Fox Chase Cancer
Center,**
p. 298
Philadelphia, PA.

Biological research on
cancer prevention and
treatment

**Furst-McNess
Company,**
p. 268
Freeport, IL.
Manufactures pre-
mixed animal food.

**G.S. Schwartz
and Company,**
p. 120
New York, NY.
Public relations firm

**Gandalf
Technologies,**
pp. 70–71
Irvine, CA.
Manufactures
ethernet bridges
for the internet

Gap, Inc.,
p. 122
San Francisco, CA.
Retail clothing stores.

Gartner, Inc.,
p. 308
Stamford, CT.
IT Industry market
research and consulting

General Cinema,
p. 292
Newton, MA.
Theater chain

**General Electric
Company,**
pp. 82, 263
Fairfield, CT.
Electrical and
electronic equipment

General Mills,
pp. 30, 143
Minneapolis, MN.
Produces breakfast
cereals and other
foods

**Girl Scouts of
Santa Clara County,**
p. 58
Palo Alto, CA.
Youth service
organization

**Good Samaritan
Hospital,**
p. 237
Cincinnati, OH.
Health care services

**Great American
Bank,**
p. 78
San Diego, CA.
Savings bank

**Great Plains-
Microsoft Business
Solutions,**
pp. 106, 164
Redmond, WA.
Manufactures
accounting software

Great Western Drilling Company,
pp. 118–119
Midland, TX.
Drilling services

GreenPages, Inc.,
p. 218
Kittery, ME.
Provides IT consulting, IT hardware and systems design

Gregerson's Foods,
p. 113
Gadsen, AL.
Retail grocery chain

Griffin Hospital,
p. 304
Derby, CT.
Medical services

Grinnell College,
pp. 158–159
Grinnell, IA.
Educational services

GTE Telephone Operations,
pp. 242–243
Stamford, CT.
Telecommunications, electrical products, laboratories

H.B. Fuller Company,
pp. 79, 93, 304, 310
St. Paul, MN.
Makes glues, adhesives and sealants

H.J. Heinz Company,
p. 41
Pittsburgh, PA.
Food processing company

Hallmark Cards,
pp. 98, 207, 326
Kansas City, MO.
Manufactures and sells greeting cards, party goods

Hardee's Food Systems, Inc.,
pp. 185–186
St. Louis, MO.
Fast food restaurants

Hartford Steam Boiler Inspection and Insurance Company,
p. 131
Hartford, CT.
Boiler and machinery insurance

Hastings Books, Music, and Entertainment, Inc.,
pp. 106–107
Amarillo, TX.
Retail media entertainment stores

Hatfield Quality Meats, *p. 121*
Hatfield, PA.
Food processing

Herbalife, Inc.,
pp. 23–24
Inglewood, CA.
Manufactures and sells natural wellness products

Herman Miller,
p. 327
Zeeland, MI.
Manufactures office furniture

Hershey Foods Corporation, *p. 56*
Hershey, PA.
Makers of candy

Hewlett-Packard Company,
pp. 33, 192, 194, 199, 212, 301
Palo Alto, CA.
Manufactures computers, servers, storage products, printers, networking equipment and software.

Hilton Hotels Corporation,
p. 65
Beverly Hills, CA.
Hotels and casinos

Microsoft Corporation,
pp. 160, 176, 183
Redmond, WA.
Computer software firm

MidMichigan Regional Medical Center,
pp. 279–281
Midland, MI.
Medical services

Mid-States Technical Staffing Services,
p. 181
Davenport, IA.
Employment services

Miller Nissan,
pp. 212–213
Van Nuys, CA.
Automobile dealership

Mini Maid Service Company, *p. 263*
Marietta, GA.
Cleaning services

Minnesota Mining and Manufacturing Company (3M),
p. 60, 257–258, 301
St. Paul, MN.
Industrial consumer and electronic products, life sciences products, information and imaging technologies, and commercial and consumer products

Mirage Resort,
p. 292
Las Vegas, NV.
Casino and entertainment services

Molson Breweries USA,
pp. 206–207
Reston, VA.
Beer brewery and distributor

Monsanto Company,
p. 179
St. Louis, MO.
Chemical manufacturer

Montefiore Nursing Home,
p. 157
Beachwood, OH.
Medical services

Moosehead Beer,
p. 134
Dartmouth, Nova Scotia, Canada.
Brewery

Morris Savings Bank (Wachovia Bank),
pp. 226–228
Charlotte, NC.
Bank

Motorola,
pp. 90, 258, 288
Schaumburg, IL.
Manufactures semiconductors,

mobile radios, cellular telephone systems, pagers

Multi-Image Productions, Inc.,
pp. 220–221
San Diego, CA.
Creates and produces multi-media products as well as executive seminars and sales meetings

Muscatine Power and Water,
p. 286
Muscatine, IA.
Utility company

NASA Johnson Space Center,
p. 35
Houston, TX.
Human space exploration

National Institute for Occupational Safety and Health,
pp. 170–171
Atlanta, GA.
Works to prevent work-related illnesses and injuries

National Office Furniture, *p. 117*
Jasper, IN.
Sells office furniture

Procter & Gamble,
pp. 165–167, 326
Paper Products
Division,
Cincinnati, OH.
Disposable diapers,
tissues, paper towels

**Professional
Salon Concepts,**
p. 222
Joliett, IL.
Hair care products
and services

**PSS World Medical,
Inc.,** p. 203
Jacksonville, FL.
Distributors of
medical supplies

**Publix Super
Markets,**
pp. 41, 325
Lakeland, FL.
Supermarket chain

**Puffer and
Associates,**
p. 270
St. Paul, MN.
Marketing and
public relations

Quad/Graphics, Inc.,
pp. 88, 119, 209, 326
Pewaukee, WI.
Prints national
magazines and
catalogues

Quantum Design,
p. 206
San Diego, CA.
Manufactures scientific
instruments

Quill Corporation,
p. 284
Lincolnshire, IL.
Office supplies and
equipment

**QuizMaster
Productions,** p. 186
Roswell, GA.
Designers and
producers of TV-style
game shows for
businesses

**Qwest Communications,
Inc.,** p. 9
Denver, CO.
Long-distance phone
services and broadband
internet services

Radio Shack, p. 244
Fort Worth, TX.
Electronics retailer

**Radisson Hotels &
Resorts,** p. 276
Minnetonka, MN.
Hotels

Random House,
p. 293
New York, NY.
Publishing company

**Randstad North
America LP,**
p. 122
Atlanta, GA.
Employment services

**Raytheon Aircraft
Company,**
p. 16
Wichita, KS.
Manufacturers aircraft
products

Reader's Digest,
pp. 71, 85, 287, 295,
297, 322
Pleasantville, NY.
Publishing company

**Recreational
Equipment, Inc. (REI),**
pp. 103–104, 116, 199,
293, 310
Kent, WA.
Camping and hiking
equipment

**Remington Products,
Inc.,**
pp. 122, 184, 298
Shelton, CT.
Personal care products

Replacements, Ltd.,
p. 146
McLeansville, NC.
Supplier of old and
new china, crystal,
silver, jewelry, and
collectibles

Republic Engineered Products, LLC,
p. 47
Akron, OH.
Steel processing

RHC (Resident Home Company),
p. 42
Cincinnati, OH.
Provides opportunities to people with disabilities

Resort Condominiums International, LLC,
p. 225
Parsippany, NJ.
Telemarketing of timeshare condominiums

Rexair, *p. 223*
Troy, MI.
Sells cleaning systems

Rippe & Kingston,
p. 69
Cincinnati, OH.
Provides services and products in accounting, technology, management, systems consulting and e-business

Road Atlanta,
p. 208
Braselton, GA.
Grand Prix track

The Robert Mondavi Winery,
p. 292
Napa, CA.
Wine company

Robert W. Baird, Inc.,
pp. 72–73, 103, 142, 183,–184, 196, 231–232, 306, 310, 316
Milwaukee, WI.
Offers wealth management, asset management, and middle-market investment banking services

Rock and Roll Hall of Fame,
p. 139
Cleveland, OH.
Entertainment

Rosenbluth International,
pp. 92, 244
Philadelphia, PA.
Travel agency

Ross Products,
pp. 273–275
Abbott Park, IL.
Manufactures pediatric, pharmaceutical and nutritional products

Rotary Club (Rotary International),
p. 78
Evanston, IL.
Social charity services organization

Royal Appliance,
p. 136
Glenwillow, OH.
Appliance manufacturer

Rush-Copley Memorial Hospital,
p. 264
Aurora, IL.
Medical services

Ryder System, Inc.,
pp. 256–257, 288, 311
Miami, FL.
Rents and leases trucks

S.C. Johnson & Son, (Johnson Wax),
pp. 144, 286, 301, 312
Racine, WI.
Manufacturer of household and personal care products

Sacramento, City of, Department of Public Works, *p. 229*
Sacramento, CA.
Local government agency

Safety Vision,
p. 216
Houston, TX.
Sells mobile cameras

manufacturing wood products packaging and paper

WinterSilks, *p. 92*
Jacksonville, FL.
Catalog winter clothing company

Workman Publishing, *p. 72*
New York, NY.
Publishing company

World at Work, *p. 95*
Scottsdale, AZ.
Compensation and related employee services association

Worthington Industries, *p. 143*
Columbus, OH.
Steel processing company, plastic products manufacturer

Worzalla Publishing Company, *p. 256*
Stevens Point, WI.
Publishing company

WS Packaging Group, Inc., *p. 126*
Algoma, WI.
Manufactures packaging and printing supplies

WRQ, Inc., *p. 146*
Seattle, WA.
Software firm

Xerox Corporation, *pp. 32, 34, 58, 147, 225, 323*
Stamford, CT.
Manufacturer of copiers, business products and systems, financial services

Ziff Davis Media, *p. 107*
La Jolla, CA.
Media company

ABOUT BOB NELSON

DR. BOB NELSON is an internationally recognized expert in management and motivation, employee recognition and rewards, and performance improvement and productivity. He is the founder of Nelson Motivation, Inc. (www.nelson-motivation.com), a management training and consulting company located in San Diego, California, and is the author of numerous books on management and motivation, including: *The 1001 Rewards & Recognition Fieldbook, 1001 Ways to Energize Employees,* and *1001 Ways to Take Initiative at Work.*

Bob is a former vice president at The Ken Blanchard Companies. He holds an MBA in organizational behavior from the University of California at Berkeley and a Ph.D. in management from the Peter F. Drucker Graduate Management School at Claremont Graduate University. He also helped found the National Association for Employee Recognition (NAER), where he still serves as an advisory board member.

Bob has worked on employee motivation with over 1000 organizations in a wide range of industries, including two-thirds of the Fortune 500 companies. He has been featured extensively in the media, including television appearances on CNN, CNBC, PBS, and MSNBC; radio appearances on all major networks, including USA Radio Network, Business News Network, and National Public Radio; and print appearances in *The New York Times, The Wall Street Journal, The Washington Post, The Chicago Tribune, USA Today, Fortune, Inc.,* and many more. He writes regular columns for American City Business Journals and Corporate Meetings & Incentive magazine, and is often featured in *Workforce Management,* as well as other trade publications.

RELATED PRODUCTS AND SERVICES

BOB NELSON and Nelson Motivation Inc. provide a wide range of products and services to help you improve and sustain employee recognition and motivation in your organization, including consulting services, training & presentations, recognition assessments for managers & employees, books, audios, videos, manager recognition kits, and training aids. For more information, contact:

Nelson Motivation Inc.
12245 World Trade Drive
San Diego, CA 92128-3770
800-575-5521 or 858-487-1046
www.nelson-motivation.com

or

P.O. Box 500872
San Diego, CA 92150-9973

Sign up to receive Bob's free Tip of the Week at www.nelson-motivation.com.

You can reach Bob directly at 858-673-0690 or on the Internet at BobRewards@aol.com.

NOTES

NOTES